John Lennon and the Jews
A Philosophical Rampage

You should especially read it if you are Jewish and (1) young; (2) think being Jewish is a bore; (3) don't, but can't explain why it isn't; (4) believe that social justice everywhere is a Jewish cause; (5) believe that saving the rain forests is a Jewish cause.... If you fall into, or close to, any of these categories, Ze'ev Maghen has written *John Lennon and the Jews* for you.... Manically exuberant, intellectually reckless and never afraid to sound zany, as a result of which it's deadly serious and perfectly sane.

Hillel Halkin, *The Jewish Daily Forward*

An intimate letter written from one Jew to his brethren, hoping to free their minds and warm their hearts, and it reminds us that, 3,000 years after God and the Jewish people first exchanged vows on Mount Sinai, Judaism remains a stunningly beautiful, vibrant, deep and often bracing experience.

Dr. Aryeh Tepper, *Jewish Ideas Daily*

I am still trying to decide if Ze'ev Maghen's *John Lennon and the Jews* is the funniest serious book I have ever read, or the most serious funny book I have ever read...Are you Jewish? Read this book.

Professor Katherine Arroues, *The ProsenPeople*

Maghen – an American-born Israeli scholar of Islamic law but also something of a general know-everything-but-not-in-an-arrogant-way sort of guy – has literally invented a new genre of writing, aptly self-titled the "rampage," which might best be described as the literary equivalent of three parts strong coffee, two parts Red Bull, and one part nuclear fusion. You pick this thing up and it practically supernovas right in your hand.... You will come out of this book more energized about your Jewishness.

Professor Andrew Pessin, *The Huffington Post*

Calculate how many great-grandchildren you are going to have, purchase that many copies of John Lennon and the Jews, and stipulate in your will that no one gets a bloody farthing until they've read this literary volcano from cover to cover. No Jew should grow up without this book!

Meredith's Monthly Choices

A book which Jews – anywhere on the religious spectrum – should pick up, read and enjoy. And then read it again.... Maghen seemingly has devoted his life to showing Jews how "awesome" it is to be Jewish.

Ronn Torossian, *The Times of Israel*

You will walk across an intersection reading this book and get hit by a car; luckily, in my case, it was a Smart car – only a sprained shoulder and some bruises, no need to worry, I'll be fine.

Zachary Foster, Georgetown University

Ze'ev Maghen

john lennon and the jews

A Philosophical Rampage

The Toby Press

John Lennon and the Jews
A Philosophical Rampage

First Toby Edition, 2014

The Toby Press LLC
POB 8531, New Milford, CT 06776–8531, USA
& POB 2455, London W1A 5WY, England
www.tobypress.com

ISBN 978 1 59264 397 4

A CIP catalogue record for this title is available from the British Library

Printed and bound in the United States

This book is dedicated to the lady
who introduced me to the Beatles and to the Jews,
and made sure that both of them were an integral part
of my upbringing and consciousness – my Mom.

Contents

My Sweet Lord 1

Shira: The Challenge of Universalism 19

Ofer: The Challenge of Rationalism 87

Doron: The Challenge of Inertia 301

About the Author 315

My Sweet Lord

Chapter One

Many years ago I interrupted a perfectly enjoyable pilgrimage to the Old Country (the USA) in order to fly out and visit some friends in Los Angeles, that sea-side sanctum of higher culture, clean air and tasteful architecture. So there I was at LAX on a balmy Friday morning, sitting in this nondescript bar nursing a black-and-white shake and waiting for my ride. Out of the corner of my eye, I absent-mindedly surveyed the vigorous maneuverings of a small but dedicated cadre of neophyte Hare Krishna, who had deployed themselves in full-court-press formation across the central concourse of the airport. These mantra-chanting devotees of the swami-whose-name-I-never-could-pronounce – festooned in elaborate religious regalia – were scurrying up and down the thoroughfare like human ping-pong balls, energetically hawking illustrated copies of Vedic texts to the few passers-by who didn't ignore them, shove them aside or spit in their general direction. This was, of course, a familiar scene to me, jet-setter that I am.

I finished my shake (such as it was – they've never heard the phrase "black-and-white milkshake" on the West Coast, and my numerous attempts to explain this simple concept to the natives were invariably futile), and made a bee-line for the exit. I guess the old quadriceps ain't quite what they used to be, though, because within seconds, I perceived a pair of dainty, be-moccasined footsteps easily gaining on me from behind. A young female voice inquired politely: "*Excuse me, sirrr, but – ehh – maybe you vould like to take a loook at zis boook*?"

I froze. Stopped dead in my tracks. I knew that accent. I'd know it anywhere. My heart plummeted into my duodenum. I put my suitcase down and turned around slowly. She was petite and pretty in her saffron sari and multitudinous bangles. She must have had auburn hair, once, judging from the stubble on her scalp. And her eyes were a deep, feline green, amplified by the dab of yellow mustard smeared ever so artfully between them. She held a tiny tambourine in one hand, and with the other extended, was sweetly offering me a psychedelic version of the *Upanishads*. We stood there smack in the middle of that broad, bustling promenade and stared at eachother for a few seconds, and when I saw she was about to repeat her practiced pitch about the book, I hastened to preempt and queried quietly: "*Meh ayfo at*?" (Where are you from?)

"*Merrramat a-Sharrron*," she answered, naturally, effortlessly, gurgling her "r" and eliding the "h" sound as people from her neck of the coastal plains are wont to do (Ramat HaSharon is a suburb of Tel-Aviv). Apparently excited by this rare opportunity to spread the Good Word in her native tongue, and undeterred by the intense suffering that must have been seared like a cattle brand all over my face, she warmed to her subject, and launched into a series of sound-bites concerning the benefits of Krishna consciousness, including especially the need to realize…to actualize…to visualize…to harmonize…to get in touch with…to remove the walls…to blend into…to meld…to merge…to coalesce…to become one….

I never even started listening (I know the lines by rote: I'm a frequent flyer *and* an erstwhile deprogrammer). "*Ekh kor'im lakh*?" (What's your name?) I asked her, still trying to get my mind and heart around this.

"*Shira*," she responded, displaying no such curiosity in return. In the meantime, the other two appropriately attired and dapperly depilated members of her Maha squad had drifted over, no doubt intrigued by the seldom encountered phenomenon of somebody actually stopping to converse, and lured by the heady scent of fresh, missionizable meat. Well, and wouldn't you know it: the *whole gang* is from Ramat HaSharon. Meet Ofer ("*Shalom*!") and Doron ("*Ma Nishma*?").

So the four of us stand there, chatting like old friends. We reminisce about the army like good Israelis do, talk about who served where and who spent more time "in the mud" and who hated it most. Shira, as it turns out, is a first lieutenant and outranks all of us, and I snap to attention and she laughs. Doron was a medic like myself, and we make a date to give each other ice-water infusions and joke about how the first thing we look at on a woman are her veins. I remind them of this kiosk on Herzl Boulevard in Ramat HaSharon where they fry up the *biggest* and *juiciest* falafel balls in the entire country, and all three nod their heads in vehement agreement and lick their lips in almost Pavlovian recollection: they know *exactly* the place I'm talking about (I've never been to Ramat HaSharon, but every town in Israel has a Herzl Boulevard, and every Israeli citizen from Dan to Be'ersheba is convinced that there is this one falafel stand in his neighborhood that makes the *biggest* and *juiciest* falafel balls in the entire country. I saw Hawkeye do this trick on M*A*S*H once, with french fries).

So we're shootin' the breeze, the three Hebrew Hare Krishnas and I, casually discoursing in the recently resurrected and unsurpassably gorgeous idiom of the biblical prophets and kings, and finally, well – I just lose it.

"What the hell are you *doing* here?!" I blurt out, diverging slightly from the pleasantly banterish tone that has informed the conversation thus far. "You are Jews! You are *Israelis*, for God's sake! What the hell are you doing *here*, in this place, on a Friday morning, wearing *these* clothes, chanting *those* words and selling *that* book?!" Now in those pious days I used to read the Torah from the pulpit every week in a Jerusalem synagogue, and since one has to rehearse continually, I never left home without the Pentateuch in my pack. At this moment, then, amazed at the extent of my own coolness, I reached back over my shoulder into my knapsack – the way I'm positive Robin Hood used to extract an arrow from his quiver – and boldly whipped out the Five Books of Moses (thwack!). "*That's* not your book," I cried, indicating the decorative and abridged *Bhagavad-Gita* Ofer was clutching to his breast like it was a newborn infant. "*This*" – and I resoundingly slapped the raggedy, worn-and-torn volume in my own hands –

"*This* is *your* book!!!"

They all stared at me sadly, with genuine pity, the way one might look at an animal caught in a trap or at someone who had just been diagnosed with a terminal illness. "No, no. You don't understand," purred Shira, her tone managing to be both soothing and patronizing at the same time. "This isn't a contest! We're not choosing one book over another, or one religion over another, we're not expressing a preference for a particular culture, nation or ethnic or social group over another. That would mean creating *hierarchical relationships* between human beings. That would mean erecting *false barriers* between people, barriers that have been responsible for so much misery and bloodshed throughout history, barriers that have prevented human beings from reaching their true potential and destiny, from achieving inner peace – and *world* peace. You and I, my friend, and everyone else in this airport, and everything that lives and breathes in every corner of this vast planet of ours, we are all of us part of a great and wonderful unity, we are all brothers and sisters, we are all linked by the same network of indissoluble bonds – we just don't *know* it yet. Krishna consciousness is about spreading that knowledge."

Zoinks! What do you get when you combine a young socialist ideologue educated in the best Israeli schools with a diluted dose of ancient Sanskrit esotericism plus a dash of the Diggers? I tried to imagine Shira haranguing conscripts in boot camp. That must have been some show.

"How can you be so naïve?" Doron chimed in, seemingly on cue. "Look around you, *habibi* – get with the program! The world is constantly imploding, getting smaller all the time. The distances between societies are diminishing everywhere, and the borders that divide us from one another are evaporating like a thousand Berlin Walls tumbling down! It's *happening*, man, whether you like it or not! The world is *progressing*, moving forward, toward oneness, toward mutual tolerance and understanding, away from the petty, archaic differences that have forever pitted us against each other. As the Lord says (and here, astonished to the point of giddiness that he had actually gotten far enough with someone as to be able to quote scripture, Doron flipped open his large-print, polychrome edition of the *Rig Veda* to a pre-marked page, and reverently recited a passage highlighted in red): '*Let all hearts be as one heart, let all minds be as one mind, so that through the spirit of oneness we may heal the sickness of a divided humanity.*'"

"Open your eyes!" he preached on, the already rosy cheeks of this juggernauted Jew turning increasingly sanguine with Eastern religious ardor. "These words are coming true! We are building a *new* reality for humankind today, and you, my friend – you are stuck, *habibi*, moored in a past of self-isolation and limitation, hemmed-in by an anachronism you refuse to let go of. But the Supreme Lord Sri Krishna can help you let go of it, can help you be *truly free*. If you'll just concentrate and chant…"

I wondered if these guys were this good in English. Just my luck to meet up with the three most articulate initiates in the entire ashram (true, not all of what they said came out of the books they were so zealously peddling, and some of it was a serious misrepresentation of "Vaishnava philosophy," but so what? They were declaiming the world according to themselves – and no doubt according to their Israeli parents' liberal-leaning "post-Zionist" progressivism – and that was more interesting to me, in any case. I wondered what their parents thought now).

"Yes, you have an antiquated attitude, my friend – a *dangerous* attitude." This was Ofer, who was so tall that I found myself mourning his loss not only to the Jewish people as a whole, but to the Maccabi Tel-Aviv basketball team in particular. He had managed to jettison pretty much every Israeli trapping that would have given him away, except the tell-tale Nimrod sandals and that really annoying hand gesture that means "wait" nowhere else on the planet except in our little corner of the Middle East. He used it on me now, as I tried to butt-in and protest my general benignity.

"Don't you see," he continued, thundering down from his nearly seven foot high pulpit, "that the Torah and its laws are no longer relevant to people's lives today? All that hocus-pocus, all those archaic stories and ridiculous rules and time-wasting rituals and impractical practices!" (This, from a guy shorn down to his cranium, with paint on his face, wrapped up in linens and dancing to a mantra beat all day long in an airport.)

"There's just no rhyme or reason to *any* of it!" he forged on. "How can such obsolete, irrational poppycock still appeal to an intelligent person like you? Now, Hindu wisdom, on the other hand, *that's* where you'll find a truly compelling reflection of reality *as it is*. That's where you'll find profound insights for the rational person, for the reasoning, penetrating, philosophical mind, insights which not only do not contradict, but actually help us to better understand and take advantage of our modern age of scientific discovery and global responsibility. But Judaism? Judaism just doesn't cut it in a thinking person's world. Sorry."

"But...what about your loyalty to...your people?" I remonstrated feebly. "You know: the Jewish People?"

That pissed him off. "Oh – now I get it: You're a *fascist*," he proclaimed, enunciating each word with conviction and solemnity, as if he were a judge pronouncing a death sentence (that was it: no more Mr. Nice Guy. Yoga and Karma and Krishna and Swami what's-his-name were long gone. For the moment, anyway, I was talking to pure Israeli leftist). "What you're preaching – it's exclusivism, it's discrimination, it's apartheid, it's elitism...it is *leumanut*," he declared, employing for his *coup de grace* a subtle nuance in Hebrew semantics that essentially distinguishes chauvinist from liberal nationalism (I doubted whether he found the latter any more palatable than the former).

"Why should people identify themselves according to this outmoded and flagrantly racist conception of yours?" he continued. "And how dare you define others based on such artificial and reactionary criteria? Human beings should be judged by their individual characters, by their beliefs and ideas, not by their national or ethnic affiliations! Why are you so prejudiced? Why do you play favorites? What, because I was born a Jew, and that man standing over there by the telephone was not, you should interact with me in a different way than you do with him? Is that supposed to make sense? Maybe he's the most upright, moral person in the entire city of LA, maybe he's calling up some charity right now to donate a million dollars!" (I glanced over at the guy. He was unquestionably Jewish, and judging from his contorted visage and wild gesticulations, was probably talking to his broker.) "And because I had the 'luck' to be born of a Jewish mother, and he didn't; because I got 'snipped' a week after coming into the world, and he didn't; for these reasons you should *prefer* me to him?! You should *care* about me more than you do about him?! Why, that's *sick*! It's downright *disgusting*!!!"

I was glad he was done so I could stop craning my neck. He might very well have been arguing as much against his own internal inclinations as he was against me – I hadn't managed to say a great deal, after all – but at any rate, Shira quickly laid a hand on his waist (you couldn't really reach his shoulder) and led him aside. I wasn't getting any closer to Krishna consciousness this way. The not-so-gentle giant inhaled half the oxygen in the arrivals lounge and rattled off three mantras at breakneck speed, all in one breath. Then he was back, calm and cool, all smiles and ready to Rama.

Shira placed a hand on my shoulder (you can reach my shoulder) and spoke to me softly. "Don't you see? All that His Divine Grace Swami Prah…is saying, comes down to this: *We must strive with every bit of our inner strength to love all people equally*. That is what these books we're distributing teach as well, and, in the last analysis, isn't that also the central message of *that* book, the one *you're* carrying?" (she pointed to the Torah).

I stood there engulfed in frustration. What could I possibly answer "on one foot" (as we say in Hebrew) – in the little time remaining to us – that would even begin to make a dent in *all of that*? I heaved a long sigh of resignation. "When was the last time you read *this* book?" was the best I could come up with under the circumstances, appealing in all directions to imaginary back-up units.

"That's not what *this* book says."

My ride showed up, and was of course parked in the red zone, which as you know is for the loading and unloading of passengers only. There was a genuinely poignant parting scene – during which, among other unexpected events, Doron pressed my hand in his and slipped me a surreptitious "*Shabbat Shalom Akhi*!" (Good Sabbath, my brother!) – and the tantric trio from Tel-Aviv waltzed off in search of easier prey. I don't know where my three semi-brainwashed but far from benighted Brahmins are now – whether they've since managed to achieve supreme bovinity, or whether they have fallen from grace and are currently putting their considerable oratorical talents to lucrative use fencing CD players on Olympic Boulevard. Either way, I sure hope I get to meet up with them again someday (yes, even if it means going back to Los Angeles). The ensuing pages contain the gist of what I would say to them, if I did.

Chapter Two

You don't have to be a disciple of Eastern mysticism or philosophy to be struck by the apparent anomaly of being a committed, involved or practicing Jew today. You just have to be pre-lobotomy. Whatever doubts I may harbor regarding their idea of a fun Friday activity or their strange notions of fashion or musical rhythm, the objections raised by my airport interlocutors are nothing to be sneezed, coughed, hiccupped, spat or in any other way eructed or expectorated at. Stripped of their atavistic, pseudo-Aryan theosophical trappings and utopian Socialist rhetoric, the positions propounded by Shira, Doron and Ofer collectively represent far and away the foremost issue and dilemma facing the current generation of up-and-coming Jews, as they decide just how Jewish they want to be, as they debate how much space and how much importance to give Judaism and Jewishness in their lives.

For the vast majority of us, after all, the poser is not: "Should I be Christian or Jewish?" or "Should I be Buddhist or Jewish?" or even "Should I be Druid or Jewish?" No. The real quandary, the fundamental inner conflict affecting and preoccupying many of today's Jewish young people – whether formulated in this manner or otherwise – is without a doubt: Should I be a modern, progressive, secular, non-denominationally affiliated American, or Canadian, or Britisher, or Citizen of the World (or alternately, just "Me" with no strings attached whatsoever)…or should I be actively and deeply and connectedly Jewish – and how much of each, or where in-between, or which elements (if any) of these two available alter-egos can possibly be reconciled? Put in an even more concise fashion, the puzzle of the hour for most of us is simply this: **Why on earth be a Jew in the (post) Modern world?**

An immediate qualifier: I am not naïve. I am well aware that in the case of a whole slew of Jews today, this issue burns inside them at about the level of a Bic lighter. Such folks are complete strangers to the inner turmoil associated with the dilemma described above, and they are of two kinds:

The first group doesn't think about this question because, in a word, *they've already made their decision*. Indeed, their decision was to a large extent made for them, long ago, by parents who for whatever reason did not expose their children adequately to one or the other of the two world-views previously delineated. Either the kids had religion shoved down their throats from age one – no doubts allowed (let alone cultivated) – and never really had the opportunity to observe the truly compelling aspects of life on the other side of the overly-protective spiritual-parochial fence; or – what is far more common – they grew up with no exposure worth mentioning to Judaism or the Jewish People, save perhaps a few years in Hebrew school, which in the majority of cases simply furnishes the poor pupil with enduring reasons to get as far away from his cultural heritage as humanly possible.

(I have to throw in just a quick kudos to my own parents here. When I was four years old – and I remember this vividly – I asked them if there was a God. Mom and Dad adjourned to the den for a progenitorial policy huddle, and emerged moments later bearing the following lollapalooza of an answer: "Go out on the porch," they instructed, "and decide for yourself." I'll never stop being grateful to them for that.)

Anyway, to you "already resolved that issue, don't bother me" types, I will say: *continuous self-re-examination* – even after having arrived at what appear to be immutable conclusions etched in stone – is the *conditio sine qua non* of wisdom, humanity, meaningfulness, relationships, progress, success and pretty much everything else worthwhile in life. So I encourage you to keep your mind open and read on.

The second group doesn't think about the question in question, primarily because...well...(how do I put this delicately?) they don't *think*. Ladies and gentlemen of this mold aren't really inclined to ponder or deliberate subjects more abstract than, say, the optimal head-height of a properly poured Heineken, the relative righteousness of the NCAA versus the NBA three-point line, how fat Oprah is this month or what T-bills are going to do over the next quarter. Issues and ideas of identity, beauty, freedom, romance, art, fantasy, justice, morality, mysticism, history, philosophy – such irrelevancies simply do not disturb or exercise the minds of these folks as they plod their pragmatic way through incurably superficial lives. Hey, you know who you are. This book has nothing for you. Just put it down, nice and easy – *there* ya go, that's right. Now go and listen to something with a lot of percussion. Crank up the bass, dude. Have fun! *Bye*!!

Where were we? The points proffered by my three Israeli amigos in the airport are not only of the profoundest relevance and legitimacy – they are also, of course, in no sense new. When universities were what they should be (and could be again, I remain convinced), long before any of us were born, our collegiate predecessors were *rarely known to do anything else* but stay up all night in meeting halls, public parks, drinking establishments, abandoned buildings, forests, caves, dormitories and even houses of ill repute, incessantly and passionately debating questions related to the epic conflict between universalism, on the one hand, and particularism or nationalism, on the other. Here, in these feverishly fought nocturnal battles of the intellect and spirit, both sides would not hesitate to haul out the big guns: Mazzini, Marinetti and Garibaldi; Kant, Hegel, Herder, Croce and Fichte; Feuerbach, Lassalle, Marx, Engels, Plekhanov and Lenin; Nietzsche and Kierkegaard, Rousseau and Jefferson, Spinoza and Hume, Russell and Ranke, all going at it simultaneously in a massive, tumultuous, WWF tag-team free-for-all slug-match of the mind.

Ah, those were the days.

Not to say that the debate is dead. Over the years, I have heard the arguments of Shira, Doron and Ofer – against attaching oneself to particularist socio-cultural cliques and clans that split humankind – advanced with conviction and passion in a whole gamut of guises by hundreds if not thousands of young Jews (not excluding, by the way, the writer of these lines). For that matter, I suspect that a whole smorgasbord of readers perusing these paragraphs right now could easily cite more than a few reasons why making the fact of their being Jewish into this big deal in their daily lives – not to mention *one of the defining characteristics of their personal identity* – why this notion might be far from compelling to them, or why it ranks rather low on their priority list, or why it is entirely ideologically untenable in their eyes, or why it's just downright stupid. I know I can.

Ever since my childhood, when I was dragged to High Holiday services once a year – where my boredom was of such magnitude that it could only be alleviated by repeatedly conjuring-up the vision of myself leaping headlong from the balcony to my own death by impalement on the spikes of the Menorah below – ever since then, I remember wondering what the point of all this was. This budding bewilderment was in no way mitigated by the edifying and intensely spiritual experience of my Bar-Mitzvah, during the course of which I learned by rote for six months how to chant flawlessly the words – without having an inkling as to their meaning – of what turned out to be the wrong *haftorah* (I kid you not). After this I took to imbibing mass quantities of Jolt soda to help me stay up all night every night for the final month, and just barely learn the right one.

I rode a souped-up Harley chopper right out of that neo-fundamentalist nightmare and into my carefree, suburban, red-white-and-blue-American teenage dream (OK, it was a Honda). I drank, smoked, won Frisbee-golf tournaments and lost my innocence. Got a girl, named Sue (really), she was terrific and a Methodist. I couldn't see one reason in the whole wide world why we shouldn't be together forever (she, on the other hand, eventually saw a reason, named Chet). I was – and remain to this day – a full-blown child of Western philosophy, intent on participating in every facet of the modern universe of discourse, no holds barred, no parameters set. I never believed Jews were any better than anybody else (now I live smack in the middle of six million of them: I can *assure* you they're not). I'm still not buying a whole heck of a lot of what organized religion is selling, and probably never will. My personal nature is such that prescriptions and proscriptions and regulations and restraints – in short, any system or institution that aspires to tell me what to do – immediately sends me fleeing for the hills, the better to organize active rebellion.

None of the above circumstances, convictions or character traits would appear at first glance to make living a full, fervent Jewish life a sensible option, let alone an attractive one, for your humble servant here. And I presume I'm not the only one in that boat.

Nor has my confusion on this score left me since moving to Israel in 1992. Several weeks ago some pals and I were patrolling the Syrian border at three-thirty in the morning (really). I was intensely exhausted, and kept nodding off and banging my chin on the safety switch of this automatic weapon comparable in size and firepower to the Guns of Navarone. Not happy with this situation, I forced our driver off the road – by repeatedly slamming my rifle butt into the back of his helmet – so that we could finally have some coffee. As I stood there, for maybe the fifteenth night in a row, bushed beyond belief, freezing my family jewels off, feeling achy and unshowered and not a little bit exposed, and marshaling the courage to quaff this ipecac-like mixture of offal and lukewarm water that the Israelis themselves refer to as "mud," I conjured up in my mind the two activities in which I had generally been engaged at this hour of the night during the overwhelming majority of my Diaspora existence: (1) ***shluffing* soundly** under my extra-fluffy, one hundred percent bona fide down quilt with the pictures of Rocky and Bullwinkle all over it; or, alternately, (2) **at Denny's**, after a full night of furious and paroxysmal partying, wolfing down some delectable pancakes with an equally scrumptious side of bacon. Let me confess to you that at that moment, right there on the threshold of a Golan Heights minefield (where there are no pancakes, let alone bacon), I rained down a hailstorm of execrations, individually and collectively, on Abraham, Sarah, Isaac, Rebecca, Jacob, Leah, Rachel, Moses, King David, the Maccabees, Theodor Herzl, and everyone else and their mother who had a hand in sustaining us, keeping us in life and allowing us to reach this season.

Who needs this?!

That is the question. Why be a Jew, a committed Jew, an involved Jew, today, under current circumstances, even if it doesn't mean trudging through northern Israel in the middle of a frigid fall night? Why bother? Everything logical, indeed, every major ideology comprising the modern, Western world-view, would appear to be solidly stacked against such a foolhardy stance. Hell, *inertia itself* is beating us, with both hands tied behind its back: like their gentile counterparts, most Jewish young people of this relatively placid and malleable generation (the sixties it ain't) are more-or-less going with the increasingly coordinated and egregiously conformist global flow, streaming away from everything the Jewish People once were, away from everything we could yet be together. Now that just darkens my eyes and blackens my soul, and I won't stand for it. So what comes now is basically me throwing everything I've got into one mighty attempt to convince you…

…to be a salmon.

One last point before we embark. Some readers may be waiting for me to lower the boom, so they can close up shop and get back to the Dodgers game. So let me reassure you at least about this much. I am not going to advocate that we stay Jewish because Doron's dispensationalist vision of a new world order where there is no hatred of Jews or anybody else is pure Hindu hallucination, whereas in reality anti-Semitism will always force us to stick together in the defensive formation of a persecuted clan. This may very well be the case – it has been more often than not in the past – but as a *raison d'être*, this particular claim has never been enough to get my personal motor running. *I am not now and never will be a Jew and a Zionist out of fear, or because I have no choice.* Screw that.

Here's what else I am not going to do. I am not going to reveal to you for the first time how if you read the last six odd-numbered verses of the tenth chapter of the biblical book of Deuteronomy backwards and diagonally, while simultaneously skipping over all personal pronouns and omitting every third, fifth and twenty-seventh bilabial plosive, it will spell out: "Read Ze'ev Maghen's book and send him a generous donation" (i.e., no "Bible codes," I promise). No exposés on how Darwin was strung out on methadone when he wrote *Origin of the Species*, no Genesis-Big Bang bull, no impartial studies on how keeping kosher increases your sexual potency and effectively prevents colon cancer, no portrayals of Semitic religion as the true font of feminism, or the real source of science, or any other such puerile bunk currently and for some time now making the rounds. What I have to say – and the manner in which I say it – might very well offend a broad assortment of readers in a wide variety of ways (you may have already noticed this). But there's one thing I promise not to insult: your intelligence.

(Finally, at this juncture I guess I should also point out that we will not be discussing the politics of the Middle East. If what turns you on is simplistic propaganda about why Israel is always right – or always wrong – there is certainly no dearth of this to be had in your general vicinity. Seek and ye shall find.)

What I *am* going to do is just spend a little time here thinking out loud, struggling with what I personally see as some of the most important issues of our time (and by no means solely for Jews), and I'd be honored if you'd tag along for a bit and struggle together with me. I'll throw some raw thoughts on the table, and you slice 'em and dice 'em like a Benihana chef (this restaurant alone is an excellent argument against Judaism). I propose to follow a "divide and conquer" format: although the several claims of Shira, Ofer and Doron – our three Hare Krishnas from LAX – are nothing if not related, we'll try and tackle them one by one.

Ladies first…

Shira
The Challenge of Universalism

"We're not choosing one book over another, or one religion over another, we're not expressing a preference for a particular culture, nation or ethnic or social group over another. That would mean creating *hierarchical relationships* between human beings. That would mean erecting *false barriers* between people, barriers that have been responsible for so much misery and bloodshed throughout history, barriers that have prevented human beings from reaching their true potential and destiny, from achieving inner peace – and *world* peace. You and I, my friend, and everyone else in this airport, and everything that lives and breathes in every corner of this vast planet of ours, we are all of us part of a great and wonderful unity, we are all brothers and sisters, we are all linked by the same network of indissoluble bonds – we just don't *know* it yet. Krishna consciousness is about spreading that knowledge."

Chapter Three

I was in junior high school when John Lennon died, and I was an absolute wreck. I grew up on my Mom's old Beatles albums, and by the time I reached adolescence, my personal classification system went, in ascending order: Billy Joel – John Lennon – God. So after that fruitcake son-of-a-bitch emptied his revolver into this consummate musician's chest on the corner of Seventy-Second and Central Park West on December 8th, 1980, I wore black to school for a month. I traveled all the way to New York and waved a candle till my arm fell off and sang "All we are saying, is give peace a chance" so many times that it really was *all* I was saying. Meanwhile, back home, I was suspended by the principal due to an unrelated bum-rap (it was Aaron Mittleman, not me, who locked our French teacher in the closet and evacuated the class), and so was conveniently able to initiate "Stay in Bed and Grow Your Hair" week – soon joined, to the principal's (and my mother's) chagrin, by some fifteen classmates – at my house in John's honor. Hell, I even went out and spent good allowance money on two Yoko albums, where she intermittently shrieks and imitates whale sounds for some eighty-five minutes straight. Now *that's* a true fan.

I tell you all this in order to establish my credentials as a veteran, fanatic and peerlessly loyal Lennon lover – because now I'm going to kill him all over again.

John was at his best as a team player, but there's no question that his preeminent *pièce de résistance*, the composition that will be forever and for all time immediately associated with his name, is "Imagine." And justifiably so: I don't care what the idiot editors of Rolling Stone think, it's a great song. Gives me gargantuan goosebumps from the first introductory adagio. The man was a genius, and this was his masterpiece. Even the words themselves are enough to make you weak in the knees:

Imagine there's no heaven
It's easy if you try
No hell below us
Above us only sky
Imagine all the people
Living for today…

Imagine there's no countries
It isn't hard to do
Nothing to kill or die for
And no religion too
Imagine all the people
Living life in peace…

You may say that I'm a dreamer
But I'm not the only one
I hope someday you'll join us
And the world will live as one…

(Tell me you didn't at least hum the melody while you were reading just now. If not, you're a freak.)

Those words, those words! They're so beautiful, so encompassing, so *right*. We agree with them viscerally, adopt them instinctively. They strike some of our deepest, most primal chords, they produce a kind of nebulous but heartfelt longing, a yearning for something better, for something perfect, something beautiful. Everything we've been taught – indeed, a decent amount of what we human beings are made of – is passionately stirred by the simple yet profoundly compelling message of John's ingenuous poetry (actually, the words were originally inspired by Yoko's verse, if you can believe *that*).

I know what you're thinking. You're thinking: "Oh, how predictable! Now this guy's gonna explain how 'Imagine' is just a pipe-dream, an unfeasible, quixotic, idyllic fantasy that's nice to sing about but has no place in our individual or collective practical planning for the future." Well, if that's what you think I'm up to…you're *dead* wrong. (If you read carefully before, you know that I've already obligated myself specifically to avoid this type of argument.)

I'm not ashamed to admit that I'm as big a dreamer as the lanky Liverpudlian himself, and when people tell me – as they constantly do, with that smug, paternalistic, ever-so-pragmatic look disfiguring their faces – that a particular unprecedented scheme or a given bold and meritorious undertaking is "unrealistic," my first instinct is generally to murder and disembowel them right then and there and leave their gutted corpses to be devoured by the birds of the air and the beasts of the field. I hate cynics.

I am not, then, challenging the wisdom of John's enterprise because I think it has no chance of succeeding – fact is, many aspects of his vision are coming truer every day. If I believed in his goal, if I genuinely desired that it be realized speedily and in our days, I would join up regardless. I'd volunteer to be his Sancho Panza, and sally forth in an unrelenting struggle against all odds toward our common objective, with all my heart, with all my soul and with all my might.

But I *don't* want John's vision to be fulfilled speedily and in our days. I don't want it to be fulfilled…*ever*. My objection to his program is not that it is overly idealistic – but rather that *there is nothing at all ideal about it*. Because John's beautiful ballad is in reality a death-march, a requiem mass for the human race. His seemingly lovely lyrics constitute in truth the single most hideous and unfortunate combination of syllables ever to be put to music. The realization of his dream – even in large part – would inevitably entail the wholesale destruction of the dreams, hopes, happinesses and *very reason for living* of yourself and every single person you know. If we – who have for so long unthinkingly admired and warbled-off Lennon's words – were to live to see his wish come true, the result would be more staggeringly horrific and more devastatingly ruinous than you or I could ever possibly…

…imagine.

(I know what you're thinking again. You're thinking: Yikes! This guy's one of them totally whacked-out, hillbilly militia types from the Mid-West who don't pay their taxes and who spend all day stockpiling high-powered rifles and fuel-air explosives in preparation for Armageddon. Listen – calm down, would you? I don't *really* mean to say that "Imagine" adumbrates the Apocalypse or that John Lennon is the Anti-Christ. It's just a device, OK? Cut me some literary slack.)

Many readers may be way ahead of me at this point. They may very well have long ago developed their own set of reasons why the ideal world sought by John Lennon – and Shira, and Ofer, and Doron and so many others like them – is in reality about as far from beautiful and wonderful as one can possibly get. Permit me, nevertheless, briefly to share with you my own take on this exceedingly crucial matter.

Chapter Four

Why do you get up in the morning?

No, really. Please stop and think very seriously for a moment about this matchlessly significant and yet for some reason rarely broached question. What is the juice that gets you going every day? What motivates you to pursue…anything? Why, ultimately, do you do…pretty much *everything* you do? What are you really looking for? What have you *always* really been looking for – just between you, me and the page?

What is the end goal – direct or indirect – of the vast majority of your activities in life? What is the one thing you need more than anything else, the one thing you just couldn't live without, the one thing you probably wouldn't want to live without? Come on: think! What is it? What do you *live* for? What do you work for? What would you *die* for? In the immortal words of the Spice Girls: Tell me what you want, what you *really*, *really* want…

(Pause to permit some expeditious introspection)

OK, I'll give you a hint: it's not any of the basic necessities – food, shelter, clothing, Hewlett-Packard Office-Jet-Pro 8600 multi-function scanner-printer-copier-fax – you already have these. Know how I know? Because you wouldn't be reading this if you didn't. You'd be out somewhere purloining bread like Jean Valjean in *Les Miserables*.

You think maybe it's your *health*? Look, I know that when two old Jewish men pass each other in the locker room on their way to or from the *schvitz*, it's a biblical precept that at least one of them has to rasp, "If you don't have your health, you don't have *nothing*." Granted. God willing the reader and her/his entire family and friends will always remain in the best of health (A-*men*!). But we don't live *for* our health, now do we? Our health is only one of those prerequisites which allow us to pursue our *real* desires in life. So, once again: What is it, that deepest, most powerful, most genuine desire of ours? *What are you seeking*??

"**Success**," you say. OK, what on earth is *that*? How do you define "success"? Of what elements is it comprised, and which is its most important and *indispensable* component part?

"**Fulfillment**." Oh, come on, enough with the word games. The same questions apply here as directly above. I'm talking about something *real*, something you can put your finger on, something you can sink your teeth into, something you crave and need and would be willing to do almost *anything* for. I'm talking about the single most important human motivation there is, and you're beating around the bush.

"OK, OK – ***Happiness***!" Oh, man: now you're *really* trying my patience. You've managed once again to beg the question: what, *what*, ***what is it***, more than anything else, that *makes you happy*?! The answer is so simple, so obvious, so clear. It's on the tip of your tongue!

All-right, here's the final clue, a Beatles clue: All you need is…

Shira: The Challenge of Universalism

LO VE

That's right, dear reader. You already knew this. And if you think it is a cliché, then it is the single most powerful cliché ever known to humankind, the one that pervades our thoughts, directs our actions, makes us move, runs our lives. *We live for love.* Love of parents, love of children, love of husband, love of wife, love of sisters, love of brothers, love of girlfriend, love of boyfriend, love of family, love of friends. *That's* what we want and need most of all, and such a vast percentage of the things we do throughout our entire lives is ultimately geared toward achieving, maintaining and increasing that one incomparably precious treasure: *love.*

Sure, there are other objectives and experiences we may strive to attain – the fascination of scholarship, the rush of artistic creation or scientific discovery, the thrill of the fight or the game, the various hedonistic pleasures – but tell me you wouldn't give up any of these before you'd give up love, tell me you wouldn't give up the entire kit-and-kaboodle of them *for the sake* of love, and I'll say it again: you're a freak. Without love (to enlist the Doobie Brothers) – *where would you be now*?

Ok, so we're agreed: no one with a brain bigger than a quark will deny that love is at least *one of* the primary motivating factors informing human endeavor.

So let's just talk a little bit about love, shall we?

Chapter Five

They asked Jesus and Rabbi Akiba – on different occasions (they lived almost a hundred years apart) – what their all-time favorite verse was in the entire Bible. And do you know what? Damned if they didn't both pick the same one: *Veahavta lere'akha kamokha* – "Love your neighbor as yourself" (Leviticus, 19:18).*

Terrific.

Now there is this fairly famous anecdote in the Talmud (Baba Metziah, 62a), which describes the following situation: you and this other chap are out for a stroll in the desert. While you are both busy admiring the various lizard species and rock formations in the vicinity, *he* suddenly exclaims: "#@$%&!!! I forgot my friggin' *canteen*!"

You quickly assess your options. One thing is for sure: there is only enough water in *your* canteen for *one* human being to make it back to civilization alive (and no, you do not have your cell-phone). You could split the water – and you'd both perish. You could give your flask altruistically to your fellow-traveler, and die a hideous death

* Jesus chose in Matthew 19:19, Mark 12:31, and Luke 10:27; Rabbi Akiba in Sifra Kedoshim 2:4 and Genesis Rabbah 24:7.

under the merciless, take-no-prisoners, desert sun. Or you could keep the canteen for yourself, and abandon your pal to the same fate (this is a slightly tougher decision than what shoes to wear to work in the morning). What do you do? *What do you do*?

Two opinions – two legal rulings – are recorded in the Talmud regarding this matter. One of them comes straight from the mouth of the aforementioned Rabbi Akiba. The other one emanates from an individual with a very strange name, who is never mentioned anywhere else in rabbinic literature: Ben-Petura. Now, I don't want to go into all the speculative etymology (Ben-Petura→Ben-Pantura→ Ben-Pandera: the fickle letter "nun" creeps in, the interchangeable "t"s and "d"s switch off, and we have the common, rather derogatory talmudic appellation for Jesus);[†] but it is at least possible that the second jurisprudent whose expertise is consulted in this passage is none other than the Christian Savior himself. We'll never know for sure whether this is so, and it doesn't really matter for our purposes today. I am only interested in utilizing this dichotomy of views as a paradigm, and the two men who espouse them as archetypes. So let's assume, for the moment, that Ben Petura is in fact Jesus – if he isn't, he's sure read a lot of the Nazarene's sermons, as we shall soon see.

Let's go back to the desert. The scorching rays of the noon-day sun are cauterizing your corpuscles, your throat is so dry you could bake a matzah in it, and you have quite a decision to make. Fast. Ben-Petura/Jesus advises you as follows: *share* the water – and die together – because you are no better than your friend. Rabbi Akiba rules differently: *you take the flask*.

Now, this is strange, because – if you will recall – both rabbis (Jesus and Akiba) chose "Love your neighbor as yourself" as their all-time favorite Torah verse. Well, what in the name of Jehoshaphat is going on here? I understand Jesus' position – his position is entirely consistent with genuinely loving your neighbor *as much* as you love yourself, which certainly appears to be exactly what the biblical commandment requires. Jesus' verdict makes perfect sense in this light.

† It might mean "Son of a Centurion."

But Rabbi Akiba? What was *he* thinking, for Chrissake?! (Sorry.) Did he *forget* that he had once put the very same verse way up high on a pedestal as "the preeminent principle of the Torah"? Had he lost his *marbles* by the time he issued the judgment in question – keep the canteen, share none of its contents, leave your buddy to expire miserably in the desert like a dog – which seems to contradict everything that that hallowed pentateuchal principle of mutual, *equal* love demands?

I don't think so. What we have here is a clear-cut case of diametrically opposed interpretations of scriptural intention (a common enough phenomenon in our sources). Jesus understands the Levitical injunction to "love your neighbor as yourself" just exactly the way it sounds (*peshuto kemashma'o*, as we say in the holy tongue). We would know this even without the whole speculative business about his possible Ben-Petura alias. Because you see, the entire New Testament is simply *riddled* with examples that leave not even a shadow of a doubt that the ideal in Jesus' – and eventually in Christianity's – eyes is at least to strive to *love all human beings equally*, granting no special, nepotistic privileges to anyone.

One day Jesus was in the middle of preaching to the multitudes – as was his wont – when all of a sudden (every Jewish kid's nightmare) his Mom showed up:

> Then it was told unto him: "Behold, thy mother and thy brothers stand outside, and they desire to speak with thee." But he answered and said unto him that delivered the message: "Who is my mother? And who are my brothers?" And he stretched forth his hand toward his disciples, and said: "Behold, *these* are my mother and my brothers!" (Matthew 12:46-49)

This and more: Jesus wanted to leave no room for misunderstanding in this matter, and turned the prophet Micah's worst case scenario – "Son spurns father, daughter rebels against mother and daughter-in-law against mother-in-law" (Micah 7:6) – into a messianic ideal: "I am come to set a man at variance against his father, and the daughter against her mother, and the daughter-in-law against her mother-in-law" (Matthew 10:34-5).

In the Old Testament, when Elisha, running after the Prophet Elijah, asks permission to "go kiss my father and mother goodbye, and then I will return and follow you," Elijah replies, "Go back!" and waits for him there (1 Kings 19:20). In what is obviously deliberate contradistinction, we read in the New Testament:

> Jesus said to another man, "Follow me." The man replied, "Lord, first let me go and bury my father." Jesus said to him, "Let the dead bury their own dead, but you come and proclaim the Kingdom of God!" Still another man said, "I will follow you, Lord; but first let me go back and say good-bye to my family." Jesus replied: "No-one who puts his hand to the plough and looks back, is fit for service in the Kingdom of God." (Luke 9:59-62)

And in case it has yet to sink in: "If any man come to me, and hate not his father, and mother, and wife, and children, and sisters, yea, and his own life also, he cannot be my disciple" (Luke 14:26).

We have not quoted verses out of context here. Christianity is a system concerned with belief, with faith, and as such it recognizes no separate national entities ("there is neither Jew nor Greek...for ye are all one in Christ Jesus"; Galatians 3:28), no tribal affiliations, not even – in the last analysis – the significance of blood kinship:

> "I tell you the truth," Jesus said to them, "no one who has left home or wife or brothers or parents or children for the sake of the Kingdom of God will fail to receive many times as much reward in this world – and in the world to come, eternal life!" (Luke 18:29-30)

> "Anyone who loves his father and mother more than me, is not worthy of me; anyone who loves his son or daughter more than me, is not worthy of me." (Matthew 10:37)

Neither exclusive familial solidarity nor distinctive national identity is Jesus' bag. Christianity is, at least theoretically speaking, the world's largest Equal Opportunity Employer, viewing as it does, without the slightest hint of bias or prejudice, all human beings as similarly deserving (more accurately: similarly *un*deserving) potential recipients of divine – and human – affection. Christian love is neither *eros* nor *amour*, but what the Church Fathers liked to call *agape*: unselfish devotion that discriminates against no one, an ardor dispensed in equal measure to all. Christianity is a thoroughly universalist – and at the same time a thoroughly individualist – religious path and creed, and Jesus of Nazareth was without doubt the foremost prophet of universal love (although nowhere *near* the only one).

OK, that's settled. Now, let's get married. Uh-huh, right this minute – you and me. I'm your beau of the ball, we've been having the most *awesome* time getting to know each other for months, and I just can't wait another second. It's time to propose. Down I go on one knee. I look dreamily up into your eyes. I reach deftly into the pocket of my Giorgio Armani blazer and pull out a rock the size of Venus. I take your two hands in mine, and, gently caressing them, I coo: "My darling, I love you. I love you *soooooo* much. I love you as much as I love...as much as I love...as much as I love that *other* woman, the one walking down the street over there. See her? Oh, and *that* one, too, riding her bicycle past the newspaper stand. I love you *exactly* as much as I love all my previous girlfriends, as well, and I love you as much as all the girls who *weren't* ever my girlfriends. I love you as much as I love *everybody else* on this planet, and for that matter, I love you as much as I love the animals, too, and the weeds, and the plankton and – Oh, *God*!! What's that searing, indescribable pain in my groin?! Hey, where are you going, my *daaaaarliiiiing*?!"

No one gets turned-on by "universal" love. It doesn't get you up in the morning, it doesn't give you goose-bumps or make you feel all warm and tingly inside, it doesn't send you traipsing through copses picking wild-flowers and singing songs about birds, it doesn't provoke heroism, or sacrifice, or creativity, or loyalty, or anything. In short, "universal love" isn't love at all.

Because love means preference. The kind of love that means anything, the kind of love that we all really want and need and live for, the kind of love that is *worth* anything to anyone – that is worth *every*thing to *every*one – is love that by its very nature, by its very definition, distinguishes and prefers. Show me a guy who tells you that he loves your kids as much as he loves his own, and I'll show you someone who *should never and under no circumstances be your babysitter*. Get this straight: he who claims or aspires to love everybody the same – simply has no idea what love means! Stay *away* from such people. Head for the hills! Whoever tells you to love all people equally – and s/he may be entirely unaware of this, and should therefore be enlightened as rapidly as possible – is really advocating *the removal of all love worthy of the name from the face of the planet.*

Sigmund Freud had a few choice words to say on this subject. True, he was evidently out performing sexual experiments on classmates during most of his Hebrew school career, because he states of the specific verse currently under our microscope ("Love your neighbor as yourself") that "it is known throughout the world and is *undoubtedly older than Christianity* [!] which puts it forward as its proudest claim" (*Civilization and Its Discontents*, p. 56). Still, somehow the Jew in Freud managed to retain a healthy aversion to the New Testament's universalist take on this eminently pentateuchal precept:

> If someone is a stranger to me, and if he cannot attract me by any worth of his own or any significance that he may have already acquired for my emotional life, it will be hard for me to love him. Indeed, I should be wrong to do so, for my love is valued by all my own people as a sign of my *preferring* them, and it is an injustice to them if I put a stranger on a par with them. But if I am to love him with this universal love merely because he, too, is an inhabitant of this earth, like an insect, an earth-worm or a grass-snake, then I fear that only a small modicum of my love will fall to his share… (p. 56)

Rabbi Akiba – and most of Judaism along with him – views this whole matter a bit differently than Peter, Paul, Mary, John, George, Ringo and Jesus. The kind of love (romantic or platonic or otherwise) that Akiba unabashedly recognizes and unreservedly encourages, is one-hundred percent biased, hopelessly *un*equal, deeply discriminatory, and incorrigibly preferential *distinguishing* love: the kind of love that plays favorites, that chooses sides, the kind of love that confers *specialness*. As a Jewish luminary, Rabbi Akiba only understood the type of love that blossoms forth from the ubiquitous Hebrew root *k.d.sh.*, which is probably most accurately rendered into English as "to declare special," or "to set apart as unique." (Thus Leviticus 11:44 – "Ye shall be *kedoshim*, for I [the Lord] am *kadosh*" – is explicated by the rabbis: "Just as I am set apart [*parush*] be ye set apart.")

When a Jewish man marries a Jewish woman, the institution is called *kiddushin*, because they *set one another apart* from the rest of humanity, because they (ideally) love each other *more* than they love anybody else (this is a far cry from the fully internally consistent Pauline-Christian attitude to marriage, which may be summed up as: "try your best to avoid it" – see Matt. 19:11 and 1 Cor. 7:1, 28 and 38). When Jews bless the wine on a Friday night, this is called *kiddush*, because we are setting apart, we are distinguishing the Sabbath day from what surrounds it and saying: I love this day *more* than any other day of the week. When Jews do that weird, Wizard-of-Oz, "there's no place like home" thing three times with their heels in the synagogue and declaim the words *kadosh, kadosh, kadosh*, this means, essentially: "Who is like unto You among the gods, O Lord?" (Exodus 15:11). We single You out. We love You best.

This is not a Jewish secret. It's a human secret. It's the way we all work, all of us, deep down inside. We all love preferentially, and that's the only kind of love we value, the only kind of love we want back from the people we love. Last week I opened my mailbox to find a card, upon which were scrawled the handwritten words: "Came by to see your smiling face and make you an offer you couldn't refuse – but alas! You weren't at home." The note was signed with a heart. I confess that my own heart started beating a bit fast (wouldn't yours?) until, that is, my neighbor happened along and opened *his* mailbox... only to pull out the self-same little missive! The handwriting, you see, was really print, and when you turned the card over you discovered that the "offer you couldn't refuse" was from a cellular phone company. My enthusiasm, needless to say, was dampened. "I wanna be loved by you," as Ginger used to sing on Gilligan's island, "*alo-o-one.*" Boop-boop-be-doop.

We all know instinctively that "Love Inflation" leads to "Love Devaluation," and ultimately, to a devastating "Love Market Crash." All those perpetually smiling, lovey-dovey, touchy-feely, swami types who appear at first glance to be all about love – and nothing else but love – of every single thing that lives and breathes, *are in reality all about stealing this absolutely essential human emotion away from you* (they've already lost it themselves). It is no coincidence that the first and most indispensable step one takes in order successfully to "deprogram" a Hare Krishna (or member of any other cult), is to rekindle his *particular* love for a *particular* someone who was once very special to him.

And all this means something else that everybody already knows, but is for a variety of reasons only occasionally acknowledged: because love is such a major deal in all of our existences, and because the love we're talking about is invariably distinguishing and preferential in nature, *human beings will ever and anon, at all places and all times, prefer hanging out in the company of some people over hanging out in the company of others.* They will always form special groups, little groups and big groups, groups to which they feel a special connection, a special sense of belonging. They will always relate emotionally to these associations in the manner of concentric circles, loving the nearer rings more than they love the farther ones. They will always seek to perpetuate these familial, socio-cultural and even national entities for as long as they can. And they will always *distinguish* between their own special circles, and those which are special not to them – but to others.

Is this because human beings are selfish, small-minded, visionless creatures who can't appreciate the lustrous loveliness and messianic morality of universal oneness? *No*. It is because they are (thank God) supremely and congenitally motivated by preferential love, and special communities of this sort are the inexorable consequence and highest, most beautiful expression of such love. It is because loving in this way is the bread-and-butter of authentic human happiness.

It is because if they *didn't* love in this way, human beings would have absolutely nothing left to live for. *Nothing*. This, to my mind, is the underlying meaning of the well-known talmudic determination: "*O khevruta, o mituta*" (loosely: Give me society, or give me death!) (Ta'anit 23a). Either you have around you a particular group of people that you *especially* love – a "*khevreh*," as modern Hebrew slang has it – or you might as well be dead.

Jesus knew this; he knew it full well. That is why he continually emphasized that "My kingdom is not of this earth." He didn't plan to – or he soon became aware that he was entirely unable to – bring about the establishment of "universal love" here in the mundane sphere. It just wouldn't work. Perhaps he even came to believe it *shouldn't* work. So he transferred it to the "Kingdom of Heaven." That is ultimately the reason why he departed (as I imagine most Christian theologians would agree). That is also where the encouragement of life-long celibacy comes in: after all, what would become of "this world" were *that* ideal ever to be attained? And this is the reason, too, why there is no parallel in Christianity to Judaism's six hundred thirteen commandments and their tens of thousands of derivatives, which are all about how to live and act and get along right down here in *this* world: Jesus relegated unto *Caesar* most things terrestrial. Early Christianity, at least, was not interested in creating a system designed for living and loving in this world. It was interested in ushering in the *next* one.

Do you know who nearly managed to pull off John Lennon's vision of no religions, no nations, no countries, *one world – right here on earth*? Do you know who almost succeeded – even if only within relative geographic and demographic microcosms – in bringing about that beautiful dream of universal love, no barriers, no walls, and no special or distinct human cliques or clans? How about these fine-feathered fellows: *Stalin*, *Mao*, *Pol Pot*. Any of *these* iron-fisted Eden makers ring a bell? Because the only way to stop people from loving preferentially and start them loving universally, is to take a page from the book of Mo Tzu – the famous ancient Chinese champion of anti-particularism – who neither hemmed nor hawed: "People must be awed into universal love through punishments and fines," he explained.

The only way to see to it that human beings do not divide up – as all people who love even a little naturally do – into distinct socio-cultural and political communities and associations, is by *forcibly ensuring that they all dress, eat, sleep, talk, sing, dance, work, play and think the same* – and killing them if they diverge. There's your "One World," John, with all the divisions and barriers erased, there's Ofer and Doron and Shira's magnificent, imploding, united Utopia, where "all hearts are as one heart, all minds are as one mind, so that through the spirit of oneness you may heal the sickness of a divided humanity."

Feast your eyes.

Chapter Six

My grandfather on my father's side was an Iranian Jew from a little town about a hundred and fifty miles south of Tehran, called Kashan. He told me this story. Once, in the time of *his* grandfather's grandfather, a Jewish merchant from Kashan allegedly overcharged a local Muslim man of the cloth (oh, believe me: he *did* it). This complacent clergyman metamorphosed overnight into the Mad Mullah, and swore upon the Holy Qur'an that he'd have his revenge, and then some. He quickly assembled and whipped into a religious frenzy all the be-turbaned ayatollahs in the entire province, and together they proceeded to the palace of the *qaim-maqam*, the regional governor. By hook or by crook they managed to prevail upon him to issue an edict requiring the conversion of every single Jewish man, woman and child to Islam by such-and-such a date, upon pain of death.

Well, the appointed deadline was fast approaching, and the Jewish community of Kashan province was in an absolute tizzy. What to do? With two weeks left, the various elders finally buried their long-standing differences, and held a solemn conference at the house of Kashan's Chief Rabbi. Prayers were offered, psalms were intoned, supplications were...supplicated. But nobody really had any suggestions worth considering. It was agreed by all present that a delegation should be sent to the governor, but no one could figure out exactly what they should say to him. The meeting was about to break up, when the Rabbi's wife – who had, of course, been bringing in round after round of sweet, samovar-seethed tea for the assembled guests – dared to address the company she had been so dutifully serving. "You leave it to me and my sisters," she enjoined confidently. "Just come back when it's time to go to the governor."

Iranian families are *big*, and soon the sound of weaving looms hard at work could be heard not just at the Rabbi's house, but in most of the courtyards surrounding it. The seven sisters worked like devils through day and night, scarcely pausing to rest, and when the elders returned one week later – on their way to petition the governor to rescind the evil decree – the Rabbi's wife laid two enormous rolled-up Persian rugs, made of the finest Kashan silk, at their feet. "Now, when you are received in audience by the governor, here's what you will do…" she explained.

A few days later the delegation of venerable, white-bearded old men – weary from their long trek through the desert on camel and donkey back – stood trembling like leaves in front of His Excellency's august presence. "You have wasted your time in traveling all the way here," he chided them, right off the bat. "There is nothing that will make me change my mind. You will all be good Muslims in time for next Friday's public prayers in the Mosque. Nevertheless, since you have come all this way, I will go through the motions of entertaining your petition. Well, what have you to say?"

The elders approached the governor's divan and bowed down to the ground. "Your Honor, before presenting our poor petition to the dust beneath the soles of your worshipful feet, we have made so bold as to bring you an unworthy gift, as a meager token of our gratitude for these many long years during which we have been privileged to live quietly and obediently under your powerful protection."

The governor liked gifts. Especially the kind one received from large delegations of rich and frightened Jewish merchants. "Enough of your pathetic truckling," said he. "What have you brought me?" The elders immediately had both of the carpets brought in and unraveled on the marble floor at the ruler's feet. "On behalf of the Jewish community of Kashan province, we beg leave to place these two humble offerings before His Excellency, and request that He choose *one* of them as our tribute."

Both carpets were broad, plush, tightly woven, and made out of the most exquisite material. The first one was covered with colorful curving calyxes in shades of gold and green and turquoise, intricately intertwined with whirling waves of purple petunias that spiraled centripetally towards the median. Splendid silhouettes of every size, shape and hue graced the corners, like an ornamental garnish surrounding a magnificent main course. The vast center was an alternately placid and surging sea of breathtaking royal blue, periodically punctuated by a cornucopia of gemlike little islands of the most elegant design, each embroidered in a different form and color and bordered by hundreds of finely interlaced, snow-white cilia, swimming softly in decorous understatement.

The second carpet was...........red.

That's all it was. The whole rug was just one sprawling, solid red mat, from warp to woof, from end to end. "What?!" cried the governor. "How dare you?! I should have you all *decapitated* for such insolence! Do you take me for a fool? What kind of choice is this? Who in their right mind would *not* choose the first carpet – and who in full possession of his faculties *would* choose the second?!"

The hoariest head of the Jewish delegation stepped forward from amongst his peers, and looked the governor straight in the eye. "The silk rugs, my Liege, are the territories under your benevolent sway – Kashan province. Today that province is filled with peoples of every imaginable culture and creed – Muslims, Christians, Zoroastrians, Manicheans, Azeris, Mandeans, Turkmen, Jews – and in this way it resembles the first carpet. Would Your Excellency, then, exchange the first carpet for the second?"

("This gimmick," concluded my grandfather with a twinkle in his eye, "plus about one hundred and seventy five thousand gold *tomans* placed discreetly in the governor's coffers, managed to avert the evil decree.")

You know I have to ask: which rug do *you* want? Which *world* do you want? The world of "Imagine," where nothing of any significance separates us, where there are "no countries and no religions," and where everybody is concomitantly possessed of the same tastes, the same loves, the same mind? The chiliastic BORGian paradise of Shira, Ofer and Doron, where all human beings blend into one-another like some kind of massive, flavorless, mud-colored milkshake?

Or wouldn't you rather live in the *diametric opposite* of these worlds? Wouldn't you rather live in a world of dazzling diversity, of independent and self-respecting societies and communities that value, retain and revel in their own uniqueness? Wouldn't you rather live in a world where *real* people unapologetically express *real* preferences for the company and society of *particular* persons with whom they have special cultural, historical and emotional bonds?

Oh, *please* stop striving so hard to be the same, in the name of all that's dear and meaningful! Please cease and desist "ever searching for the One" (you guessed it: the Spice Girls again). You'll never get there, of course, but you'll destroy so incredibly much of what makes life interesting and mysterious and exciting and beautiful along the way. Read up on your biology: it is *mitosis* which is the engine of creation, it is the proliferation of internal *heterogeneity* which is the substance and process of human life – of *all* life. It is increasing *diversity* which is the hallmark of growth, of evolution, of progress – not approaching ever nearer to the great, all-encompassing One, but rather…*fleeing it headlong like the plague.*

Move over to your psychology notes, and peruse your Piaget. This famous Swiss shrimp-shrink explained time and again how the deepening ability to distinguish between the self and others – and between others and others – is the most powerful indicant of infant maturation. In this manner, declared he, we go forward step by step, distancing ourselves further each day from our original, *non*-distinguishing, fetal disposition (called "indissociation" in his nomenclature), that all-engulfing oneness experienced by newborns that Freud dubbed "Ocean Consciousness."

So what is it? Is *regression* your bag? Is life so bad and growth so scary that you want to turn around one-hundred-eighty degrees and head right back where you came from? (That's it: go to your womb!)

Divided we stand, my friends – *united we fall.*

Chapter Seven

"Ok," you say, "I get the point. But it isn't exactly a *new* point, now is it? You're simply preaching 'multiculturalism,' that's all. A day doesn't go by when I don't have *that* concept shoved in my face! And truth be told, I pretty much support it." Good. So do I – with all my heart. And I think you will agree, that in order to promote and maintain authentic, polychromatic, humanity-enriching multi-culturalism, it goes without saying that we simply *have* to preserve and cultivate *multiple, coherent and distinctive cultures* the world over. There's only one thing that the vast majority of young, fiery, and so very often Jewish advocates of the modern multicultural approach almost *always* seem to forget: that one of the foremost examples of such cultures *is their own.*

For heaven's sake, what kind of sense does it make when Jewish-born intellectuals espouse the toleration, nay, the *celebration* of the "international cultural mosaic," while at the same time ignoring and neglecting almost everything remotely Mosaic? (Good one, eh?) Have they then no desire or responsibility to contribute *their own tiles* to the overall design?! Is it not astounding – along similar lines – that the same Jewish post-modernist professors who have for three decades and more now decried "Western Cultural Imperialism" of every conceivable type, are in the overwhelming majority of cases themselves the very *personification* of the unconditional surrender of what is perhaps the most ancient and enduring non-Western culture – *their own Jewishness* – at the feet of that very same "Western Cultural Imperialism"? And what is going on in the hearts and heads of Jewish students who ostensibly support constructive dialogue and illuminating interaction between different ethnic, national, cultural and religious groups – but identify only peripherally (if at all) with their own? How on earth can people be expected to tolerate, respect and eventually learn from each other's socio-cultural differences...*if they don't have any*?

The Global Village is getting me down. I buy an outrageously expensive airline ticket, board the plane in New York and squirm around uncomfortably in my seat for ten hours, the bird lands, I "deplane" (doesn't really matter where) and – lo and behold – *I'm right back where I started from*. The same English language plastered all over the storefronts, the same Calvin Klein jeans plastered on everybody's behind, the same rap music as back in the States issuing ever so rhythmically from the taxi driver's radio (even though neither he nor his passengers could ever possibly decipher a word of it – which makes them very lucky people, if you ask me). E. M. Forster lamented this eventuality way back in 1909, when it was still science fiction, in *The Machine Stops*:

> No one left home anymore, because thanks to the advance of science, the earth was alike all over. What was the good of going to Peking, when it was just like Shrewsbury? And why return to Shrewsbury, when it would all be like Peking?

When I was a kid, my parents taught me with relentless vigor to *be myself* – indeed, to be almost deliberately different from those around me, to stand out, to stand apart, to be a *non-conformist*. I guess that's why I have so much trouble understanding why so many people today are driven by this lukewarm, lemming-like, perennial search for sameness, why they wouldn't rather prefer being themselves – both individually *and* collectively.

Am I advocating that nations and cultures should insulate themselves, digging in behind an ethnocentric and xenophobic fortress and erecting all types of intellectual and ideological tariffs, the better to maintain their separate group identity, their "cultural purity"? Not on your life. *Au contraire*! I am specifically and passionately advocating that the various socio-cultural units of the world interact and share, that they challenge, stimulate, edify, surprise, enlighten, influence and *open the eyes* of one another. As Rudyard Kipling once wrote: "What do they know of England, who only England know?"

But don't you see? In order to share, you have to have *what* to share, you have to cultivate, and become knowledgeable about, and rejoice in, and build upon *your own unique, accumulated heritage*. You need to cherish and nourish specifically the *distinguishing* traits and characteristics that make you different and fascinating, and place you in possession of desirable gifts to bestow upon others – things they don't already have! (Who wants to bring home a Bruce Lee or Michael Jackson T-shirt as a souvenir from *Morocco*? And yet, these and a tassel-cap were the only three examples of Moroccan fashion memorabilia available at the Abu'l Hadi and Sons souvenir shop of Fez when I visited there not long ago.) If you grow rutabaga and I sow kumquats, we certainly have every impetus to trade with one another; if we both plant kidney beans – what's the point?

A couple of years ago, when Israel and Jordan were still semi-friendly, they used occasionally to hold these get-togethers for adolescent "scouts" of both nationalities. I remember listening to the radio after one of these events, as the returning participants from our side were interviewed. "Wow, I really learned a *lot*," repeated Sabra scout after Sabra scout. "I thought they would be all weird and – you know – *foreign*, but as it turns out…they're *just like us*! They love the Burger King Whoppers we brought 'em for lunch as much as we do – did you know that there are *fifteen* Burger Kings in Amman?! Their favorite band is U2, and so is ours, and the Number One Hero of everybody on *both* sides is Michael Jordan. So where are the gaps, where are the differences?"

Where, indeed? Would not this scouting-outing have been ten times more educational and adventurous, a hundred times more profound and eye-opening (and fun), had the Israeli kids come back *blown away* by the largely unfamiliar and hauntingly beautiful tones of the Arabic musical instruments oud and qanoun; by the strange and different dress – *jalabiyya, qalanswa, kafiyya, jilbab* – of their Semitic peers from across the river; by the strange smells and tantalizing tastes of Arab cuisine; and by the beliefs, customs and stories of Islam? Would it not have been a far more meaningful and horizon-widening contribution, had their Jordanian counterparts returned home to Amman piled high with tapes of Israeli rock and folk, enriched by stories from the Midrash and Yiddish literature, and turned on by Israeli games, dances, food and drink? Well, the scoutmasters didn't think so. Indeed, nobody thought so. It's so much easier, after all, to be a cookie-cut; so much less bother to go for the lowest common denominator. So much simpler to join the international herd.

I guess, like most people, my general ideas about "the way things should be" are to a large extent the product of my childhood – which, by the way, was idyllic (I call my Mom and tell her this every Mother's Day, and she says: "Maybe for *you*"). My suburban Philadelphia block was made up of about ten separate houses with ample space between them, all of which formed the peripheral ring around this huge, green, common lawn in the middle. The families inhabiting these houses – the Ciartes, the Fitzgeralds, the Popowitches, the Hing-Yips, the Rosenbergs, the Sanchezes – were as incurably and pridefully diverse as the architecture of the houses themselves. Visiting each other – as we often did – was a mind-expanding *tour de force*: the unexpected smells, the strange conventions, the vastly different notions of internal decor (for years I begged my parents to paint the inside of our house pink and green like the Ciartes had).

The wide, long, grassy courtyard in the center of the block was daily the scene of some of the best times we all probably ever had. There we kids would play – on top of the standard soccer, football and our own version of ultimate Frisbee – this unending variety of the wildest and weirdest games that everybody's Mom and Dad had imported from God knows where (Chun Hing-Yip taught us this game where all the kids ran and hid, and nobody looked for them. I still don't understand this game). At least three times a week in summertime, most of the families would gather together on the green for varying ethnic versions of the traditional back-yard barbecue – or at least hang out after dinner on this large conglomeration of carpets, bean-bags and lawn chairs – and the adults would talk about everything under the setting sun, sometimes arguing so loudly that we kids (in a defiant reversal of generational roles) had to ask them to please keep it down, we couldn't concentrate on the game.

Now, what if someone had taken all these families, and somehow convinced them that it was a waste of space, all these separate houses; a waste of crockery, all these diverse dishes; a waste of artistic effort, all these varying internal and external decors. Everybody should move into one big, humungous house and do all that stuff together and uniformly. Then everything would be hunky-dory – and *far* more economical – and look how much closer and more unified everybody would be!

How would you like to live in *that* house?

We need our separate houses. It's the only way we can be good neighbors. It's the only way we can avoid *butchering* each other with chain-saws and Ginsu knives in a matter of two-to-three days, tops. And it's the only way that the interaction between us – nightly on the grassy knoll, or daily in the world of work – can bear any fruit and *be any fun*. Just as you, dear reader, no doubt live your personal life within a given community *as an individual*, self-confidently sporting your own singular and special trademark qualities – so nations and ethnic groups need to actively participate in and contribute to the world order and the totality of human civilization as proud, particular, peculiar, *unique* socio-cultural entities, each boasting a brash and defiant attitude of "national individualism," each – as it were – building, decorating and living in its own distinctive cultural and political home within the overall neighborhood of nations. Here is Woodrow Wilson's simple yet crucial insight: the need for "self-determination." Here is Samuel Coleridge's "most general definition of beauty – Multeity in Unity."

"*Gotcha*!" That's you talking, a self-satisfied smirk spreading speedily across your visage. "All you've been pushing for quite a few pages now is the direct-ratio relationship between waxing heterogeneity and human progress, between expanding diversity and a life that's worth living – and now, you've thrown the loaded term "individualism" into the pot, to boot. Very well: by *your* logic, then, we should none of us affiliate with *any* association or community or nation or even family. Rather, we should focus solely on our own, independent, individual *selves* ("I, me, me, mine," as George Harrison, may he rest in peace, describes this attitude in an awesome song) – renouncing loyalty to or prejudicial affection for any one particular group – and thereby provide the world with the largest amount of variety and individualism possible! Think of it: *six billion* different and unique colors!"

Not so fast, pal. Wipe that smile off your face. This is indeed the conclusion that has been reached – consciously or unconsciously – by a great many members of what is often (correctly) referred to as "alienated" Western society. But I put it to you: this approach is not one iota different from the "universal oneness-or-bust" frenzy we've been striving to dethrone and debunk thus far. *If you love everybody you love nobody – and if you love nobody you love nobody.* It's a big circle, and you've come full 'round it. You are talking about eradicating preferential love again – or at least severely restricting its scope and outlets to yourself and perhaps a few intimate relatives and acquaintances (is that all the love you've got?). You are talking about eliminating the special community – the "*khevreh*" – which the Talmud rightly says it is not worth living without.

And consider, if you will, the humble Persian carpet from my grandfather's story: suppose the elders of Kashan had unrolled before the governor not two rugs, but three. The first of elaborate and colorful design, as described; the second, just plain red; and the third, made up of literally tens of thousands of tiny pixels and knots, each dyed with its own unique tint, and with no attempt at thematic organization or color coordination whatsoever. Do you know what *that* rug would look like? Like *drek*, that's what. It would look the way an orchestra with a hundred musicians each playing his own separate composition on his own unique instrument would sound; just as the *all-red* rug would look like the *entire* orchestra playing the *identical* melody on *one and the same* instrument would sound.

Neither full-blown universalism nor full-blown individualism makes for a beautiful or melodious world. Only that world which is based upon a structure and conception planted firmly *between* these two poles can ever be called truly beautiful.

For God's sake, *be* an individual – and an individualist! I for one certainly lay claim to such a title – with a vengeance. It is *because* I am an arrogant, uncompromising, incorrigible individualist, and I know like I know my own bed-sheets that nobody can ever take my "me-ness" away from me without a sawed-off twelve-gauge shotgun or some such – it is because of this that it never occurred to me to be afraid that I would lose myself in a crowd; and it is because of this that I am able and willing to provide myself with the incredible privilege of being an integral participant in that unparalleled, nearly impossible phenomenon...called the Jewish people.

Chapter Eight

Let's make a quick pit-stop for a few important reminders and clarifications. First off, remember: the above generalizations about the positions taken respectively by Christianity and Judaism on the issue of love of – and affiliation with – national, cultural, tribal and familial collectives, are just that: generalizations. And I have no doubt they could become the target of virulent and often justified assault, at least on some counts. Again, however, I don't think anyone knowledgeable about these issues would dare to deny that non-Jewish creeds from Bahai to Buddhism, from Islam to Secular Humanism, from Christianity to Communism, are at least far stronger supporters of universal love than Judaism ever was or ever will be. This, I think, everyone will grant. It is true if for no other reason than that none of the other faiths or doctrines mentioned above lays claim in any way to being the cultural-ideological constitution of a particular national or ethnic group. Indeed, such an imputation would be an insult and anathema to the most fundamental principles of every single one of them!

Judaism, on the other hand, makes *specifically* this claim, and the Jews have traditionally seen the Torah as their own, special, *personal* possession and guide (there are a few eschatological prognostications emanating from the mouths of the Prophets and Rabbis that might be construed as contradicting this, but even here, the daily Jewish expression of gratitude to "He who separated and distinguished us" – *HaMavdil* or *Asher Bakhar* – remains at all times the dominant motif). We Jews are and always have been not primarily adherents to a set of spiritual dogmas, but *members of an extended family*, of a nation, and of a "tribe." We have never referred to ourselves anywhere in our sources as "*Emunat Yisrael*" (the Faith of Israel) or "*Dat Yisrael*" (the Religion of Israel). Indeed, the first time the designation "*Dat*" – a non-Semitic word in fact derived from ancient Persian – was used in our connection, it came out of the mouth of none other than Haman the Wicked. Rather, we have always denoted ourselves throughout our long history by the significant cognomens "*Am Yisrael*" (the Nation of Israel), "*Klal Yisrael*" (the Totality of Israel), "*Knesset Yisrael*" (the Assembly of Israel), "*Beit Yisrael*" (the House of Israel) and "*Benei Yisrael*" (the Children of Israel). You see where the emphasis lies, right?

The point is, however, that I promised to utilize the purported positions of these various religions and ideologies regarding questions of love and oneness *solely as a paradigm* – and that, I hope you understand, is the only thing I am doing. If all the learned rabbis in the entire State of Israel were to assemble in my living room tomorrow and – prior to excoriating and excommunicating one another for various perceived heresies – prove to me chapter and verse that the attitude to love and oneness that I have ascribed above to Judaism is completely foreign to Judaism; and then a parade of padres filed past in their wake and demonstrated to my satisfaction that it is specifically *Christianity* which happens to see such issues in that way (those seeking ammunition to support such a position may apply, for example, to John 11:5 and Ephesians 5:28) – this wouldn't matter even a *smidgen* to the argument on behalf of which I am so vehemently expostulating. I would *still* advocate the particular positions I am advocating, regardless of which theology or philosophy is privileged to be used or abused as the paradigm. It is the attitude *itself* (preferential love, socio-cultural diversity) that I am pushing with all my might – *not* one religion over the others. I love and prefer my family the Jews, whether or not their "ism" or religion is "best."

Oh, and another piece of – related – business: "chosenness." The chosenness or lack thereof of the "Chosen People" has been a bone of contention between the Lord-only-knows-how-many Jewish philosophers and theologians over the past hundred years or so. I am certainly not going to try to resolve such a sticky problem here, if for no other reason than I cannot imagine where anybody gets off thinking they have enough information about the overall dynamic of the cosmos to make decisive statements about which group is "chosen" and which group is not. And frankly, I just don't give a hoot. I never got chosen first for basketball in elementary school, whereas Seth Lapidus (that bastard) invariably did. Now I'm a professor and he wraps fish.

I will venture this, however. The notion of the "Chosen People" says as much, if not more, about the Jews' conception of the Divine as it does about their conception of themselves. God it is, after all, who is purported to have done the choosing. And that's just it, you see: in the earliest Israelite literature (the Bible, the Talmud, the Midrash), the Lord above is portrayed time and time again *as a chooser*. Our sources have always presented Him as a *distinguishing* Deity. Like all lovers worthy of the name, He loves *preferentially*:

> Because He loved your forefathers, and He therefore chose their seed after them...You are a special people [*am kadosh*] to the Lord your God: the Lord has chosen you to be His own treasured people, out of all the peoples upon the face of the earth. It is not because of your numerousness that the Lord set His heart upon you and chose you – for you are the smallest of all the nations. Rather, it is because of His love [*ahava*] of you, and His fulfillment of the oath He made to your forefathers. (Deuteronomy 4:37-7:8)

> You shall be unique [*kadosh*] unto Me – for I, the Lord, am unique; and I have set you apart [*va-avdil etkhem*] from all the peoples, that you should be Mine. (Leviticus 21:26)

> Israel is beloved unto Me more than all other nations, for they are My peculiar treasure: upon them have I set My love, and them I have chosen. (Midrash Tanchuma, *Ki Tisa*, 8)

Not very ecumenical, huh? Few issues evince more clearly than this one the fundamental divergence between the Jewish and Christian conceptions of God and His overall approach to things. And this dichotomy of views is doubly important for our purposes, because in classical Semitic theology, *divine* behavior is the pre-eminent paradigm for *human* behavior:

> It is written, "You shall walk in His ways" (Deuteronomy 6:8) – just as He is merciful, be ye merciful; just as He clothes the naked, clothe ye the naked; just as He comforts mourners, comfort ye mourners… (Sota 14a)

It's all rather chicken-and-eggy: the qualities attributed to the Master of the Universe by Judaism and Christianity alike, simultaneously reflect *and* influence human ideals. What God does, and how He does it, is really all about what *we* should do and how *we* should do it.

Now, bearing this paradigmatic perspective in mind, let us note yet again that the "Jewish" God of the Hebrew Scriptures spends a large chunk of *His* time doing one very particular type of thing: *judging, discerning and discriminating*. Not just in the matter of "choosing Israel from amongst the nations," either, but in a hundred other fields. Indeed, the biblical Deity's single most famous and lasting accomplishment – Creation itself – was the end result of a lavish, all-you-can-eat, six-course smorgasbord of unrehabilitated "distinguishing":

> And God said: "Let there be light." And there was light. And God saw the light, that it was good. And God *distinguished* the light from the darkness.… And God made the firmament, and *distinguished* the waters underneath from the waters up above the firmament…and God said: "Let there be lights in

> the firmament of the heaven to *distinguish* the day from the night..." (Genesis 1:4, 7, 14)

Creation is a function of delimitation: waters are next divided from land, permitted fruit trees from forbidden fruit trees, the seventh day from the other six, species from species, woman from man, holy from profane, life from death, languages from languages, Levites from Israelites, pure from polluted, ox from ass, linen from wool... for Heaven's sake: milk from meat! The Jewish God is a fanatical, unstoppable, obsessive-compulsive *distinguisher*. And this predilection of His for...predilection, carries over into the Lord's relationships with His creatures – He is avowedly sweeter on some of them than He is on others:

> The word of the Lord to Israel through Malachi: "I love you," saith the Lord. And ye ask: "Wherein dost Thou love *us*? Is not Esau Jacob's brother?" And the Lord answereth: "Yet I love Jacob, but Esau I hate." (Malachi, 1:1-3)

The God of the Bible's divinity is tainted – by favoritism (and hatred!).

Not so Our Father Who Art in Heaven as depicted in the New Testament. This Deity is a *lot* less chauvinistic and prejudiced – and a great deal more accepting all around. Let's quickly compare and contrast the "personal example" set by each version of the Almighty in this matter, according to the founding texts of the two separate religions. We begin with a brief and much-acclaimed excerpt from Jesus' Sermon on the Mount, as recorded in the Gospel of St. Matthew, 5:43-45:

> You have heard that it hath been said: "Thou shalt love thy neighbor, and hate thine enemy." But I say unto you: "Love your enemies, bless them that curse you, do good to them that hate you, and pray for them that persecute you. That ye may be children of your Father who is in Heaven: for He maketh His sun to rise on the evil as well as the good, and sendeth rain down on the just no less than on the unjust."

Jesus was as awesome an orator as John Lennon was a singer-songwriter. These are evocative, soul-stirring words, and you can easily imagine their powerful effect on the apostles and the surrounding crowd. Just as God shines His heavenly light and sheds His heavenly tears upon *all* His creatures, equally and without distinction (exhorts the charismatic speaker, employing the traditional Semitic "emulate the Divine" device) so should *ye* bestow *your* bounty and sympathy upon all your fellow human beings: *equally and without distinction.* And now that's a truly moving picture: friends and foes, sinners and saints, arm-in-arm and swaying sweetly to the mellow strains of Jimmy Taylor (with a twist): shower the people you love – *and the people you hate* – with love. Beautiful.

Only some folks just can't appreciate genuine beauty when they see it. Here comes the stodgy, curmudgeony, pettifogging, *judgmental* Author of the Old Testament, to spoil this whole euphonious and egalitarian fondness-fest with some of His typical hair-splitting. First, in the matter of indifferent precipitation:

> And it shall be, if you hearken diligently to My commandments…that I will send down the rain of your land in its season, the former rain and the latter rain…but beware, lest you go astray, and you worship other gods and prostrate yourselves before them. For then will the Lord's anger be kindled against you, and He shall shut up the heavens and *there will be no rain*…(Deuteronomy 11:13-17)

> And it shall come to pass, when [the evildoer] shall hear these words of warning, that he may fancy himself immune, saying: "I shall be safe, though I follow my own caprice, *for the parched land shall be drenched together with the moist land*"… The Lord's anger and passion will rage against that man, until every sanction recorded in this book comes down upon him… (Deuteronomy 29:18-20)

Rain à la Torah, it would seem, is a bit more selective in bestowing and withholding its favors than the disinterested drizzle of the New Testament. It pours down – or stays up – based on that really square, super old-fashioned set of criteria they used to call the "merit system" (and when "all flesh had corrupted its ways upon the earth," it kept on coming for forty days and nights – and drowned the lot!).

The remainder of the Hebrew Bible is certainly no different in this respect: Solomon warns of a time when "the heavens will be shut up and there will be no rain, because they have sinned against Thee" (1 Kings 8:35); as a result of Israel's transgressions, God "withheld the rain for three months before harvest-time" (Amos 4:7); Zechariah predicts that "any of the communities of the earth that does not make the pilgrimage to Jerusalem to bow before the Lord of Hosts shall receive no rain" (14:17); etc., etc. It is certainly more than just ironic, that the specific weather element employed by the New Testament as a metaphor for the *lack* of divine discrimination, is the very same meteorological phenomenon the Pentateuch, Prophets and Writings (and Talmud) adduce more regularly than a quartz clock as the *preferred instrument and preeminent symbol* of divine discrimination.

And while Jesus is unquestionably right that in 99.99% of cases the sun also rises on the wicked man, even here, the Jewish Bible is at pains to show at least some occasional bias on the part of the flaming orb that rules the sky:

> Arise, shine, for thy light is come, and the glory of the Lord is risen upon thee. For behold, darkness shall cover the earth, and thick clouds the peoples, but upon thee the Lord will shine. (Isaiah 60:1-2)

> On that day, when God routed the Amorites before the Israelites, Joshua addressed the Lord; he said in the presence of the Israelites: "Stand still, O sun, at Gibeon, O moon, in the valley of Aijalon!" And the sun stood still, and the moon halted, until a nation was finished wreaking judgment on its foes… Thus the sun stopped in mid-heaven, and did not press on to set, for a whole day. (Joshua 10:12-13)

It takes some doing, but it seems that if you are really, *really* bad – like the Egyptians or the Amorites – then even Elton John's hands are tied: the sun *will* go down on you (or *not* go down on you, as the case may be). Indeed, even way back "In The Beginning," as we saw, the Creator made an extremely big deal out of "*distinguishing* between the light and the darkness," and divine manipulations of the "Day's Eye" in connection with human moral behavior range from the case of King Hezekiah – for whom the sun performed a veritable *volte face* (2 Kings 20:11) – to that of the wicked – whom it will roast on a spit at the Eschaton:

> Then shall ye *discern between the righteous and the wicked*, between him that serveth God and him that doth not – for behold, a day cometh, blazing like a furnace, and all the arrogant and all the doers of evil shall be straw, and the day that cometh shall burn them to ashes…but unto you that fear My name, a sun of righteousness shall arise, with healing in its wings. (Malachi 3:18-20)

The stern and partial God of Judaism, so it would appear, simply never tires of judging, discriminating and preferring – come rain *or* shine!

I'm not just playing verse football here. You see, the Nazarene himself – and the New Testament after him – made a very big deal out of a particular declaration found in the biblical book of Ecclesiastes: "For there is not a just man on earth, that does good and sins not" (7:20).

Jesus and Paul extrapolated from this "realistic" evaluation of the human condition – penned when Solomon was a tad depressed – that behold, sin croucheth at the door; and unto thee is its desire; and guess what: it is going to *kick your bloomin' arse* straight through the fiery gates of hell – no matter what you do! Sin is like Tiger Woods, says Christianity: unbeatable. The only way to avoid spending eternity playing sheath to a pitchfork is to "believe on Jesus," history's ultimate sin-offering. For the same reason, says the Bethlehem-born Redeemer – consciously opposing himself to the

Lord of the Pentateuch – "I pass judgment on no man" (John 8:18). In Christianity's eyes, *everybody* is guilty and should be, by rights, consigned to damnation. So why bother with fine distinctions?

And this leads us back to the *first* verse we quoted from the Sermon on the Mount, which contains what is perhaps the Only Begotten Son's most famous line ever: "**Love your enemy.**" *Love* him. Because when all people are hopelessly iniquitous, your enemy can't *really* be all that much worse of a fellow than you are, now can he? Doesn't matter *what* he does. You still share with him that common human condition. Nor can you, in the end, be much better than him. More importantly: when one preaches and practices universal, non-distinguishing love – as opposed to biased, preferential love – loving one's enemy should, indeed, come just as naturally as loving one's best friend (or one's mom). As the world-renowned twentieth-century Christian theologian and ethicist Paul Ramsey explicated this verse: "Be ye therefore entirely indifferent to the qualities of character in particular men which usually elicit preference or lack of preference for them." Now this really makes me blow my stack.

I don't know about you, dear reader, but *my* love is worth a whole *hell* of a lot – to me myself, and hopefully to whomever is on the receiving end. My love is *real*, and it's *valuable*, dammit, it is the single most valuable thing I have! Do you think I can afford to just throw it away indiscriminately and without reflection on every Tom, Dick and Saddam Sonofabitch Hussein who happens across my path or tries to nerve-gas my family? Should I just "put out" emotionally for…*everybody*? Bosom buddies, bitter adversaries, people I've never met, the entire high-school football team? That would *debase* love. That would *blaspheme* love. That would make love – that "richest ornament of heaven and earth," that magnificent and overwhelming feeling like no other, that most noble, rare and precious of gifts – into a cheap, gaudy, mass-produced trinket. Not to mention what it would make *me* (promiscuous – to put it politely). Bottom line: if love is worth anywhere near as much as I think it is, then not everybody is worthy of it (and certainly not in the same degree!). I'll reserve my love, thank you, for those I feel *deserve* it. They'll appreciate it lots more that way.

Let's stop again, and strive to be fair: I'm in Jesus' head even less than I am in John Lennon's. Maybe all of the above *isn't* in fact what the Son of Man had in mind – regardless of how most Christian theologians have since interpreted his words. And for that matter, if this *is* what he meant, it is more than likely that he drew at least some of his ideas on the subject from Jewish sources. After all, Jesus was as immured as anyone could be in the environment, lifestyle and discourse of rabbinic Judaism, and the ethos of this last was by no means monolithic. The "ideology" of the Talmud is in reality a choir of thousands of voices, not always in harmony, often deliberately dissonant, many of them raised to a fever-pitch of impassioned hyperbole to drive home a particular point or momentary imperative. Rabbinic literature is an immense, cavernous, boiling cauldron of "controversy for the sake of heaven," in which polar extremes coexist and duke it out in what proves to be a delicate and – to my mind – incomparably fruitful "balance of power." Within this dynamic and eclectic arena, almost every polemical position along a wide variety of spectrums can easily be found, including not a few of those espoused by the protagonists of the New Testament (there is even a rabbi who uses almost the same rain metaphor as Jesus – see Ta'anit 7a). Nor is sympathy for the "enemy" a complete stranger to Jewish sources (although it is largely drowned out by exhortations to pummel the living you-know-what out of him). In short, the intellectual and ideological cosmos of the Talmud is a coat of many colors, and it would indeed appear that much of nascent Christianity's power came from a *focused amplification* of certain specific "stripes" of that coat. The point being, again, that neither the positions praised nor those criticized in this book thus far can be confined or exclusively ascribed to one particular religion.

For this reason, I wish to stress once more for the record, that while I *do* feel that the preceding does indeed represent a defensible analysis of Christianity's and Judaism's overall positions on the issue at hand, we are *still* dealing here only with paradigms. Loving and forgiving the enemy who perpetrates horrors upon you and yours, being kind to the cruel, "turning the other cheek" – this general attitude has had a long and winding career, professed as it has been not only by Christians but by folks hailing from *all types* of backgrounds and creeds. Indeed, few would deny that the Christian world itself has been rather remiss down the centuries in consistently practicing this, its own proclaimed ideal – although it is currently doing an excellent job, I must say, of preaching it with great vehemence to us over here in Israel. Like last week, for instance, when we committed the horrific atrocity of sending in our special forces to take out this terrorist who has dispatched suicide bombers into Israel that have killed and maimed some thirty-five Jews, and who has announced both in print and on the air that he is heading right on over to kill more of our kids just as soon as he can free himself up from some really pressing engagements. In response to this stimulus – can you imagine? – we neither loved him, forgave him, prayed for him nor offered him our other downy cheek. We fired a missile from a helicopter into the rear window of his Mercedes. For this heinous crime we have since been assailed in the European and American press by literally dozens of writers and columnists, among them one Vincent Cannistraro, "former chief of counter-terrorism operations at the CIA," who not only chastised us in the *New York Times* for failing to provide the mass murderer in question with "due process" (alas – the miscreant ignored his subpoena!), but went on petulantly to whimper that the projectile we employed to vaporize the bastard was purchased from none other than the good old US of A (all of which, one certainly hopes, has at least something to do with why Mr. Cannistraro is *former* chief of counter-terrorism operations at the CIA).

It's OK, though – we're used to it. We get this "turn the other cheek" advice rather often, both from others and from ourselves. At the height of the Holocaust, Mahatma Ghandi helpfully recommended that the Jews "offer their throats to the butcher's knife" as a sort of non-violent protest against the treatment being meted out to them (thanks for the suggestion, Bapu). Twenty years later, when we captured, tried and convicted one of the men who implemented that same "Final Solution" – Adolph Eichmann – the famed Jewish philosopher Martin Buber fervently pleaded with Israeli judges and politicians that the Nazi's sentence be commuted to…*picking oranges on a kibbutz* (I'm not kidding).

And so we come back to *Imitatio Dei*, Sinai style: the mirror opposite of the Sermon on the Mount. The God of the Jewish Bible, you see, does indeed care about *all* of humanity (and so should we). All of humanity, that is, except for the really, *really* bad people – mass murderers, terrorists and the like – whom He fiercely and avowedly *hates*, and whom He promises rather regularly in His Number One Bestseller to hunt down and "trample to a pulp" (Malachi 3:21) – *and so should we*. And on top of His general affection for all that lives and breathes and refrains from suicide-bombing, the Deity of the Old Testament also unapologetically harbors *particular* inclinations toward *particular* folk who happen to strike His fancy for *particular* reasons (*and so should we*!!).

"One God through Israel, and one Israel through God" (effuses the Midrash): monotheism and election as a dual celebration of the "Joy of Choosing," as two intertwining aspects of the same passionate embrace, as a mutual expression – not of universally equitable *agape* – but of everlasting, unapologetic, and 100 percent partial *amour*. The Jewish holiday that commemorates the giving of the Torah at Mount Sinai is called *Shavuot*, which literally means "weeks." The rabbis ask us to read this name differently, omitting a measly vowel: *Shvuot*, which means "oaths." For on this momentous occasion, out there under the desert stars, the Jewish people and the Lord their God exchanged vows: We swore we would never replace Him with another god; He swore He would never replace us with another people.

Just as, according to the Jewish literary tradition, the Lord in Heaven *prefers* individuals and groups, and singles them out for special lovin' – either on their merits, or because for whatever romantic reason He has simply "set His heart upon you and chosen you" (Deuteronomy 7:7) – just so, urges the God of the Hebrews: prefer and single *ye* out individuals and groups! Single them out because they're *good* people, single them out because they're *your* people, single them out solely because *that is where your heart's compass points*! And then love 'em, dammit: love 'em *hard*. Not all of 'em – just *some* of 'em. *Discriminate*…for I, the Lord, am the Father of all discriminators!

And so, while I confess to full-fledged ignorance and indifference regarding which religion or nation – if any – is "chosen" in some absolute sense, I do disagree strongly (as everything above should serve to indicate) with the prevalent contemporary universalist notion that *no group* should see itself as chosen. I would much rather live in a world where *every group* sees itself as chosen (*by* itself!), because it is in love with itself to *that* degree. Thus, I am not saying – with Nietzsche – that "Men are not equal, and they should not become so, either." I am saying that men may indeed be more-or-less equal, objectively speaking (unless they forfeit that equality through heinous deeds). But I am also saying, at the same time, that they should never, *ever* become equal *in each other's feelings*. I am saying that the preservation of *that* type of inequality is the blueprint and cornerstone of all human happiness and prosperity.

Chapter Nine

A few issues, however, are still troubling you deeply, no? For instance: isn't the world I am asking for perforce a world forever doomed to experience incessant violence and desolating warfare between peoples, all of whom love "their own" with a passion and hate everybody else with the same? Universalists regularly resort to this rebuttal when up against the wall: distinction and preference make for a history of bloodshed. Well, let me say this about that.

First of all, hey, don't try to out ☮ me, man. My Mom had her hoola-hoop earrings *ripped right out of her lobes* by the National Guard while marching on Washington against the Vietnam War. As kids, my brother and I were expressly denied the use of toy weapons, and had to participate in the bi-weekly game of Cops-and-Robbers wielding sticks. So whereas Albert Ciarte would show up toting a shoulder-fired, magazine-fed, gas-operated, fully automatic Kalatchnikov 7.62 millimeter assault rifle with optional laser scope and barrel-mounted flashlight, when Alex and I would emerge from *our* carefully chosen ambuscade firing wildly in all directions like Butch and Sundance, the other kids would say: "that's a stick" – and blow us away. During my freshman year of college, some friends and I were arrested and briefly jailed for trying to depart the Limerick Nuclear Facility disguised as a nose-cone. Many years ago, I got into a heap of hot water when Israel's *HaAretz* and *Ma'ariv* newspapers published a particularly frothing op ed piece I wrote in favor of the IDF getting the hell out of Lebanon yesterday. And I have supported the creation of a Palestinian State in the West Bank and Gaza Strip since the age of fifteen, back when Shimon Peres was still a hawk.

All right, I'm skirting the issue. Look, even assuming that the One-Worlders could ever bring us peace – which they most definitively cannot – it would only be at the price of a terrorist, totalitarian, socially engineered nightmare that would make George Orwell and Aldous Huxley wet their pants. That is the only possible, earthbound consummation of the words: "Imagine all the people, living life in peace…" (stop humming). If you've got no will, no emotions, no preferences and no special ties left to speak of, I guess that'll take the fight out of you pretty good. Lao-Tzu (no relation to Mo) sums it up: "When there is no desire, all things are at peace."

Contrary to the well-known and oft-cited last utterance of the early Zionist hero Joseph Trumpeldor – "It is good to die for our country" – I gather you would agree with me that there isn't the slightest thing good about dying for your country, your nation, your religious beliefs or whatever. It *sucks.* I don't wish it upon anybody (except maybe Mahmud Ahmadinejad. I hope he is privileged to die for his country – soon). What I *do* wish, however, upon every single person still persevering through these pages, is that **you *do* have things in your life that are dear enough to you that you would be *willing* to die and possibly even kill for**, if it ever – God forbid – became absolutely necessary. Says John: "Nothing to kill or die for…" Says me: in that case, nothing much to live for, either.

There is another important subject to be addressed in this connection, however, a subject that we left dangling more than thirty pages ago. Back then we were trying to figure out the motives of Rabbi Akiba for apparently contradicting himself, by lauding the precept "Love your neighbor as yourself," while at the same time ruling elsewhere (in the case of the forgotten flask) that when it comes down to choosing between your life and that of your neighbor – *your* life is paramount. We have tried to show that as a Judaic scholar, Akiba was reared on the principle of preferential love, and thus he was forced to rule as he did. But we still haven't resolved the glaring disagreement between his ruling and the explicit scriptural prescription he praises so highly. Let's try to do that now.

A while ago I was sitting in this Yemenite restaurant in Jerusalem reading a book and munching my *malawakh* (a delicious Moroccan doughy dish). At seven PM, the air was shrilly pierced – as it is every hour on the hour – by those six long beeps that some sadistic socialist functionary from the early days of pre-state broadcasting decided was an appropriate way to introduce the news. After a run-of-the-mill item – a foreign dignitary's helicopter had been hovering on the brink of Israeli airspace for the last three hours and was about to plunge into the Mediterranean Sea because officials of the Foreign and Defense Ministries were quarreling over whose prerogative it was to issue the entry permit – the anchorperson announced that two hundred and thirty people had been killed in an airplane crash in Indonesia.

"That's *terrible*," I thought, and proceeded to cut myself another large, juicy morsel of *malawakh*, drench it in my side-dish of *hummous*, and loft it lazily into my watering, hangar-like mouth. Yummmmm. "That's really *awful*" – oh, there's a nice big piece of chicken smothered in delectable *kharif* sauce, come to *papa*...mmmm, yummmm...

And then I stopped. I was actually a little angry at myself for being unable to get sufficiently upset about those two hundred and thirty Indonesians and their poor, grief-stricken, destroyed families to have it affect my appetite even for *five seconds*. So I tried an experiment. I took the headline I had just heard on the radio, and changed only one or two words. Now it read:

TWO HUNDRED AND THIRTY ISRAELI SOLDIERS
DIE IN PLANE CRASH OVER NEGEV DESERT

"Oh. Oh, God. Is *that* what it feels like? Like *that*? Jesus – that really *hurts*. It physically *hurts*. As if someone punched me really hard in the stomach. It's nearly *faint-inducing*! Tell you what, I'm not thinking about my next bite of food anymore, that's for sure! Hell, I'm pretty close to being nauseous. Oh, *man*. So now I know. Now I have some inkling at least of what those crushed, devastated, innocent families are experiencing right now, as the news reaches them one by one that everything they ever lived for is gone. Dear *God*..."

You may not believe this, but I actually got up and left without finishing my *malawakh* (and there was *at least* a third still sitting there on the plate). I know, I know: my momentary abstinence really helped those Indonesian families. That's not my point. Let me give you another example.

A couple of years ago I was under Manhattan, riding the One Train downtown to South Ferry. Round about Sixty-Sixth Street, the door on the end of our car slid open, and a man with no legs came through, propelling himself with his arms and carrying a bucket in his teeth. He didn't say anything (obviously), wore no explanatory sign, but I guarantee you this: by the time he made it to the other end of the car, there was easily upwards of fifty more bucks in that bucket. Now people give for all types of reasons, granted. But I know what made *me* at least reach for the paper and not the change. It wasn't "altruism" – whatever that is. It was really a much simpler, more compelling deal: as I would imagine most other people did on that train, I looked at that indescribably miserable man and instinctively said to myself: "My God: what if that were *me*? What if that were *my* father, or *my* brother, or *my* son?"

Preferential love is the most powerful love there is, the only truly *motivating* love there is. **It is *by means* of that love – the *special* love we harbor for those who are closer to us – that we learn how to begin to love others, who are farther away.** Genuine and galvanizing empathy for "the other" is acquired most effectively and lastingly through a process that involves – first and foremost – immersion in love of self, then of family, then of friends, then of community... and so on. It is via *emotional analogy* to these types of strong-bond affections that one becomes capable of executing a sort of "love leap" (yes, I'm disgusted with myself for coining that term), a hyper-space transference of the strength and immediacy of the feelings one retains for his favorite people – smack onto those who have no direct claim on such sentiments. (How does King Priam finally pry open the long-locked heart of Achilles, and win his son Hector's body back for burial? "Remember your *own* father," the Trojan monarch pleads with Peleus' pitiless son – and this alone does the trick.)

Let's try a little experiment. There is a famous characterization of the Tao Master recorded in Lao Tzu's ancient Chinese spiritual classic, the *Tao Te Ching*. It reads: "The Master is detached from all things, therefore he is at one with them." Nice. Now, let's transpose the two predicate clauses in this description, and see what we get. Ready?

> The Master is at one with all things –
> therefore he is *detached from them.*

Surprise, surprise: it's amazing what a little rearrangement will do to clear things up. If you don't love your own *best of all*, we said – but rather somehow manage to feel "at one with all things," *equally* tied to everyone everywhere – then you really have no idea what *genuine* love is. And if you really have no idea what genuine love is, then your chances of learning to feel for people in Indonesia or Syria or Tajikistan or Wyoming, your chances of learning to care about people in far away places or contexts (or on the other side of a tense border, or in the opposite camp of a *kulturkampf*), are pretty slim indeed.

Here, then, is (my guess at) Rabbi Akiba's exegesis of the much-touted verse: "Love your neighbor as yourself." In his eyes, it doesn't mean: "Love your neighbor *as much as* you love yourself" – Rabbi Akiba doesn't believe in such artificial love, we know that from the flask story. To him it reads (and the Hebrew supports this tolerably well): "Love your neighbor *in the same fashion* as you love yourself." **Use the feelings you have toward yourself *as a guide* for how to feel about *him*.** You will never love him *as much* as you love yourself – you *should* never love him as much as you love yourself – but you will *learn* to love him at all, in the first place, solely through your overwhelmingly powerful love of yourself and your own. It is to this process and no other that the Torah refers when it urges – in over twenty different versions of the same statement – "Love the stranger: for you were strangers in the land of Egypt" (Deuteronomy 10:19).

Peace, man. If you are looking for a common denominator, a unifying factor, a "hug-the-world" kind of feeling to tie you to all people everywhere – well, I got one for ya: a *real* one, not this sloganeering "Love the whole world equally" nonsense. All you need to do, see, is pull off the following most human of deeds: *love the ones you're with.* Love them like nobody's business, circle your wagons around them if necessary, protect them from harm, make them *number one* on your priority list! (I'll bet you already do this.) Do *that*, and you will be as human as they come, a card-carrying member in good standing of the incredibly impressive species we are capable of being: because there are few things more characteristically human than loving your own. (*Don't* do it – *don't* love discriminately – and you will gradually become *in*human…not to say *inhumane.*)

Prefer your family, and you will have something *genuinely* in common with all decent, caring, feeling, loving human beings the world over, an experience to share with almost everyone. Imagine all the people…*showing each other pictures from their wallets*! Sting put it well (much better than Lennon), when he sang near the end of the Cold War: "I hear the Russians love their children, too." *Their* children, you see – *not ours* – but…"too." And there's the real common ground for you: we all love preferentially. There's the real basis for cross-cultural understanding. There's the only potential for peace.

The world of preferential love and distinct socio-cultural and political entities certainly need not, then, be one of hatred and interminable warfare. What is Isaiah's vision? "*Nation* shall not lift up sword against *nation*, neither shall they learn war anymore" (2:4). It may, in fact, be the *only* system available to the human race that will ever have a chance of breeding genuine global empathy and tolerance.

Chapter Ten

You are still not happy. "OK," you say, reluctantly. "I'll concede – *for the moment*! – the following points: (1) I accept that the kind of love that means the most to me is preferential, distinguishing love – I want it, I need it, I can't live without it; (2) I'll give you that the world should optimally resemble a tapestry of distinctive families, or groups, or peoples, or nations, that's cool by me; and (3) I'll even grant you that I personally – for the sake of my own happiness and for the general good of humanity – should connect myself in a vigorous and loving fashion to one of said groups. Fine. What you haven't really told me is…

…*why on earth that group should be the Jews*?!"

Good point. After all, you might claim (and I don't want to assume anything, but just for argument's sake) that you've had little or no exposure to Judaism or the Jewish community, so what's it to ya? Or you might explain that what meager exposure you *did* have was not exactly tantalizing, and you can't see much point in going back for seconds; or you might (finally) ask this extremely excellent question: why shouldn't I adopt as my "special society" all the members of the intramural hockey league I play in? Or all the guys I go bowling with? Or all the fighting feminists of the world? Or everybody who digs Celine Dion? Or all the people who live in the same city I do? Or all the people who live in the same *country* I do (I'm as good a patriot as the next fellow!)? After all, I probably have a great deal more in common with *them* than I do with your average Jewish person walking down one of the streets in another part of the world. Why not *these* groups as my first loves?

I'll tell you (in the immortal words of *Fiddler on the Roof*'s Tevya the milkman): .... *I don't know.*

Because here we stand on the threshold of things that are not really rational: they are emotional. It is very hard – indeed, it is well nigh impossible – to logically argue something that does not belong to the realm of logic, but rather to the kingdom of the heart.

For you see, dear reader: although you and I have never had the pleasure; and although you may harbor opinions and inclinations as different from mine as the sky is from the earth (and I'm assuming that if you've read this far you're either Jewish, or you have a *lot* of extra time on your hands); and although you are probably sitting there reading this over seven thousand miles away from where I am sitting here writing it – *we've still got something going, you and I, now don't we*? Oh, I admit, I can't know for absolute certain that it is requited from your side, but as for me, well, what can I say? I am *smitten.* Head over heels. Nuts. *You are my family and you mean everything in the entire world to me.* I would lay down my life for you – hell, I *do* lay down my life for you – *and I don't even know who you are*!

As you can see, this whole business is a bit clouded over – or, rather, illuminated! – by some serious emotion, making rational discourse on the subject a difficult feat. Nevertheless, I will give it my best shot. So back to our question: *why join the Jews*?

I could start by telling you how much *we* need *you*, and how much what you personally decide to do with your life has earth-shattering consequences and ramifications for your whole extended national clan, wherever they sleep and dream, wherever they wake and work, wherever they fight and fall. The Midrash tells this terse tale: there are twelve people in a boat. One guy, he starts drilling a hole under his seat. When everybody gapes at him in dismay and astonishment, he looks up and says: "What's it to ya? I'm only drilling under my *own* seat."

The idea is, of course, that we Jews are all in the same boat, so your particular actions or inactions naturally attract our interest and concern, whether you like it or not – because they are inextricably bound up with our collective prospects and welfare. Make no mistake about it: whether you are aware of this or consider it a cliché or not, *the future of the Jewish people is as much up to you as it is up to the current Israeli prime minister*. But this is too close to a Jewish guilt trip, and I'm just not into that. A brave and brilliant Zionist revolutionary by the name of Vladimir Jabotinsky always made it clear to his cohorts and disciples that if a Jew chooses to opt out of his nation's ongoing struggle and experience, there is certainly no effective or morally defensible way to force him back in. If he wants to go, *gey gezunderheit*! More matzah-ball soup for the rest of us.

Very well. I could also advance the proposition that you ought to join us with a passion and a fury for the following very simple reason: **you are a Jew**. You are a Jew, and *another* Jew – the heart that was huge enough to imagine the State of Israel, and then bring that imagination down here to earth, Dr. Theodor Herzl – once declared plainly: "**The greatest happiness in life, is to be that which one is**." I couldn't agree more. And my Daddy always used to say to me, he would say: "Son, never do anything half-assed." So I figure, if you *are* going to be who you are – a Jew – well then, *do it up*. Don't be a "by-default Jew," a "checkbook Jew," a "High-Holiday Jew," a "peripheral Jew," or a "marginal Jew" – *Yuk*! Be a "bold, breathless Jew," be a "wild, wanton Jew," be an "I'm going to milk this cultural identity thing for *everything its got* Jew," – be a knowledgeable, thirsty, caring, daring, *actively involved* Jew.

This is not a bad argument (if I must say so myself). But it is far from lacking holes through which the esteemed reader could slip if s/he chose to do so. Although I certainly don't intend anything of the sort – far from it! – it is possible that a certain tinge of traditionalism and conservatism could be read into a thesis that suggests: "Be what you are – because that is what you are." It could conceivably smack of an attack on human mobility – a concept as dear to me as it is dear (in my humble interpretation) to the Torah itself. Besides, you might easily parry by claiming that "being who you are" at this point in your life entails being a feminist, or a vegan, or a Bostonian, or a Celine Dion fan, or a bowler, far more than it does being a Jew, which is "what you are" only due to an accident of birth. So this contention doesn't pass muster, either.

In desperation, I could fall back on the oft-repeated asseveration that Jewish theology is absolutely true (and I can *prove* it: just look at these cleverly encrypted Bible codes…) and everybody else's is patently false; and that the Jewish legal and behavioral system is morally superior to that of any other religion, culture or ideology. Both of these claims partake of the particularly rampant and regrettable trend of Thomistic apologia and polemic currently in fashion (again) among Jews, Christians, Muslims, Sikhs, Confucians, Jains, Scientologists and almost every other religion or "way" running around. Sure, this might be the unavoidable nature of the beast, but that doesn't mean you – or I – have to accept such rationalizations or support such simplifications. I, for one, am not clinically brain-dead yet.

I personally happen to believe – after a respectable amount of round-robin investigation – that Judaism as a lifestyle and *Weltanschauung* has a good deal more to recommend itself than many other ready-made systems available to people for the adopting and practicing – but that's just me. I also happen to think there are a lot of *less*-than-palatable provisions to be found in the dos and don'ts of Judaic jurisprudence, and besides: who says we should conduct every aspect of our existence according to a pre-fabricated plan purveyed to us by our illustrious predecessors? We were given minds, I would venture, for the purpose of judging and evaluating each and every instance and episode in our lives independently, on a case-by-case basis – not so that we should know how and where to look up the proper response to every single stimulus in the pages of a book. So this argument goes down the tubes as well.

Let's try a different approach. Again, the gnawing question: Why not choose my bowling buddies, or the people on my block, or the International Society of Vegans, or who knows what other coherent entity as my spiritual center and the object of my primary affections? Why is the Jewish people a better candidate for this exalted position in my thoughts and in my feelings than these previously named options?

Let's hum along with Dr. Winston O'Boogie – Lennon's favorite nick-name – once again: "Imagine all the people, living for today…" **Living for today**. Oh, John, my main *man*, what it *is*? Did you *think* about this wish before you made it, before you put it to such awesome, persuasive music?! Granted, this line suffers a number of possible interpretations, but they all more or less connect to the problem I would like to raise here. Come with me, please.

We have already discussed the ugliness and emptiness engendered by the modern Western ailment of exaggerated individualism and utter non-affiliation. The symptoms of this disease are sequestration and isolation from a whole concentrically constructed solar-system of potentially enriching relationships on the *horizontal* – or *spatial* – plain. In a word, this is the affliction of "**living for yourself**."

Well, one thing is for sure: being Jewish cures *this* affliction, like no antidote I've ever seen. As a Jew, you literally have millions of people all around you, right this very second, throughout the world, with whom you share a secret, with whom you can exchange a knowing glance, at whom you can wink (use your judgment). These people are *your* people, they feel tied to you, they are pulling for you, they are *on your side* (travel tip: this does *not* mean you will not get ripped off by Israeli cab drivers – that's *their* way of saying "I love you").

I don't know if this special relationship is a product of the historical and international uniqueness of the Jewish phenomenon – we are neither a "nation" like the French, nor a "religion" like the Christians – or whether it is because as a group, we are not too big (like the population of America) and not too small (like the number of tenants in your apartment building), but just the right size to elicit that super-family feel, that combination of transcendence *and* immanence, of greatness *and* closeness. Or maybe it is just because the rest of humanity has always been so kind to us. I don't know exactly *why* there is this powerful electricity constantly coursing and pulsating between Jews the world over – I just know it's there.

Many years ago, just before one of my stints in the Israeli army reserves, I was in New York City blading with my brother down the lower West Side promenade hard by the Hudson, and we stopped to rest near the World Trade Center. This guy a few feet away from us was attempting to pick up a young lady by aggressively and intimately massaging her dog, and Alex and I switched to Hebrew in order to comment upon his original method. As we were talking, this be-suited fellow sitting on the bench opposite – clearly taking a five minute lunch-break from an action-packed morning of corporate raiding – kept staring at us. Finally, he rose, walked over, and stood rather awkwardly dead center in front of our bench. I looked up at him, and he faltered, gestured, fumbled, hesitated, and then just stammered, "Um……uh……*Shalom*!" I extended my hand and he shook it warmly and smiled. Still flustered, he half-saluted us goodbye, and went back to merging and acquiring.

What he really wanted to say was: "Hey – I'm Jewish, too." What he really intended by "Um…uh…*Shalom*," was: "I embrace you, my brother, member of my tribe from a faraway place. We share something tremendous and indescribable, something ancient and exalted, something wonderful and mysterious. We were soldered together, you and I, by the fires of hell on earth, and our bonds are since unsunderable. I'm glad you are in the world, and it gives me strength and pleasure to see you. Here: have some genuine affection." He meant all this, and more. He had been momentarily lifted out of the prosaic mundanity of his daily drudge, into a sphere that was powerful, exciting, fathomless and beautiful. He wanted to close that circuit and tap into that energy flow. He just wasn't sure how to do it. Neither am I, most of the time. We need a secret handshake.

The modern Western sickness of living solely for oneself, however – for which Jewish identity is such a powerful serum – is usually accompanied by another malady, which, as we noted above, Lennon and so many others aspire to infect us all with: living solely for today. This second disorder – let's call it "time hermitism" for lack of a better term (is there a *worse* term?) – emaciates our psyches by disconnecting us from a vast and fascinating potpourri of mind- and soul-expanding elements on the *vertical*, or *temporal*, plain. You can be alone in space, and you can be alone in time. I'll explain.

Over one hundred years ago, a British author by the name of Edwin Abbot penned a wonderful little work entitled *Flatland*, in which – as you may know – he arrays before the reader a two-dimensional world, literally speaking, a world in which there exist length and breadth, but not depth. The story's protagonist – one of the inhabitants of this pancake universe – takes us on a tour of his tabloid society, explaining that his fellow citizens are all geometric figures, the social station of each of whom is determined by the number of sides s/he was blessed with at birth. The lowest class is peopled by the isosceles triangles, whose sharp-angle point confers warrior status, whereas the elite is composed of pentagons (physicians), heptagons (landed gentry), and finally the clergy, who are possessed of so many sides that they pass themselves off as purely circular. And our narrator – a properly businesslike bourgeois tetragon – elaborates upon the complex methods whereby denizens of this duo-dimensional realm distinguish between members of different social strata. For without looking from above or below – and they are entirely bereft even of the *concepts* "above" and "below" – how is one to ascertain the number of sides belonging to the geometric figure sidling up to greet you at a given moment (all you see is a line!)? And how is one therefore to know whether to behave toward this individual with haughtiness and condescension or, as Richard Gere put it in *Pretty Woman*, to engage in "some major sucking-up"?

Now, at a certain point in the midst of our hero's horizontal adventures, an event takes place that is not only unexpected, but, from his point of view, quite impossible: he encounters a *three-dimensional* figure! Of course, our stolid square is at first unaware that he has to do with such an inconceivable entity; his slits-for-eyes still perceive nothing more than a line. But a few signs betray the voluminous nature of his newfound acquaintance. For instance, the stranger reveals to his quadrangular comrade immediately, without recourse to the traditional means and methods of Flatland, exactly how many sides are sported by each and every approaching countryman, a task easily accomplished, of course, by peering from above or below. Since, however, the Flatlanders are incapable of even *imagining* such notions as "above" and "below," the new kid on the block is taken for a magician or prophet in their midst…and thus the story continues.

Now, let us attribute a different allegorical purpose to this not-so-tall tale than that intended by Abbot (the book was meant to be a satire on British society of his day). Let us say, that the horizontal environment of Flatland – the right, left, forward and backward – symbolizes the spatial interrelationship between ourselves and all those surrounding us in the *present*; and let us posit further that the third, the vertical dimension – imported into Abbot's squashed oecumene by the protruding intruder – represents the chronological or temporal relationship between us and all those who came before us and will arise after us in the *past* and *future*, our connection to all that was and all that will be.

Well, in terms of this analogy, isn't it crystal clear? The best and brightest of the Beatles is in point of fact the *official travel agent for Flatland* – step right up, folks: he's just "waiting to take you away!" How so? Simple. John aspires to a world where "all the people live for today." That is to say, his dream – which is being realized at a dizzying pace in the present generation – is, as it were, a dream of "liberation." John has come to set you free: to *unfetter you* from the vertical tie that binds you to what came before you and what will arrive after you; to *lighten your load* by jettisoning the unbearable onus of eternity and dulling the acute pain of historical perspective; to *relieve you* of the heavy burden of the past and the even heavier responsibility for the future; and to *break the chains* that ensnare and enslave you to the knowledge, the feelings, the stories, the dreams, the experience, the power, the mystery, and the spirit of humanity's generations one and all. John Lennon desires that you live in *space*, but not in *time*, in *breadth*, but not in *depth*, he urges you most melodiously to shed all profundity and become two-dimensional, he pleads with you to be superficial, to be skin-deep, to be…flat.

Ah, but he doesn't stop there. Our lilting limey has a further destination in mind, on the way to which "two-dimensionality" is a mere "*Nachtysl*," a caravanserai on the road to the messianic Promised Land of – you guessed it – **one-dimensionality**. For it is, after all, only the *vertical plane*, only the *commonly shared history* – the legends, the literature, the adventures, the symbols, the suffering, the achievements, the images, the references – which allow us to communicate on a deep and meaningful level with those surrounding us *in the present*, on the *horizontal plane*, and create special relationships with them, connecting to their souls and building together with them associations, communities, cultures, nations. He who would deny you the former – the temporal connection – perforce denies you the latter – the spatial connection.

Thus, Lennon's two dreams – "Imagine all the people living for today," and "Imagine there are neither countries nor religions" – are mutually consistent, are in truth *one and the same dream*. And that dream is in fact the most awful nightmare the Bible can cook up: the curse of *karet*, of the soul that is "cut off" both "temporally" and "spatially." John Lennon wishes upon you the Bhagavad-Gita's famous "disengagement," in this case from both the vertical *and* horizontal planes of human interaction and enrichment, leaving you to live out the rest of your superficial and circumscribed existence – ignorant of how very much more there is to be had in life – stuck inside the four walls of isolated and ever-contracting one-dimensionality. How did John himself put it in a later solo song? "I don't believe in [long list of everything and everybody] – I just believe in *me*" (afterthought: "…Yoko and me").

You may say that he's a dreamer – but he sure as *hell* isn't the only one. Indeed, perhaps the single most salient characteristic of the (post) modern period is just this: *discontinuity*. Public life over time as an unconnected collection of random points, and history viewed and re-construed in the same fashion. This is the inevitable price of progress – so we are told by the many slavish and unthinking mouthers of slogans, who have forgotten the simple fact that genuine "progress" is solely and exclusively the result of *building upon what came before*. Otherwise, each generation would have to start from scratch, could not benefit from the accumulated wisdom and experience of all of its predecessors, would be the intellectual, emotional and cultural equivalent of a troglodyte. Would be, in short, a "post-modernist."

Decade after decade, "artist" after "artist," pseudo-intellectual professor after pseudo-intellectual professor, contemporary high society has chipped away at the links in the chains binding each generation to its predecessors. For these links are the insidious components making up historical continuity, and are thereby guilty of the unpardonable crime of "essentialism." These links dare to *tie things together*, to make *new* things the result of *old* things, to instill a sense of temporal "responsibility," to "tune in" and "turn on" big time – but *not* to drop out! Worse still, these links to the past allow and encourage us to indulge in the unforgivable perversion of *communal awareness in the present*: how does a leaf on one side of a tree know it is related to a leaf on the other side of that same tree – if it doesn't look down at the trunk? Our ties to our past are our ties to each other.

But today's anti-essentialist "progressives" can't stomach *any* of that: for them, "all things which give perpetuity are mischievous." In order to eliminate "exclusivist" communal identity and solidarity across the "horizontal plane" in the here-and-now, they strive to erase any possible basis for it, by severing our connections along the "vertical plane," to all that once was. Like the declaration on the cover of the old *Dada* magazine, they "don't even want to know that any man has lived before me." With Marx, they complain that "the tradition of all the dead generations weighs like a nightmare on the brain of the living." After Shelley, they cry:

O cease!
The world is weary of the past,
Oh might it die,
Or rest at last!

Poor fools. Remember Ben Jonson? No, not the Canadian almost Olympic gold-medalist track-and-field junkie. I mean the early seventeenth-century English dramatist and poet (and bar-room brawler). He put it best, I think, when he said: "They spring farthest, that fetch their race the longest," which in proper American English means: if you want to sail a good five meters in the long jump, you have no choice but to *start out really far back* (stanozolol steroids also help). Same with quarterbacks: the further back you cock your arm, the further forward you throw the football. *Same with life and human history*. Too bad Ben Jonson wasn't around to coach his twentieth-century namesake. Too bad he isn't around today to break some bar stools over the heads of all these obviously inebriated post-modernists.

But old Ben Jonson's slightly more famous contemporary is where you have to go if you want to hear some *real* anti-post-modernist invective. Like this here, from King Lear:

> That nature which contemns its origin
> Cannot be border'd certain in itself
> She that herself will silver [sever] and disbranch
> From her material sap, perforce must wither
> And come to deadly use.

Deadly use, indeed. The product of all this "disbranching" is a contemporary Western generation today that lives in what Eric Hobspawm called an "eternal present," a generation that can't be bothered with all that "useless remembering." The end result of this burgeoning, "progressive," anti-essentialist ideology and its inevitable cultural and commercial manifestations is a flat, shallow, uni-layered society that (like Ronald Reagan) "simply cannot recall." Were John Lennon alive and with us now, there would certainly be no need for him to "imagine all the people living for today." Most of those people are already doing just that.

Did you ever see that *Star Trek* episode where they strap Captain Kirk (William Shatner) down into a big, black, padded chair, and beam this memory-erasing light at his head, such that after a few minutes he would have been emptied of all recollection? (I can't remember how he escaped, but whatever he did, I'm sure it was far more manly than anything that Shatner's so called "successor," Jean Luc Picard, could have managed, that uncaptainly wiener.)

Now, suppose we strapped you, dear reader, into that chair, and erased your entire memory – everything you did throughout your entire life, everything you felt, everything you learned, everything you treasured, everything you daily and constantly reference. What, do you suppose, would be left?

A turnip, that's what. "You" are simply the accumulation of your experiences throughout your life. Growing and living and enjoying and fulfilling is all about the interaction, combination and application of those past experiences – which constitute the greater part (if not the whole) of your consciousness – to what it is you are thinking, feeling and doing at the present instant. If all you know and all you feel is what you know and feel *today* – or this week, or this year – well, you aren't going to get invited to a lot of dinner parties, I can promise you that.

So your *personal past* is important and dear to you, it plays the central role in the creation of your psyche, in the forging, expanding and deepening of your personality and consciousness; it is the very foundation of your existence as a thinking, feeling, acting human being – you wouldn't part with it for the world!

Ah, but why settle solely for your *personal* past? Because along the same lines, "you" are – or at least could be and should be – much, *much* more. You have the opportunity to expand your horizons further than any normal eye can see, further than any detached intellect can perceive, further than any untouched heart can feel. You can sink your roots down deep into the nourishing earth, you can extend your grasp way beyond the waters and across the deserts and into the remotest canyons surrounded by the most distant and imposing mountains clambering upward toward the furthest stars. You can reach beyond your individual, birth-and-death-bound walls and palpate immortality. You can draw on, you can *gorge* upon, the accumulated experience, inexhaustible knowledge and inextinguishable fire of the manifold ascending centuries that preceded you. You can stand higher than Everest on the shoulders of five hundred generations, and thereby see light-years farther into the future than those who have grounded themselves at sea level, and cannot see past their noses in any direction. In a word: you can be HUGE.

How does one do all this? The answer, I promise you, is not available from the ever-multiplying gaggle of "self-awareness" seminars. It's rather like this: see, *you personally* were born quite recently. You haven't existed, built, climbed, fallen, lost, won, wept, rejoiced, created, learned, argued, loved and struggled for thousands of years. Nevertheless, you, my dear friend, happen to have lucked out. You are a distinguished member of a nation that *has* done all these things, and then some. You have special eyes, eyes that can see for miles and miles. If you only will it – enough to work at it – you can extend your arms and touch the eons and the millennia, you can suck in the insights and bask in the glory and writhe in the pain and draw on the power emanating from every era and every episode and every experience of your indomitable, indestructible, obstinately everlasting people. As if in deliberate contradistinction to Marx's "tradition of all the dead generations weigh[ing] like a nightmare on the brain of the living," the Talmud compares the Jews to a vine: just as the vine itself is alive, but is supported and nourished by the dead wood beneath it, so the nation of Israel is alive and flourishing specifically *because* it is so deeply rooted and derives so much of its sustenance from those very same "dead generations" – from its past, from its "material sap," from the innumerable and profound traditions that are its very *source of life*!

Tapping into this vast and plumbless resource is not an ability acquired solely through learning or reading (although this is a *major* ingredient, I hasten to emphasize); it is first and foremost a function of connection, of belonging, of powerful love. If you reach out and grasp your people's hands – *you were there*. You participated in what they did, in all those places and all those times, you fought their battles, felt their feelings and learned their lessons. You tended flocks with Rachel, and slaved in Potiphar's house with Joseph; you sang in the wilderness with Miriam, and toppled the walls of Jericho with Joshua; you carried first fruits to the Temple Mount in Jerusalem, and were mesmerized by Elijah on the slopes of Carmel; you brought the house down on the Philistines with Samson, and bewailed your virginity in the mountains with Jephtah's daughter; you fought the chariots of Hatzor under Deborah, and danced before the ascending Ark with David; you went into exile with the prophet Jeremiah, and hung your harp and wept by the rivers of Babylon with the Judean exiles; you defied the divinity of Nebuchadnezzar with Daniel, and vanquished the might of Persia with Esther; you sought communion with the infinite with Simon Bar Yokhai, and studied law and lore in the vinyards of Yavneh with Elazar ben Arakh; you were with Judah the Maccabee at Modi'in, with the Zealots at Masada, with Akiba in the Roman torture chamber, and with Bar-Kokhva at Betar; you devoted your life to Torah at Sura and Pumpedita, and philosophized by the Nile in Fustat with the men of Maimonides; you were crucified for refusing the cross in the Crusades, and were turned into ashes for your stubbornness at the *autos da fé*; you were exiled from the shores of Spain by Isabella, and chased down and raped by the hordes of Chmielniki; you went out to Safed's fields to greet the Sabbath bride with Luria, and went in to Galicia's huts to seek the ecstasy of the fervent Ba'al Shem Tov; you ran in terror from the Black Hundreds across Russia's taiga, and sailed past Liberty and Lazarus onto the shores of the *Goldeneh Medineh*; you sought secrets in Fez with the luminous "Light of Life," and fled the murderous *Farhud* between Iraq's ancient rivers; you filed into gas chambers at Bergen Belsen, and were hurled living into the flames at Matthausen and Sobibor; you parachuted into Hungary with Hanna Senesh, and fought back at Warsaw with Mordechai Anilewitz; you were shot with your family in the forests of Poland, and dug a mass grave and perished there at Babi Yar; you revived your dead language, you resurrected your sapped strength, you returned to yourself and renewed the lapsed covenant, you arose like a lion and hewed out your freedom on the plains and the mountains of your old new land.

Throughout all this and so much more, *you were there with them* – and they are here with you. This is the thrust of the Passover Haggadah when it exhorts: "In every generation, a person must see her/himself as if s/he *personally* left Egypt." This is the intention of the Talmud when it whispers – based upon a strongly suggestive biblical verse – that we were *all* present and accounted for at the foot of Mt. Sinai in the desert, over three thousand years ago. This, I would venture, is the deepest meaning and ultimate emotional motivation behind the Jewish-originated concept of the Resurrection of the Dead in the End of Days: you see, I think that in certain ways we loved one another so much, so damn much, that we simply couldn't *bear* the notion that we wouldn't all – all of us, from every place and every Jewish generation throughout our entire history – eventually have the opportunity and pleasure of meeting one another face to face, and just spending some quality time. Not to worry, crooned the rabbis of the Talmud (with the Supremes): *someday, we'll be together…*

I am a Jew, and I am tied to teleology as well as to history. I live not just "for today," and not even just for all that has *led up* to today – I also live for a thousand tomorrows. I do not know what will be in ten centuries from now, but I know that I want Jews to be. Because through them *I* will be, through them I will *touch* what will be, through them I will *create* what will be. You and I, dear reader, we are members of a unique, extended family, extended in *time* as well as in space, extended into the *future* as well as into the past, a family whose members look out for one another across centuries no less than across continents. My noble ancestors will pardon me for the odious comparison, but it is like having access to a vast Internet of Existence, like being plugged-in and logged-on to forever. In the words of Leo Tolstoy (not that we need his approval or reinforcement, he just happens to be the world's most talented writer, and he put this – and everything else – rather nicely):

> The Jew is the emblem of eternity. He whom neither slaughter nor torture of thousands of years could destroy, he whom neither fire nor swords nor inquisition was able to wipe off the face of the earth, he who was the first to produce the oracles of God, he who has been for so long the guardian of prophecy, the pioneer of liberty and the creator of true civilization, and who transmitted all these to the rest of the world – such a nation cannot be destroyed. The Jew is as everlasting as eternity itself.

Thanks, Leo. What I am trying to communicate here is this: you need not live the impoverished life of the "space recluse" nor that of the "time hermit." You, dear reader, my sister or brother, daughter or son of Sarah and Abraham, you are invited to take pen in hand and add with a flourish a new and beautiful stanza to the "the greatest poem of all time" (as J. G. Herder once called Jewish history). You are blessed with the opportunity to connect with and benefit from a sprawling, boundless, spatial *and* temporal network, suffused with the deepest mysteries of the ages, and humming with the love of countless generations, a love that was always and everywhere channeled directly and unhesitatingly…at you.

By tying into all of this – while *ferociously* maintaining your own, stubborn individuality (I beg you) – you indeed achieve a great deal: you add innumerable new intellectual and emotional dimensions to your life, as you absorb, melt-down and re-fashion in your own image the fruits of untold centuries of evolving Jewish thought and churning Jewish tumult; you teach yourself the syntax and vocabulary of a timeless language, which you can use to communicate with all that went into creating you, and with all that you will one day create; you partake in a four thousand year-long journey of savage struggle and jubilant exultation, of unimaginable sacrifice and ineffable beauty, an adventure recently rekindled in a phoenix-like flash of incandescent splendor the likes of which human history has never seen; and eventually you burn, my brother and sister, you burn with the light and the fever and the strength and the passion of the magnificent and undying people of Israel, the bush that burns, but is never consumed.

Try getting that from bowling.

Ofer
The Challenge of Rationalism

"Don't you see that the Torah and its laws are no longer relevant to people's lives today? All that hocus-pocus, all those archaic stories and ridiculous rules and time-wasting rituals and impractical practices! There's just no rhyme or reason to *any* of it! How can such obsolete, irrational poppycock still appeal to an intelligent person like you?…

"…Why should people identify themselves according to this anachronistic and flagrantly racist conception of yours? And how dare you define *others* based on such artificial and reactionary criteria? Human beings should be judged by their individual characters, by their beliefs and ideas, not by their national or ethnic affiliation! Why are you so prejudiced? Why do you play favorites? What, because I was born a Jew, and that man standing over there by the telephone was not, you should interact with me in a different way than with him? Is that supposed to make sense?"

Chapter Eleven

Judaism is nonsense.

I intend here by the term "Judaism" – just so there should be no mistake – the hallowed, millennia-old belief and behavioral system prescribed by the Pentateuch, preached by the Prophets, elaborated by the Talmud, codified by medieval scholarly literature, articulated by latter-day rabbinic responsa and realized – even in the face of the most adverse circumstances, indeed, often at peril of very life and limb – in the tenacious inner faith and pervasive daily practice of countless Jewish communities from the remotest antiquity all the way down to the present time. *Unadulterated hogwash, the entire business.*

Exhibit A: "*Pan*-ic."

For the past several months – as the reader is no doubt aware – Israelis have been living in abject terror. Especially in Jerusalem and its environs, but throughout the remainder of the country as well, the Jewish population of the Jewish State has once again come to understand – as so often before in the long and tragic history of our beleaguered nation – the true meaning of the word fear. No one is safe. No haven is to be had. Our anxiety mounts daily, and when night descends we toss and turn, awakening in a cold sweat. In our streets and in our neighborhoods, in our very homes where our children sleep, security has become a stranger to us. We quiver, we shiver, we shudder, we quake, we cast furtive glances at every corner, search suspiciously under each item of furniture, constantly glancing over our shoulders, ever on the alert, prisoners of an acute, torturous and exponentially snowballing paranoia.

...*Help*!!!

Wherefore do we tremble so? What has engendered this ominous atmosphere of malaise in our ranks? What threat, what force, what ghastly foe has cast consternation into our hitherto brave and placid bosoms? Is it Palestinian gunmen? Hamas terrorism? Islamic Jihad suicide bombers? No.

It is bread.

Passover is here again, dear reader, that heady holiday when spring is in the air, the flowers are all a-blossom, and hundreds of thousands of observant Jews in Israel and the Diaspora go irremediably and uncontrollably *out of their minds*. Seized by violent, existential panic over the possible presence anywhere within the confines of their ultra-sanitized domiciles of a micro-fraction of a subatomic particle of yeast-contaminated dough, it is not long before these leaven-leery lunatics leap into action. See them strap on their armor and do decisive battle with all feloniously tumescent cereal products, wiping out wetted wheat where it stands, boldly summoning bloated barley to single combat, lancing in their pious fury the puffed-up pride of panis! Thrill to their exultant, whooping cries, as they swoop down unannounced on scandalous scones, give cringing crumpets the *coup de grâce*, hold public pumpernickel *autos da fé* (toast in hell!), yes, cheer them as they banish bagels, slaughter sandwiches and pillory pop-tarts, massacring muffins with not a hint of mercy, crucifying croissants with ne'er a care!

Deep in the throes of their annual fermentia, these Hebrew crumb hunters run amok, trashing their residences, switching their dishes, changing their wardrobes, replacing their dog-food, confiscating their children's Play-Doh (play-*dough*), manufacturing special Passover deodorant (sans the *grain* alcohol), purchasing kosher-for-Passover telephones (plosives with the mouth full can lead to irretrievable food particles lodged in the receiver), and generally scrubbing the self-same surfaces time and again like open-and-shut-case obsessive-compulsives, scraping, scouring, scalding, buffing, polishing, burnishing, sandblasting, blowtorching – everything short of full-tilt thermonuclear saturation bombardment – then hermetically sealing these sterilized exteriors under twenty-three layers of nylon, rubber, tin foil, Kevlar and God only knows what other agents of insulation, and finally – unsatisfied that all of these operations together have sufficed to extirpate every last vestige of the lethal Staff of Life from under their consecrated roofs – throwing up their hands, abandoning their homes altogether and fleeing pell-mell to resort-hotels in the mountains. An entire nation of purportedly intelligent and clear-minded people wages an annual international holy war of ruthless extermination…against a legume.

(Perhaps you find the traditional attitudes and activities described above to be somewhat humorous. That is what my cousin Kevin thought, when he had a deep-dish pan pizza delivered to my Uncle Joe's house during the family seder [yes, *of course* it was pepperoni]. He was grounded for a month.)

Amongst my people I do dwell: I cannot claim to have stood entirely aloof from this year's collective paschal psychosis. Permit me to share with you just a few highlights from my own participation in the latest installment of this three thousand year-old insanity, an involvement that began a good week before the actual inception of the festival. On this date, I was forced to cut short a lecture at the Hebrew University at five-thirty in the afternoon sharp. Turning a deaf ear to my students' anguished pleas ("No! You *can't* stop teaching us!"), I flew like a tornado down to my waiting wheels, hopped in and revved up the engine, jammed my "Meatloaf" disc down the player's throat, juxtaposed pedal to metal and hightailed it on out of there with tires screeching and rubber burning like the opening sequence of the good ole' *Dukes 'a Hazzard.*

What was the rush, you ask? Had a crisis occurred? Maybe a medical emergency, God forbid? Did the *Mossad* need my services urgently *yet again* that week? No. Nothing quite so trifling as that. As my '82 Volvo tore up the road, treating traffic lights as if they were works of modern art (that is, ignoring them), I knew that I was not alone. At that very moment, at least five other stalwart co-conspirators were themselves leaving the sound barrier behind, speeding wildly and irresponsibly through the narrow streets of Jerusalem in the direction of the city limits, all of them heading, like me, for the identical destination. Watches having been synchronized earlier (in the business we're in, anything short of Prussian punctuality spells irreversible disaster), my dedicated comrades and I were scheduled to rendezvous in precisely twenty-seven minutes at the mouth of a secret cave, reportedly located half-way down the face of a sheer cliff somewhere out in the undulating expanses of the Judean mountains compassing the capital.

Our mission? Matzah.

Let me explain. As the esteemed reader is no doubt aware, the production of grain-derived victuals requires an admixture of water – and matzah is no exception. In stringently controlled conditions that make your average laboratory look like civil war in Yugoslavia, said water is carefully combined with flour during the first stage of matzah manufacture. For the third year in a row, then, our courageous little band was being honored with the privilege of scouting out a natural spring and fetching that water – enough of it to make matzahs for an entire city block. And unlike on the two previous occasions, when we had simply dumped off the requisite fluids and gone our merry way, this time we were to follow the matter through to the bitter end, and *bake* the matzahs to boot.

"What was wrong with that nice little bubbling brook we went to last year – you remember, the one that *didn't* involve rock-climbing, rappelling, spelunking, and other typically Jewish activities that my mother would definitely have me assassinated for if she knew about?" Thus, with my back pinned to a jagged boulder and refusing to budge, did I remonstrate with our Orthodox team leader, Itzik, successful hi-tech entrepreneur, father of six, and deputy commander of an elite paratrooper unit (reserves) who has absolutely no respect or patience for those of us who think of motion as a primarily horizontal phenomenon.

"That position has been compromised," came the typically gruff reply from down-cliff. "The Radzyner Hassidim found out about it – it's gonna be a mob scene over there. Now stop that infernal whinin' and move your yellow-bellied arse. We're a full two-and-a-half minutes behind schedule!"

My question was answered. But you have a *better* question, now don't you, dear reader? It's a question that somehow didn't occur to me until I found myself dangling from the end of a thirty-foot rope lowered into the midst of a pitch black grotto, trying (and miserably failing) to fill a five gallon jerrican with one hand, and doing my best to disregard the various sliming, slithering, swimming and swarming creatures that called this place home and were in no mood to disregard me: *why not just use tap water*?

Was that it? Was *that* what you wanted to ask? Hah-hah: you fool! Do you *think* there was tap water in *talmudic* times? We obviously have to use the *same* type of water upon which the rabbis of blessed memory based their meticulous fermentation calculations two thousand years ago! And besides: what about…*Rosh HaShanah*? Did you *forget* that only a little more than half a year earlier, during the festivities of the Jewish New Year, Israelites of all persuasions had proceeded to rivers, streams and lakes throughout the country for the purpose of *tashlikh*, a traditional ceremony that entails the tossing of bread crumbs (symbolic of our sins – surprised?) into bodies of water as an expression of atonement? Now, what if one of those crumbs somehow managed to survive for six months, was buffeted about by the waves until it reached a reservoir, eventually wended its doughy way into the pipes of our water system and thence via the faucet… directly into our matzah-mixing bowls! What then, huh? I'll tell you what: *Armageddon*!! (What were you thinking?)

"Dammit, Scotty – I need that *water*, and I need it at warp speed!"

"I'm fillin' as fast as I *can*, Captain!" These subterranean rivulets seem personally bent on demonstrating the Chaos Theory of Turbulence. They simply *won't* flow calmly and quietly into my jerrican. But you have another question, don't you (go on, ask – I promise not to bite your head off this time): what is Itzik hurrying me for? Why is there a *time limit* on the obtainment of this water?

Ahem (you're going to be sorry you asked): let us recall that the eventuality one wants to avoid like the plague in matzah-making is known in Passover parlance as "leavening" (an etymological first cousin of words like "levitate," "lift," "lofty," "Levant," "Lufthansa" – all of which denote *raising* or *rising* – not to mention "Bye, bye, Miss American Pie, drove my Chevy to the"...*raised* embankment). Right. So you basically want to steer completely clear of any and all "leavening" or dough distension when bringing a matzah into being. Now, one of the innumerable factors affecting the pace of the swelling of dough is obviously going to be the temperature of the water used to create it – right? Heat rising as it unfortunately does, the rabbis of old wisely prescribed the use of "chilled" water (*mayim tzonenim*) for the purpose of matzah production, thereby largely sparing us the ugly task of iron-fisted batter suppression, and helping to postpone the advent of that apocalyptic catastrophe with which the reader is by now familiar: *chametz*! (Hebrew for "leaven".)

OK, so we need *cool* water from a natural source. Now, when do you suppose we should draw such water, hmmmm? What was that? During the *day*, you say? Noooohh sirrrreee! Daytime is, after all, the inalienable province of Sol Invictus, that glorious lamp of heaven that beats down upon the myriad pools and ponds of our fair planet and warms them up but good. "Sunshine," warbles Stevie Wonder, "on the *wa*ter, looks so *loooove*-lyyyyyyy" – but also means you cannot obtain fluids of the requisite nippiness from natural sources during the day.

Well, then: *after midnight*, you correct yourself. Preferably closer to dawn. *That's* when the water would be coldest. Draw the water *then*, you say. That would be the *logical* thing to do, you say.

Ha-hah – strike two! Here is what you did not know. The Talmud (Pesachim 94b) records a debate that took place around the first century before the Common Era between some Jewish rabbis, on the one hand, and a bunch of Greek scientists, on the other. The issue dividing these parties was the nature of the "solar system," or more specifically, the nagging conundrum: where does the sun disappear to at night? The rabbis opined that during the day the sun *swoops down under* the clouds and shines its invigorating light upon us and then, at the approach of nightfall, it climbs back up *over* the clouds from the other side. Their Hellenist interlocutors accepted the general principle of quotidian periphrastic helio-circumambulation (that's "daily solar orbit," for you non-astronomers), but, contrary to the rabbis, insisted that in the morning the sun *soars up above* the flat, discus-like earth, and in the evening dives down *below* it again at the opposite rim. And what's more, the Greeks had proof: at night (so they claimed) underground springs get hotter – for the obvious reason that the sun is down under there playing stove to the spring's kettle.

In the face of such unassailable evidence (rabbis have better things to do than hang out at underground springs in the middle of the night), the Jews were gracious enough to back down and concede this point to their opponents. On the basis of this new information, then, the talmudic sages (or their medieval successors) went home and decided that the best time to draw the coolest water for matzah baking is…*at twilight*, when the sun is neither overhead nor underground, but way out there "on the edge," posing the least thermal threat to our spring. And since the sun spends a relatively infinitesimal amount of time "rounding the bend" prior to embarking on its torrid track back toward our location, the matzah-water procuring "window" is rather small, and alacrity is of the essence (all of which serves to illustrate, once again, Galileo's famous admonition: "Religion is there to tell you how to go to heaven – *not* to tell you how the heavens go").

Ten minutes later, with my dazzling coordination and I having managed to fill less than two-and-a-half jerricans, I was summarily hauled up out of the hole by my zealous and more capable companions and transferred to donkey duty: shlepping already-filled jerricans (twenty-six of them) up to the waiting vehicles. That miscasting rectified, the operation now proceeded with more or less military efficiency, with the exception of a brief hydro-conflict that emptied three whole containers before Itzik could step in and reestablish discipline. Altogether you could say that we got in, got our water and got out, with a minimum of casualties and the sun – trailing a fanned peacock's tail of scarlet magnificence in her wake as she plunged demurely below deck for the evening – not a word the wiser.

Now, it was Miller time.

What?! God *forbid*, Miller time! Miller beer – and beer in general – is made from yeast-fermented barley, and is therefore an out-and-out Passover nightmare on roller skates. Besides, this was no time for dipping the snoot: we had matzah to bake.

Or so I thought. Arriving in a seedy part of town, we carried the whole sloshing mother-load up the stairs of a dilapidated old building, the entire third floor of which had been purged and deterged beyond all recognition in preparation for its new incarnation as temporary matzah factory. Lugging my jerrican with difficulty, arms threatening to go on strike any minute, I tried to take comfort in the well known talmudic adage: "If you cannot be a scholar yourself, at least carry water for scholars."

"Go on home, now, boy, and get some shut-eye!" bellowed Itzik, as he whizzed by me up the stairs toting *two* jerricans as if they were helium balloons. "We've got a big day tomorrow!"

Tomorrow? What happened to tonight? Why not just keep the ole' matzah momentum rolling and bake those Paschal patties *right now*? We're here already, aren't we? What's with the procrastination?!

I put my question to Itzik, who duly banished the darkness of my ignorance with the lantern of explanation: we have to wait until tomorrow, it seems, because the water we use to bake matzah must be…*mayim shelanu*.

"Ooh, ooh," you interject effusively, keen to participate. "*I* went to Hebrew school. '*Mayim shelanu*' means '*our* water'! OK, so I get it: we wait a day before getting underway, in order to give any and all potential claimants a chance to challenge our ownership of the water we've drawn, and then, and only then – when a reasonable period has elapsed, and we are assured that the fluid is indisputably '*shelanu*' or 'ours' – do we go ahead and bake with it. Well, now, that's certainly rational and enlightened!"

Geez. Isn't it, like, a *super-groovy* feeling when something you learned all those years ago in after-school religious school can help you to comprehend a new notion you encounter today? Too bad that's not the case here. *Mayim* does indeed mean "water" in the holy tongue, but in the particular phrase under scrutiny, the *second* term – '*shelanu*' – does not signify "ours," but rather derives from the Hebrew verb *lan*, meaning "to spend the night" (whence *malon*: hotel). We can bake matzah, according to Jewish law, only with *mayim shelanu* – water that has "slept over." And *why* must the water "sleep over," you may ask? Well, that's obvious: so that it has a chance to cool down overnight before it comes into contact with the flour.

"*Cool down*? But you just spent *five long pages* explaining how – "

Exactly, perplexed reader. You see what I mean? Irrationality incarnate.

Please forgive me if I offer here only a skeletal outline of what took place the following evening. Severely traumatized, I am still in therapy and would rather not dredge up painful memories. Suffice it to say that this whole hair-raising, nerve-shattering, blood-curdling ordeal could have easily been avoided had we simply remained slaves to Pharaoh in Egypt.

The Matzah Bakery. How to make you understand? Picture a large, powerfully lit room with a low ceiling, slightly longer than it is broad, with what looks like the very jaws of hell (the monster oven) occupying the entire wall at one end. On the opposite side, where the whole operation will momentarily commence, envision a division: two separate, sealed-off compartments, one in each corner, with an alcove in between them. The first of these compartments is called the *vasser tzimmer*, Yiddish for the "water room" – whither we had delivered the previous afternoon's hydro-haul. The second is the *mel tzimmer* or "flour room." (While our little posse had rode off on its sacred quest for low-temperature H_2O, other temporarily *non compos mentis* Jews had marched out to the fields clad in overalls and bearing scythes, looking for all the world like an old Soviet propaganda poster, and with their very own city-slicker hands had reaped, gleaned, threshed, winnowed and finally – back in basements across Jerusalem – actually *ground* enormous quantities of raw wheat using old-fashioned, hand-rotated mills, all of this the better to guard the grain in question from contact with *Der Teufel* himself – a.k.a. moisture – at every stage of the game.)

Back to the bakery. In the nook between the water and flour rooms, enthroned upon a sturdy tripod, rests a large aluminum bowl, presided over with much solemnity by the *funnemmer* (the "taker"). The *funnemmer* will soon demand and receive valuable and dangerous contributions from the chambers on either side of him, thereby initiating the momentous liquid-solid miscegenation process.

The fellow at the water post occasionally emerges from his room for a quick breather. But no one has ever even *met* the flour guy. He goes into strict sequestration in his *mel-tzimmer* corner cell long before anyone arrives, bolts the door and never comes out. They say he has it all in there: library, telephone, Internet hook-up, DVD, facilities for responding to the call of nature – you name it. Just so long as he stays put. This policy of rigid apartheid is more than justified, given that the "flour guy" handles the matzah-baking version of pure grade plutonium: were the tiniest speck of unsupervised wheat-flour inadvertently to be trekked by a heedless *mel-mann* into the main room and there to encounter the minutest droplet of unaccounted-for liquid trickling somewhere around the premises, well – *chametz* (leaven) could conceivably come into being, and then, of course, the entire universe as we know it would be sucked back into the Cosmic Egg.

Proceeding further down the floor of the factory, we enter the fearsome domain of the *finners*, eight bruiser-class mastodons of the palooka variety who together resemble nothing so much as the backfield line-up of the Washington Redskins, and whose job description is basically to beat the bleeding bejazus out of the *funnemmer*-furnished proto-dough, rendering it soft, malleable and submissive. Moving beyond these prodigious personages, we arrive at the center of the factory, which is dominated by the *tish*, a massive table made of stainless steel and literally glistening with vestal immaculacy. Around the *tish* stand thirteen *velgerers* ("rollers") – ten of them laymen (including the present writer), two "skilled workers" and a supervisor – whose collective duty it is to fashion by means of assembly line a round sheet of dough (*real* matzahs are round, machine-made matzahs are square) so flat and thin that you can barely see it from the side, lest any part of the innards escape unbaked.

Onward to the penultimate station, staffed by a lone *reddler* or "perforator," who effects the Passover fare's notorious punch-card look (another method of preventing dough expansion) using a three-pronged, hoe-like device that he cleans every thirty seconds with a blow-torch. Finally, two *shibbers* ("shovers") and four *bakkers* ("bakers") hold sway over Dante's Matzah Inferno at the back wall, which is partitioned off from the main ward lest it escalate room temperature by a sliver of a mini-micro-nano-degree, and thereby accelerate the rising process. These highly trained (and no less highly remunerated) "specialists" are charged with the unenviable double task of ensuring, on the one hand, that the wafer-thin matzah-frisbees are not immediately burnt to a crisp and rendered inedible by the immense heat, while at the same time seeing to it, on the other hand, that not a single square millimeter on any of the thousands of large-circumference patties that will be flung into the oven over the course of the evening escapes the full effect of the roaring flames. For were it to remain uncooked, that mite-size morsel of matzah could conceivably continue to decompose, react and rise...and we all know what *that* means. Altogether, theirs is a nerve-racking navigation between the Scylla of incineration and the Charybdis of fermentation that less lion-hearted folks tend to shy away from – which explains why the *shibbers* and *bakkers* get the big bucks.

Every one of the above-mentioned participants is subjected to a full body search upon ingress, and then either dons a surgical mask (really) or takes a vow of silence (I am *not* making this up), so that no possibility of expectorated saliva alighting upon unsuspecting dough need be feared.

Major domo of this whole Kafkaesque menagerie was Itzik: stopwatch in hand, whistle around neck, his anxiety-ridden features showing the toll of the inordinate responsibility placed upon his shoulders, as he made a final round of inspection and engaged in last minute consultations with talmudic commentaries, medieval super-commentaries and even one or two manuscript discrepancies. All eyes were upon him. The atmosphere was choked with that thick, electric silence that precedes a violent storm. At long last the moment of truth arrived. Drawing in a deep breath, Itzik locked eyes meaningfully with the supervisor of the central table or *tish*. Giving him a grave, barely perceptible nod, he issued forth the command:

"Flour."

"Flour!" seconded the supervisor with voice raised, turning in the direction of the Goliathan *finners* at their anvils.

"Flour!" thundered the *finners* as one man, swiveling to face the stern-looking *funnemmer* in his alcove between the two corner cubicles.

"Flour!" barked the *funnemmer*, master of the silver basin, addressing his order to the partitioned-off *mel tzimmer* on his right.

And then…nothing. All waited with bated breath. After an excruciating ten seconds that seemed like an eternity, a lone hand emerged through an aperture in the wall of the flour room, clutching a paper bag filled with exactly one kilo of the precious yet perilous substance. Stretching itself out to full length over the *funnemmer*'s bowl, the hand hesitated slightly, and then, with a practiced flourish, emptied out the contents of the bag into the bowl with not a hint of refraction or even a cloud. The hand immediately withdrew into the wall. An audible sigh of relief greeted the successful maneuver.

"We have *flour*!" shouted the *funnemmer*, keeping his masked mouth as far away from the silver basin as possible.

"Flour on deck!" bellowed the Brobdingnagian *finners*, preparing to pound like jack-hammers.

"Flour on the main deck! Look alive!" echoed the *tish* supervisor, unable to conceal the rudiments of a satisfied grin.

This, however, had been child's play. Now things would get sticky – literally. The *funnemmer* shifted his stance and positioned himself just so behind his bowl. The *finners* flexed their elephantine forearms. The *tish* was tense. Itzik raised his eyes heavenward and mumbled a hasty supplication. Then, consigning himself to the will of the Almighty, he gave the order:

"Water!"

"Water!" repeated the *tish* foreman.

"Water!" roared the *finners* in unison.

"Water!" cried the *funnemmer*, turning this time to the *vasser tzimmer* on his left, a shadow of genuine worry flitting across his determined visage.

Out from a tiny window in the wall of the water room came a second hand. Quavering with obvious trepidation, it extended itself toward the silver bowl, slowing to a halt at its rim. For a horrific moment the hand wobbled, but then it regained its composure, and ever so carefully – the years of experience serving it well – overturned a small pitcher, pouring out its fluid contents into the *funnemmer's* basin without spilling so much as a drop.

And that's when all hell broke loose.

According to the Talmud, from the moment you cease kneading matzah-fated dough, you have "the time it takes to traverse a Roman mile" before the criminal fermentation process kicks in and the big beige blob in your bowl begins to rise. It seems, however, that Roman people moved at a rate that would make Usain Bolt look like a snail on barbiturates, because once flour-water fusion had been achieved in the *funnemmer's* vessel, the resultant concoction – and hundreds of others like it, hurled at us in an unrelenting fusillade over the next six hours straight – was the proximate cause of factory-wide pandemonium, with portions frenziedly catapulted out every which way to be pulverized, steam-rolled, rounded, massaged, tossed, twirled, sliced, mashed, smashed, squashed, skewered and burnt alive, at the incredibly punishing pace of exactly *seven minutes from bowl to oven* and with the utmost attention paid to all legal minutia and special strictnesses along route. One false move, one miscalculation, one minor fumble, and you were liable to be sent up to the Big House (*Leaven*worth, I presume). And all this organized mania went down to the accompaniment of Drill-Sergeant Itzik's splenetic, dithyrambic and – as the evening wore on – increasingly rabid harangue:

"Just between you and me, *funnemmer*: are you a lily-livered leaven-lover? Are you a slimy, good-for-nothing, yeast-infested, commie-pinko *deadbeat*? GET THAT LOUSY BRAN-GOOP UP AND *OUT* OF THIS BOWL BEFORE I IMPALE YOU ON A SERRATED BROOMSTICK, YOU SPACED-OUT, LOTUS-EATING GOLD-BRICKER!"

"Well, well – and what have we here? It appears that *finner* number four is being dainty with his dollop. Why you gentle giant, you! Here's my cell-phone, cream-puff. Perhaps you'd like to call up the Pillsbury Dough-Boy Municipal Shelter for Battered Batter – and volunteer? Maybe you want I should demonstrate the concepts 'pummel' and 'bludgeon' with this here five-kilo mallet on your *twelve-inch thick skull*? I SAID BASTINADO THE LIVING *CORN-JUICE* OUT OF

THAT INFERNAL BALL OF WHEAT-PULP, YOU SPINELESS LEVIATHAN *PANSY*!!!"

"Tell me, *velgerer* – is this pathetic excuse for a Passover patty your idea of 'flat'? You *shikker*! This matzah has a profile like Barbara Streisand! I want a *two-dimensional* sliver, dammit, and I'm gonna get it if I have to – wait a minute…WHAT IN THE NAME OF SOLOMON'S SEVEN HUNDRED AND SEVENTY SEVEN SQUEEZES – IS *THAT*?!?"

About four hours into the program, the unthinkable had happened. Itzik and everyone else stopped whatever they were doing and stood with mouths agape, staring at a single gob of heretofore ignored matzah-dough, lounging in self-complacent solitude near the north-east corner of the *tish*. The Lord alone knew how long it had been lying there, left to its own devices, just sitting pretty and quite possibly…*fermenting*. That's when things got ugly.

"OH MY *GOD*! RED ALERT! RED ALERT! GO TO DEFCON 3! MELTDOWN! MAYDAY, MAYDAY! CALL OUT THE NATIONAL GUARD! *ABANDON SHIIIIIIIIIIIIIIIIIIIIIP*!!!"

The stress of the last few days had taken its toll: Itzik had clearly left lucidity behind. Desperate measures were required. We lured him outside and dumped a five-kilogram vat of flour over his head, bringing to a forced conclusion his part in the performance. *Sic semper tyrannis.*

What I am trying to say here, dear reader, is that if you have never experienced the joy of matzah baking – don't start now. It is a truly grueling affair, and not suitable for the stout of heart, let alone the weak. The famous eighteenth-century hassidic rabbi, Levi Yitzchak of Berditchev, once visited a matzah factory, and emerged visibly shaken. "It has always been charged against us, that matzah is made with the blood of Christians," he commented afterwards. "This is not true. Matzah is made with the blood of Jews."

Dear reader, let's be honest with each other: have you ever encountered an equally certifiable band of totally raving *loons*? Can anybody point to the rational, sensible, explicable side of this meticulously prescribed and punctiliously executed *derangement*? Is this the way straight-thinking, pragmatically oriented people spend their time? Well – *is* it?

I daresay it is not.

All of the above took place, you will remember, several days *prior* to Passover. Now that these and other complex preparations were quite behind me, I looked forward to a relaxing, halcyon holiday with no surprises up its sleeve. Man proposes, however – and God just laughs His head off.

This year, I was slated to celebrate the Passover Seder at the house of close friends in Ramat-Gan (next door to Tel-Aviv), people who are – as far as I can tell – perfectly normal and mentally balanced throughout the rest of the calendar year. Liora is a sociology professor at a nearby university. Her husband Dan is what's known in Israel-speech as a "*shushu-ist*," because if you ask him what he does, he deftly and imperceptibly changes the subject to your tie-pin or the fortunes of a local sports team. We think he goes to foreign countries and kills people for a living. Anyway, the two of them are also tremendous gourmet cooks, which explains why long before I even arrived at their high-rise abode, my mouth began to water in anticipation. More than anything, I was dreaming of my favorite item on the Passover menu, the humble broth that over the centuries has justifiably achieved legendary status, that simple stew of delicious, melt-in-your-mouth oval orbs that long ago became the emblem of everything good and sweet about Jewish domesticity. I refer, of course...to matzah-ball soup.

I love matzah-ball soup. I pine away for *knaidlach* (the dish's Yiddish alias) all year long. There's something about the *sui generis* look, smell, taste and texture of the floating matzah-ball that just... sends me. It is without doubt an utterly indispensable element in the creation of that special Seder-eve ambience. Moreover, fantasizing about forthcoming matza-ball soup is all that sustains me through the exceedingly lengthy pre-feeding section of the ceremony, and lends a certain one-track-mind quality to the proceedings. Why is this night different than all other nights? That's easy: matzah-ball soup. What did the wise son ask? He asked: Where is my matzah-ball soup? What was the third plague with which the Lord smote the Egyptians? Off to bed without matzah-ball soup. When dinner rolled around at last, I was fairly frothing at the prospect of my beloved bouillon.

(While we wait for the much-touted *pottage* to be served, let us pause for a brief digression on the taxonomy of matzah-balls and their role in Berenson-Segal family politics, as told verbatim by my mother: "There are two kinds of matzah-balls, the 'fluffy' kind, and the 'bullet' kind. When I was a little girl, both my grandmothers used to make matzah-ball soup for the Seder. It was kind of like a competition. My mother's mother always made the 'fluffy' kind, which in our minds was associated with the fact that she had come to America from *Podolia*, a place with a soft-sounding name. My father's mother always made the 'bullet' kind, which was also fitting, because she was from *Chernigov*, a place with a hard-sounding name. One year, when I was about nine, my cousin Robert lobbed a 'fluffy' matzah-ball across the table at my brother Mickey. It landed with a harmless 'poof' on his arm and disintegrated. In retaliation, Mickey – who was already a star Little League pitcher – plucked one of the Chernigovian 'bullets' out of his soup and whipped it back at Robert. It missed Robert, but hit Harvey smack on the nose, causing him to fall over in his chair and be taken to the hospital with a concussion. The two sides of the family didn't speak for weeks.")

Back to Ramat-Gan, and Liora and Dan's table. Matzah and bitter herbs dutifully consumed, two homemade Gefilte fish crammed down the gullet and out of the way, the path was now cleared for the glorious advent. Ah, here came the soup – I could smell its heady bouquet wafting in from the kitchen. Liora ladled, and soon a large, steaming bowl was placed before my face. Senses reeling, I reached for my spoon, plunged it into the semi-pellucid consommé, and… wait a minute – *what was this*? Something was definitely wrong. Oh, it was matzah-ball soup, all right. Only lacking in one rather seminal ingredient: *the matzah-ball.* Thinking myself the victim of a simple and forgivable oversight, I surveyed the soups of my neighbors. *Sacre-bleu*! The deficiency was universal! Noticing my growing agitation, our hostess inquired in the most solicitous of tones whether there was anything at all she could get for me.

"Ball?" was all I could manage, pointing an accusing finger at my soup, my facial features screwing up in that "I'm about to have a seizure" look. "*Ball*?!"

"He's upset about the missing matzah-balls, honey," interjected Dan the Hit Man. "Sorry, pal – not this year. Matzah-balls are *shruya*."

So it was true: Liora and Dan had decided to take upon themselves a particular Passover stringency that was all the rage of late in their neck of the woods. This supererogatory strictness is referred to in the professional literature as "*shruya*" or "*gebrochts*" – Hebrew and Yiddish respectively for "soaking" – and entails the prevention of all potential contact between matzah and liquid of any kind, throughout the entire eight day-long Passover holiday. You remember all the care we took back there in Itzik's matzah sweatshop to make quintuply sure that absolutely *no part of any matzah* could possibly have escaped its own personal baptism of fire? In vain, all of it! Useless! Wasted effort! Because Liora and Dan (and hundreds of thousands of other members of our daffy tribe) are so completely petrified of the most infinitesimal trace of what might conceivably be related to a distant cousin of an adopted nephew of a great-great grandmother of something barely resembling leaven – *that they just don't trust us*! That's right: you can't be too careful these days! Whoever made their matzah might just have missed a spot after all, leaving it not fully cooked, and that damned spot would therefore still be susceptible to expansion upon contact with liquid, and we would then have a *chametz situation*, now wouldn't we?! Matzah-balls being made out of matzah-meal, they are accordingly not allowed – as per this particular stringency – anywhere near the broth. Hence: no matzah-ball soup.

I swear, if I could have called in an air strike on that location, I would have. Did you ever hear of anything crazier? Banning matzah-balls from the Seder table is like…it's like…it's like prohibiting beer at a frat party. It's like taking away Lance Armstrong's bike. It's like telling Tiger Woods he can't play the US Open. It's pure *anti-Semitism*, is what it is.

"Oh, don't worry," Dan reassured me. "When you see what's in store for the main course, you'll forget all about the matzah-balls!"

As if! Not the least bit consoled by these half-baked diversionary tactics, and acting as any self-respecting human being would under such dire circumstances, I sought to compensate myself for this grievous loss via the simple and innocent expedient of cracking off a piece of matzah and dunking it into my soup. This – as you may have already guessed – was a mistake.

You know those slow-motion scenes in movies when someone is about to inadvertently activate a booby trap or accidentally push a button that will obliterate a mid-size country or some such, and the camera keeps panning back and forth between the unwitting perpetrator's finger approaching closer and closer to the cataclysmic apparatus and the muffled scream rendered at 10 RPM of the guy trying to intervene before the worst happens: "*N-o-o-o-o-o-a-a-a-a-a—u-u-u-u-o-o-o-o-o*!!!" You know what I'm talking about? Well, it was worse than that.

Dan was already halfway around the table by the time Liora – up until that second a polite, reserved, not to say diffident woman – let out a piercing howl and more or less dove across the table with arm outstretched in a desperate attempt to foil my nefarious project in time. But it was too late. Matzah hit soup. There was a collective gasp from the assembled guests. Before I knew what was happening, Dan had pinned my left arm to my right scapula, and Liora had grabbed the bowl, raced across the living room rug toward the window, and (I have fifteen witnesses to this) summarily defenestrated its contents twelve floors down to the sidewalk (luckily, the entire nation of Israel was then at Seder, so it's safe to assume that no one was hit by the fall-out from this plummeting lethal compound). Hyperventilating and visibly shaken, Liora then carried my compromised utensil back into the kitchen, whence were subsequently heard sounds of disinfection, fumigation, and finally just plain smashing to smithereens. Everybody glared at me. I wanted to jump out the window after the soup. I drank the third cup of wine early, and the fourth, and the fifth. A few hours into the holiday, and I was already a Passover pariah.

The ensuing days of the festival did not see any alleviation of this enigmatic behavior on the part of my cuckoo co-religionists. On the second night of Passover (unlike you wanderers in the Exile, we here in the Homeland have only *one* Seder, on the first night), I was invited to a gala repast at the house of some extremely wealthy hassidic acquaintances in Herzliyah – another appendage of Tel-Aviv on the north side – who made their not inconsiderable bundle in the diamond trade (they're not called "*jew*els" for nothing). Fine. So we get there, and everything is as opulent and elegant as can be: Francis the First sterling silver flatware, embossed Limoges porcelain dishes, sparkling Waterford crystal glasses, elaborately carved napkin rings – the works. Real aristocratic, old-world class.

Summoned to tableside, we each sat down gingerly, not neglecting to transfer the hand embroidered linen serviettes to our laps. Various delicacies were already spread before us on the French lace tablecloth: paté de foie gras, boeuf Wellington, clear consommé in a silver tureen, white asparagus tips marinated in a rich vinaigrette sauce. *Mon Dieu*! An appetizing array! It was like supping at Versailles. At this moment, two formally dressed waiters entered, each carrying a large tray draped in silk. Circling the table, they proceeded with much pomp and ceremony to dispense to each and every one of the guests and family… Glad trash bags. Yes, you heard me. Every one of us around the table was provided with his or her very own tied-up, plastic pouch, in each of which were to be found five or six broken pieces of…matzah.

Party favor? Pre-dinner doggie bag? Feed the birds, *tuppence* a bag? What the *hell* was going on?! I looked around to see what other people were doing. When the proper benediction had been pronounced ("…*hamotzi lekhem min ha-aretz*"), host and guests all brought bags up close to faces, carefully thrust a hand in, took a broken piece of matzah and cautiously placed it in their mouths. I'll leave you to imagine what this looked like.

Could it be, I thought, that they had somehow been informed of my embarrassing fiasco of the night before, and were therefore taking extra precautions to protect their viands from me, the diabolical matzah moisturizer? No, no, I was reassured: the tradition of affording such extra protection to their unleavened bread – lest it be exposed to anything damp or humid, the good Lord have mercy – had been in the Katzenellenbogen family for generations (did they have trash bags in the Shtetl?).

I had a flash of brilliance. This quaint custom of my hosts started my mental gears a-grinding, and soon an idea occurred to me whereby

I would – in a single, deft stroke – add a dash of levity to the situation, save the face I had so ignominiously lost the previous evening, and show myself *au courant* with the latest Jewish legal developments. All this I proposed to achieve by raising one minor, neglected issue. Putting on my most pious, "more Polish than the Pope" expression, I turned and addressed my fellow feeders. "Stop!" I cried, my hands outstretched in a gesture of dire warning. "*Stop*, I say! What in *God's* name are you all doing?! Your mouths are simply *submerged* in saliva, and your stomachs are a regular *reservoir* of digestive juices! You weren't actually planning to force your matzah to run such a fluid-filled gauntlet, were you?! *Saints be praised*! Why, we're talking pure leaven-heaven, my friends, a regular *chametz* convention waiting to happen!! Now, where *I* hail from, what *we* do, see, is to swallow the matzah *still wrapped in the bag* – you know, like your basic transatlantic cocaine courier? That way it stays dry as dust from esophagus to intestines!"

No one spoke to me for the rest of the meal.

On the third day of Passover, much bewildered and deflated, I went to eat with distant relatives who live in Beit Shemesh or "The House of the Rising Sun," a burgeoning little city about half-way between Tel-Aviv and Jerusalem. Aryeh and Rachel are both architects, and they and their four kids live in this beautiful, split-level structure made mostly of picture windows, so that you can watch the sun rise from pretty much anywhere. Anyway, they are rather religious people, and by now I was ready for anything. Would they spray their matzah with silicone? Have separate rooms for eating and drinking? Perhaps reduce the temperature in their apartment to twenty degrees Fahrenheit so that all potentially menacing liquids would freeze over? Whatever the case would be, I made sure to bring along my own bag, just to appear hip to the scene.

The bag turned out to be unnecessary. Dinner began, proceeded, and entered the homestretch, and the matzah never showed up. "Uh...please pass the matzah?" I ventured.

"Matzah?" replied my host. "You must be kidding." Dear reader, I know you're not going to believe this – so I'll swear on whatever you like – but Aryeh went on to explain to me how, according to most Jewish jurisprudential schools of thought, the divine injunction to consume matzah on Passover applies only to the *first night* of the festival. Since, therefore, it is not absolutely *obligatory* to eat matzah on the remaining days, then why take the unnecessary risk of having this vulnerable, hazardous substance hanging around at all? Better safe than satiated.

"But the Bible itself specifically instructs: '*Seven days* shall ye eat matzah!'" parried I, in high dudgeon, deftly adducing Exodus 12:15.

"Now look," shot back my host, growing impatient with my casuistic nitpickery. "You have the *whole rest of the year* to eat matzah, OK? Just *not on Passover*!" It was at this juncture that I began seriously contemplating conversion.

By the fourth day of the festival I had reached the point where nothing could surprise me. Or so I thought. Lunching at my friend Omer's house down the block, we were just finishing the main course and embarking on dessert (Jewish holidays, you may have noticed, are primarily gastronomic affairs – or, as someone once aptly summed up the whole phenomenon: "They tried to kill us, we won, let's eat!"). Coffee was brought in, but I wanted tea. "Where are the tea bags?" I queried, heading for the kitchen.

"First cupboard on your left," answered my friend. I have an old, incurable dyslexia problem with rights and lefts, so I opened the wrong cabinet. I reeled backward in utter shock. Piled high on each and every shelf of the cupboard, sitting there plain as day in all their fermentative finery, were examples of every kind of fully risen bread you can possibly imagine: white-bread, rye-bread, pumpernickel, whole-wheat, bagels, baguettes, challah, pita – you name it, it was in there. Enough to feed a division.

"Alright," I said to myself, trying to remain calm. "Just back away and close the door. Nobody needs to know about this." The words of Isaiah unconsciously worked my lips: "Who among us is righteous and hath not sinned?"

"It's not mine," said a voice from behind me, startling my limbs into a palsied leap. Noticing my extended absence, Omer had followed me into the kitchen.

"Rrriiiiiight – of *course* it isn't. I didn't suspect for a moment…"

"No, no – really. It isn't mine. I sold it."

"You…*sold* it?"

"Yeah, I sold it. On the Internet, to this Protestant guy in Australia."

"Uh-huh. Um…he comin' to pick it up anytime soon?"

"No, idiot. He's gonna sell it *back* to me at the end of the week."

The ban on leaven during Passover applies to three basic "relationships" with this substance: you can't ingest it, you can't benefit from it in other ways (say, using a hot-cross bun as a paperweight), and you can't own it. Omer had solved the latter problem by retailing his entire collection of leavened goods to an online Crocodile Dundee.

As it turns out, he is far from alone. Multitudes of Jews sell their *chametz* to non-Jews during the Passover holiday, and then buy it back – at a slightly cheaper price, of course, in order to make a *bisel* profit (just kidding) – at the conclusion of the festival. In fact, every Passover, the chief rabbi of Israel sells all government-owned leaven products in the entire country to this one Arab family in the Galilee (really).

By the way: this "mercantile" solution has spread to other spheres of Jewish practice, spheres that have nothing whatsoever to do with Passover, but that constitute no less instructive illustrations of the truly exiguous role afforded to rationality in the Judeo-classical worldview. For instance: did you know, that all of the thousands of feathered, furred and otherwise epidermally encapsulated animals in the Jerusalem Municipal Zoo were recently purchased by a retired taxi-driver named Menahem Cohen…for the equivalent of *three bucks*? I kid you not.

It works like this (stay with me here): before one eats fruits, vegetables and grains – at any time, all year round – Jewish law prescribes that a kebillion-zillion tithes and duties (OK, two tithes and duties) be removed from the produce in question and set aside for the nutritional upkeep of the *cohanim*, members of the priestly class, descendents of Moses' brother Aaron. Once separated out and earmarked for this sacred purpose, no one else may touch this specially allocated food, called *terumah* in Hebrew, save members of that same priestly class, to whom it shall forthwith be remitted. So far, so good.

Here's the snag. The *cohanim* or priests are enjoined by the Bible to eat their allotted *terumah* provisions in a state of untainted "ritual purity." Problem is, in order to obtain such a pristine state, you kind of need a red cow (you heard me: *you need a red cow*). This cow – which must be the epitome of heifer perfection in every way, with not a blemish on the lass and not more than *one* non-red hair discoloring her entire bloated chassis – needs to be slaughtered, sacrificed and burnt. Her blood is then sprinkled seven times outside the camp, her ashes mixed with cedar wood, hyssop roots and some unidentified vermilion stuff ("double, double, boil and trouble…"), and this whole appetizing decoction made into a concentrate and then poured into a large tub of spring water. A priest who has come into contact (or even just been under the same roof) with a dead body – the "father of fathers of all impurity" – then immerses in this bovine bubble-bath on the third and seventh day after exposure to the deceased, follows up with a visit to a properly constituted *mikveh* or purification pool (a dissertation in itself), and lo! – he is cleansed of his death-induced defilement (whereas the folks involved in the various stages of *preparing* this decontaminating formula all become *impure* – don't ask). So the priest is purified and may partake of his *terumah* food, and all's well that ends well.

Except that there's a premium on carrot-top cows these days – they are *really* hard to come by. This kibbutz in the north claimed they had bred one about a decade ago, and a billion rabbis with magnifying glasses and cattle-prods converged on the place overnight to get a closer look. She was indeed a lovely specimen, mooing demurely on the meadow, but soon the unmistakable scent of Clairol hair dye cast a slight pall on the proceedings. In the end, the only thing truly red on that kibbutz turned out to be its ideology. Sad fact is, there haven't been any bona fide crimson kine found for going on a couple thousand years now. No red cows, no pure priests (most ground in the world was burial ground at *some* point in history, and priests perforce walk over it, thereby contracting "corpse pollution"). No pure priests – a lot of wasted *terumah* food! What to do?

Well, as it turns out, there is *one* more category of consumers besides the *cohanim* themselves who are entitled by talmudic law to eat the priest's portion, and this group is *incapable* of contracting ritual impurity as long as they live: we are talking about the *priest's pets*. Animals owned by the *cohen* may eat the food set aside solely for his consumption, especially if he can't chow down himself due to temporary or permanent ritual pollution. Now are you starting to get the picture? That's right, dear reader. We sold all the lions and tigers and bears in the Jerusalem Municipal Zoo to Menahem Cohen the retired taxi-driver priest for the price of two subway tokens, so that – in their new capacity as his personal possessions – they could be fed all the tons and tons of tithed and "offered" food separated out by the giant Israeli agricultural concerns before marketing their produce.

Aren't we clever? (Aren't we *nuts*?)

There is one more area where this legal fiction of lending-qua-vending comes in handy, and that is the institution known as *shemita*, or the Sabbatical Year. The Bible expressly commands: "Six years shalt thou sow thy land, and gather in the yield thereof; but in the seventh year thou shalt let it rest and lie fallow" (Exodus 24:10). We Jews handled this somewhat problematic statute just fine during our lengthy sojourn in the Diaspora, primarily because (a) we weren't exactly big farmers, and (b) the prohibition on planting in the seventh year applies only to the fields of good ole' Canaan Land.

Difficulties arose, however, when we began returning home in trickles and then in droves to the Land-of-Milk-but-No-Money in the latter half of the nineteenth century, and decided (as the Zionist guru Aharon David Gordon put it so nicely) "to open up a new account with nature." Making the desert bloom and living off your own agricultural economy is tough enough, without the added nuisance of losing one out of every seven years of harvest. To rectify this problem, famous *fin de siécle* rabbis found a loophole: the Bible commands that we not farm *our* land during the Sabbatical Year. If, however, the land doesn't belong to us; if it is, officially speaking, *somebody else's* land; then hey: rev-up those John Deeres and get a plowin'! All of which goes a long way to explaining why – depending on what year it is when you are reading these lines – the entire State of Israel may currently be owned by a nun.

I won't burden you with the wild and wacky escapades of the remaining half of this year's Passover festival, except to say that the neurotic bread-dread I had encountered during the earlier part of the holiday only intensified as the days wore on. Israeli television has one of those "ride with the police" true-crime features, and on the sixth night of the holiday they documented a raid on a restaurant on Judah the Maccabee Street in Tel-Aviv, not far from my house. And I do mean a raid: the Ministry of the Interior's anti-leaven SWAT team poured out of the back of a truck, complete with "smart spatulas" and other highly sensitive yeast-detecting equipment, not to mention a fully ordained rabbi in tow. The entire country jeered the maître d', captured on video screaming back to the kitchen, "Oh, no – hide the bread, *hide the goddamn bread*!!" If the film had been a bit grainier and the accents slightly more Hispanic, you would have sworn you were watching the movie *Traffic*: "Ju ain' got *nothin'* on me, gringo. Dis place is *clean*!" Cop emerges from kitchen holding up a roll. "Clean, huh? Then what do you call *this*, Pedro?" The restaurant was fined what amounts to $500. Are you registering this? An eating establishment in the twenty-first century had to lay down five hundred smackers because their customers wanted to dine *au bon pain*!

I won't even bother to tell you about my country's milch cows, which are denied all yeast products over a *month* before Passover, to preclude the possibility of any leaven-lactose mingling; or about the incident of what can only be described as "pano-terrorism," reported in the paper just before the holiday, in which an irate housewife took five bags of the Israeli version of "Shake-n-Bake" and – with the help of everyday gardening tools – catapulted their contents severally through each of her neighbor's windows. I think, by now, the picture is basically clear.

Now, don't get me wrong. There is, of course, an entirely rational and sensible explanation underlying all of the seemingly frenetic Paschal behavior described in the last twenty pages. Here, then, is the entirely rational and sensible explanation:

About three thousand five hundred years ago, this family of seventy people moved from the Land of Canaan to the Land of Egypt. There, it seems, they were "fertile and prolific and multiplied and increased and waxed exceedingly" (Exodus 1:6). So much so, in fact, that not four generations later they already numbered "six hundred thousand men on foot, besides the women and children" (Exodus 12:37), which unprecedented pullulation they achieved (explains the Talmud) via the highly plausible and commonly employed expedient of every woman giving birth to sextuplets each time she got pregnant. The indigenous Egyptians reacted to this alarming population explosion by enslaving the teeming newcomers, as well as by giving all their male infants neo-natal swimming lessons in the Nile River, which they failed. All but one, that is, who was floated downstream in a little basket, fished out and raised by a princess, grew up and ran away to the desert where he was rumored to conduct long interviews with foliage and was ultimately commissioned by a flaming shrubbery to go back and redeem his nation from bondage, toward which end he promptly marched into Pharaoh's court and turned his rod into a snake. The Egyptian King's royal wizards also turned *their* rods into snakes, but our snake was...snakier, ate up their snakes without so much as burping, and we won round one.

Wielding this triumphant, gorged ophidian that had meanwhile reverted to an inanimate stick, our deliverer then metamorphosed the entire Nile River into a regular Red Cross wet dream of streaming hemoglobin. This feat was followed in rapid succession by other eminently logical and credible phenomena, such as ice hailstones that were so blisteringly hot they spontaneously combusted, three days of pitch darkness in some neighborhoods while it was perfectly sunny in others next-door, a nation-wide amphibian epizooty, and finally a plague in which all the firstborn (and *only* the firstborn) sons of the Egyptians (and *only* the Egyptians)...croaked.

Unable to stand up to such a relentless onslaught, Pharaoh finally decided to Let Our People Go, announcing that after some two hundred years of slavery, we had exactly *eighteen minutes* to pack up and get the @!%#$& out of his country. Never going anywhere without a little nosh, the newly manumitted Israelites whipped up some dough, but had no time to let it rise before baking, and so took it with them flat, thereby also saving space in their suitcases for all the incredible last-minute bargains they had squeezed out of the cowed and gullible Egyptians. Meanwhile Pharaoh, regretting his hasty decision, gave chase to the departing Hebrews with his entire army of chariots. The Red Sea, alive to the fact that that it constituted an obstacle to the progress of such a meritorious and well-connected band, had the good grace to step aside – to the right and to the left – and allow the escapees to cross through it on dry land without so much as getting their ankles wet, but refused the same right of passage to their pursuers, who were mercilessly drowned to a man. Thereafter, our valiant ancestors followed a mysterious pillar of cloud as a guide during the day and a blazing pillar of fire that lit up their road late at night, deep into the forbidding wilderness, where they were wined and dined on a desert menu of food that fell from the sky and water wrung from rocks.

Hey: *just like real life.*

You think maybe the Passover story and its resultant commemorative praxis is perhaps an irrational exception, some kind of fluke in an otherwise calm, cool and logically collected system? Think I chose some sort of extreme example within the overall scheme of perfectly reasonable narratives, precepts and customs making up the totality of the Judaic ethos? Sorry, Bub. You got another think coming. I chose Passover as an instance of such illogical comportment, solely because I just experienced it less than two weeks ago, and the wounds are still fresh. You want to talk about *other* areas of the Jewish religion that are no less crazy? OK. Let's discuss a wound that is *not* so fresh – and not so metaphorical (I think most of the gentlemen in the audience already know where I'm going).

When I was a freshman at the University of Pennsylvania, I dormed with three really nice guys named Jan, Carlos and Dave. Jan was from Denmark, and had spent most of his teenage life scanning every inch of his body for virginal spots that had managed to escape the tattoo artist's needle. He was a walking Sistine Chapel.

Carlos was from Chile. Preppy and studious during the day, at night he would get all gussied up in leather pants and spiked boots, do ten lines of speed and go out slam-dancing with two office-size safety pins jammed through each cheek.

Dave was from Zimbabwe. His real name involved a series of laryngeal clicks that sounded like an alien eating Sigourney Weaver, so we called him Dave. On tribal holidays, Dave would go into the bathroom, and come out with both his earlobes stretched all the way down to his shoulders. I won't even tell you what he then proceeded to do with his bottom lip.

My friends used to say to me: "Damn! You live with some real mutilated freaks." This always made me smile wryly. Because we all know – now don't we, dear reader – who the *most* mutilated freak was in suite 711 High Rise North all those years ago. I mean, come *on*. It's one thing to decorate, puncture, extend and otherwise modify or manipulate various bodily tissues or protuberances, but **hey**: *stay away from Mr. Happy* – know what I mean? What sensible rationale could *possibly* exist for pinning down a hapless tot at eight days of age and...never mind. Let's change the subject.

You see, there's just no logic to any of it. Judaism is like that famous old joke you're not supposed to get, with the two guys in the bath-tub and one of them says, "Hey, man, pass the soap," and the other guy responds, "Sorry, pal – *no soap, radio*!" By rational, empirical and logical standards, this religion of ours is just one long series of discombobulating *non sequiturs*: Why can't I wolf down this succulent lobster? Because lobsters have no fins and scales. Why can't I savor this delicious rabbit stew? Because rabbits don't have split hooves. Why can't I devour this scrumptious soufflé for dinner? Because you had a chicken sandwich for lunch. Why can't I chow down on...*anything* today? Because you are the firstborn son. Why can't I send this urgent business e-mail? Because today is Saturday. It's raining – why can't I open an umbrella? (See previous answer.)

Hello?

Or then there is the minor episode from my grad school days entitled: "Why God Owes Me Four Hundred and Seventy Five Bucks." Half way through my first year at Columbia University, I landed a swell job *laining* (Yiddish for "reading" or chanting out the weekly Torah portion from the scroll to the congregation) at this super-chic Modern Orthodox synagogue on the Upper East Side. I was highly pleased to be able to play my altruistic part in the melodious diffusion of the Lord's Holy Writ, and was not, of course, in the least bit motivated by the eighty-five-dollars-a-pop honorarium that just happened to come along with the position. Anyway, this particular synagogue was quite the formal affair (the rabbi and cantor wore top hats) and I had to buy me a suit. Fine, so I go down to Moe Ginzburg's in Chelsea and get myself this really dapper Yves St. Laurent double-breasted dark-blue pinstriped thing, with which I am eminently pleased, for two hundred and fifty dollars. I bought an orange and pink silk tie to go with it (thirty five dollars) and had it tailored just so (twenty dollars). So now we're up to a subtotal of three hundred and five dollars, all invested for the greater glory of His illustrious Name.

Terrific. I prepared the reading diligently throughout the week, and finally Saturday morning rolled around – my debut. I donned my new duds with pride, and wended my fashionable way across Central Park, strutting like Beau Brummell himself. Having slightly miscalculated the walking time from 114th and Broadway, I arrived a tad later than the beginning of the service (although long before my own part came up), and was wrathfully received by two anxious, crusty *gaba'im* (sort of sextons) in tails. While the first one berated me for my tardiness, his partner critiqued and subsequently undid the knot in my tie. As he replaced it around my neck, he suddenly rasped, "Hey, Sam – better come have a look at this."

"Whadya got, Jack?"

"Check out the label on the jacket."

Sam comes over and all but grabs me by the scruff of the neck. He examines the label, and his face visibly reddens. "Follow me!" he barks, and – ducking into what turned out to be the cantor's dressing room – he slams the door shut behind us. "Take off that suit!" he yells.

"What?"

"You heard me, kid – *strip*!"

Now this was too much. "Would you mind telling me what's going on here?" I demand.

"What's to tell? Your suit constitutes a flagrant violation of Torah law – and you're about to read the Torah wearing it?! What the hell do they teach you up there at that college of yours, anyway?"

"Um – what exactly did my suit do?" I inquire, nonplussed.

"Can't you read, boy? Your suit is made of fifty percent linen, fifty percent wool – *sha'atnez*!"

It's pretty simple, really. *Sha'atnez* is a weird biblical word referring to a garment composed of the two above-mentioned materials, and the book of Deuteronomy makes its position rather clear, decreeing in no uncertain terms: "Thou shalt not wear clothing made of wool and linen combined" (Deuteronomy 22:10).

"What could possibly be harmful about a combination of wool and linen?" I make so bold as to ask. "Are these materials mutually reactive? Is my suit going to explode?"

"Listen to him, the big *chochom* over here! Next thing he'll be asking why you can't eat milk and meat together!"

"Well, I *have* always kind of wondered what possible basis…"

"Because you CAN'T, that's why! You see, Jack, I *told* you they were all Communists up there at Columbia – now shut yer heretical trap and put this on already, will ya? The cantor's about your size."

The cantor was a booming bass, with the bodily proportions to match. He was *not* my size, to put it mildly, and I walked up to the stage looking every bit like a Charlie Chaplin film. Tuesday next I marched mournfully over to the Salvation Army depot, gave away my brand new suit (are you getting this?), and headed downtown to buy another one, this time gray and one hundred percent cotton. Now, the way I see it, either God explains this entirely irrational, completely arbitrary law to me, or else He owes me three hundred and five dollars for the suit, the tailoring and the tie (because, as everyone knows, orange and pink clash with gray).

But that was not, unfortunately, the end of the matter, and the Lord's liability to me was soon compounded. The following Sabbath I decided to make a gesture in compensation for the previous week's imbroglio, and showed up really early to synagogue – so early, in fact, that I got there the night before, for the Friday evening *Kabbalat Shabbat* or "Welcoming of the Sabbath Queen" service (please note that this presence of mine was an entirely unsalaried freebie). The Sam-and-Jack team was there, of course, and immediately approached to give me the once over. "Hey, Sam," said Jack, grabbing and squishing my cheeks between his fingers. "Kid used a knife."

"That true, kid?" asked Sam, twiddling his *tzitzis*.

"Is *what* true?" I fumed, already exasperated.

"Did you shave with a blade this afternoon? Well…*didja*, kid?"

"Wha – of *course* I shaved with a blade. What did *you* shave with – a banana?"

Sam shook his head. "*I* shaved with an *electric shaver*, kid, like a good Jew is *supposed* to. Thank God my Jeffrey never went to college. Otherwise he would've turned out to be a complete *bonehead*, like you!"

I *am* a bonehead. It was news to me at the time, but as it turns out the Bible addresses this issue head on: "Thou shalt not 'cut' the corners of thy beard," it exhorts plainly (Leviticus 21:5). The rabbis ultimately interpreted this verse to mean that you can't shave with a one-blade cutting action, but – and here's the fun part – you *can* shave with a *dual* blade *scissors* action, which just happens to be the difference between the way your average stainless steel razor operates and the way most electric shavers get the job done.

To make a long story short: I went out to Rite-Aid – the previous incarnation of Duane Reade – and purchased a Norelco triple-head rechargeable 875RX electric shaver, for which I shelled out forty-nine clams. This turned out to be Torquemada's official torture device. While half an hour of letting that thing ravage my face and neck did help produce some of the most creative and emphatic strings of curses I have ever heard come out of anybody's mouth, it still left me looking like Yasser Arafat. It, too, found its way to Salvation Army Headquarters, where it will torture a homeless person. I went back to the store, finally put my money where my facial hair was, and procured – in exchange for *eighty five dollars* – the only brand on the entire market that really works: a Braun shaver (a product that my younger brother – still obsessing about certain irregularities in the German treatment of Jews during one of the wars in the previous century – insists on referring to as the Eva Braun shaver).

Can someone please clarify to me why – as if it were not already difficult enough to be a Jew – I have to forego the manly pleasure of lathering up, and suffer from five o'clock shadow in my 9 am class?! *Is there some rational explanation for this arbitrary ban on clipping my whiskers any damn way I please*?!

So God, if you're reading this (hey: I read *Your* book, at least three times), then get a pencil, 'cause here's how it tallies up:

One Yves St. Laurent suit:	$250
Tailoring:	$20
Yellow and Purple silk tie:	$35
Norelco Triple-Head Shaver:	$49
Eva Braun Shaver:	$85
Pain and Suffering:	$50
Graduated Interest:	$62.39

What? What do you mean, "Thou shalt not charge interest" (Ex. 22:24)? Are you sure you're a *Jewish* God?

Chapter Twelve

OK – that's enough. I've been regaling you with tawdry tales of Judaic rain-making for quite a few pages now, and could go on doing so, I daresay, for quite a few more. The point I've been trying to hammer home with the help of all of this anecdotal infotainment is the same one I stated so baldly at the outset of this section: Ofer, the mantra-chanting human skyscraper from LAX, was right. *Judaism is nonsense.*

Judaic doctrine and deportment may perhaps have made a certain amount of sense in the eyes of a certain number of people when it first appeared on the world scene several millennia ago. But in our *own* enlightened day and age? Unmitigated malarkey! The Jewish religion is quite simply a big old fraying suitcase stuffed to the bursting point with endless examples of the most unrelieved and unrepentant *irrationality*. It propagates dogmas and conceptions that have no empirical or logical basis whatsoever (at least not anymore), and demands of its adherents untold acts of commission and omission that can boast no conceivable utilitarian justification or practical benefit to speak of. There is simply *no compelling rational reason* why a modern, pragmatic, busy, productively occupied individual should disrupt or complicate his already challenging daily struggle – let alone *run his entire life* – according to all the anachronistic rules, obsolete regulations, outlandish stories and bizarre credos contained in that highly unreasonable institution known as the Jewish faith.

All right – let me qualify that slightly before I get barbecued by a lightning bolt. I don't mean to say that Reason and Judaism are total strangers. It cannot legitimately be claimed, for instance, that there was no element of sound syllogistic thought or step-by-step deductive argumentation informing the deliberations of the talmudic rabbis. *Au contraire*! The lion's share of the literally hundreds of thousands of pages of the Talmud, its commentaries and super-commentaries, consists of an uninterrupted flow of some of the most impressive feats of discursive logic, rigorous reasoning, scintillating ratiocination and dexterous logomachy ever recorded in the intellectual annals of humankind. Proposition and refutation, hypothesis and verification, synthesis and analysis, inferences, proofs, rebuttals, parries, ripostes, arguments a priori, a posteriori, a fortiori – they're all in there, by the oil tanker-load, and are proffered for our consideration (and participation) with incomparable exigency and matchless gusto. Judeo-classical literature is jam-packed to the gills with multifarious examples of the most trenchant cerebral pugilism to be found anywhere, and is simply *peerless across the planet* for the cultivation of the critical faculties – both way back when, and at any time since. A little Talmud study will, I think, convince almost anyone of this truth.

And while no one should be caught dead underrating the preternatural dialectical prowess of the pre-Socratics, or the staggering genius of the Stagirite (Aristotle), nevertheless: were we somehow to find ourselves ringside at an All-Star Battle of the Titans between ("in this cawna, wearing the white and gold togas and the laurel leaves...") all the paragon personalities of Greek philosophy from Thales, Pythagoras and Anaximander down to Plato, Aristotle, Zeno and Diogenes – on the one hand – and ("in *this* cawna, wearing the blue and white striped four cornered garments with the fringes and beanies...") a choice assortment of the chief tannaitic and amoraic luminaries of the Talmud, beginning with Hillel, Shammai, Rabbi Akiba and Rabbi Meir, and wrapping up with the likes of

Resh Lakish, Rabbi Huna, Abbaye and Rava – well, it would be a tough fight, no question about it, but still: I sure as hell know where *my* money would be (let's just say you'd unquestionably see a lot of laurel leaves and bits of torn toga strewn across the arena). Socrates is lucky he didn't have any of *these* guys as interlocutors – the Platonic Dialogues would have gone a *lot* less smoothly. When it comes to disciplined, razor-sharp reasoning, absolutely *nobody* can touch the talmudic rabbis.

So what? They were smart – but they were wrong. There was undeniably, for instance, a healthy dose of logical thinking involved in the aforementioned Hellenic-rabbinic determination that the sun zooms around the pancake-like earth and takes a simmering snooze every night down in the terrestrial basement. Logic's first step (as every big-time cogitator from Lucretius to David Hume has pointed out) involves a processing of sensual stimuli garnered from the surrounding environment. The joint Greek-Pharisaic astronomical think-tank made perfectly reasonable inferences based upon what they had observed in nature (the sun sinking below the horizon, the springs supposedly heating up at night) and then the rabbis derived – no less logically – legal-ritual conclusions from these same inferences (cool water for matzah-baking must be drawn at dusk).

So "A" for intellectual effort, guys, really – thanks for playing! It's just that I'm afraid you *bungled it beyond belief*, see? A major howler, ninety three *million* miles wide of the mark! Nor is this the only example of its kind. Basing themselves upon similarly unassailable inductive methodology, the rabbis of the Talmud – in a plethora of other contexts throughout the tractates of this millennia-old magnum opus – posited the existence of demons, bought heavily into astrology, peopled the deep with mermaids, assumed the Ptolemaic-geocentric universe, claimed that rats are spontaneously generated from the earth, and ascribed a host of telekinetic and other supernatural powers to Torah scholars that the Avengers would have killed to get their hands on. The Talmud asserts that "grafting" watermelon seeds onto an apple-tree will get you pistachio nuts; that a baby's brain and bones come from the paternally donated "white substance," its flesh and blood from the maternally contributed "red substance"; that some birds actually grow on trees (yet nevertheless require ritual slaughter); that lions gestate for three years (it's really three months) and vipers for *seventy*; and that lice are not born of sexual congress but are rather products of perspiration (quite often, these scientific "facts" formed the bases of religious legislation, as for instance – in the latter case – the ruling that lice, unlike other pests, may be done to death on the Sabbath). On these as well as dozens of other questions, the rabbis thought well, but ultimately – how you say in English? – they blew it.

The science of the Greeks didn't fare much better (indeed, their many mistaken notions often served as launch-points for talmudic theorizing, sending the rabbis on not a few wild-goose chases). I mean, no offense intended, but I'll pass on submitting to open-heart surgery performed according to the intricate diagrams and detailed instructions found between the covers of the second century Alexandrian physician Galen's *Anatomical Procedures*. And whereas Aristotle was unquestionably an egghead of colossal proportions, nevertheless, let's face it: the man's entire life's work – set down on thousands of sagely pages filling up scores of encyclopedic tomes that continued to provide the pivot for nearly all scholarly and popular thought regarding the nature of the world around us for a good twenty centuries – the whole impressive oeuvre may pretty much be summed up in one word: *oops*!

There is, of course, no shame in being wrong. Both the Hellenic and the rabbinic thinkers (as well as those of many other ancient cultures and civilizations) did their unflagging damndest under comparatively difficult conditions, evincing an indefatigable curiosity and taxing their amazing brains to the max in an endless quest to slake their chronic thirst for knowledge and understanding – and given the data and equipment available to them at the time, they generally did one helluva job (if it had been me back then, we would still be brushing our teeth with flint rock). Indeed, were it not for their tireless odyssey of trial and error, we today would not be anywhere *near* as far along as *we* are. And for that matter, how far along *are* we? After all, much of our present day science might appear no less off-the-wall to the folks of the future than primitive science does to us (in a hundred years, if you want to call a guy an idiot, you might say: "Come on, Harry – stop being such an *Einstein*!").

All of this is true. We owe the ancients our respect – nay, our awe – as well as our gratitude. Yet the obvious point remains: there is nothing rational about *behaving today*, about living our lives and conducting our communal activities, based on the erroneous conclusions derived from the impressive but nevertheless faulty reasoning of our venerable foreparents.

But the problem with Judaism specifically goes far deeper than that. Suppose the rabbis of the Talmud *had* been vouchsafed some sort of proto-Copernican inspiration, and had actually managed to get the whole solar system thing right. And suppose they had therefore sent us out – not at eventide – but 'round about 4:30 in the morning to fetch that coolest of all possible matzah waters. Would it make any more sense under *those* circumstances to carry out their directive? (Do you *want* to get up at 4:30 in the morning?) It wouldn't, of course. Because the very *underlying premise* that led to this whole eminently logical and soundly scientific discussion regarding the sun and the earth and the water and the time and the temperature; the *seminal motivation* and the *ultimate goal* of this entire series of mathematical measurements and astronomical calculations; beneath it all and behind it all and before it all nestle aspirations that are – at least from the point of view of the modern mindset – irrelevant, wasteful, ludicrous, impractical and even just plain bonkers (in this particular case: devoting hours and days of your precious time, energy and mental and physical elbow grease to the extremely worthy cause of… *dough-rising prevention*).

I mean, jeez, man – don't you have anything *better* to do? Wouldn't you rather spend any given segment of the depressingly short amount of time allotted to you in this once-around Vale of Tears, engaged in pursuits that are empirically useful, that are utilitarian and pleasurable, rather than – say – spending five consecutive hours scrupulously examining the stem of your citron (*etrog*) with an electron microscope to determine just how closely your particular specimen of this fruit approximates the Universal Platonic Form of unblemished "Citronness," and whether it may therefore be efficaciously employed on the holiday of *Sukkot*, in a ceremony where grown people repeatedly shake elaborate palm branch arrangements at one another? Is *that* your idea of optimal time management?

Wouldn't you rather (to take another instance) be busy diversifying your investment portfolio or skiing in Switzerland than conducting a three-day-long, exhaustive investigation to find out whether your neighborhood is properly encompassed by an unbroken border or – if it isn't – ringing it round-about with a string threaded tautly between poles and tied, just so, to nails banged into the tops of said poles (a demarcation known in the nomenclature as an *eruv*), all so that if you wish for some odd reason to take off your sunglasses and place them in your shirt pocket whilst strolling down the street in front of your house on a *Saturday*, you won't inadvertently kindle the inextinguishable wrath of the Lord against you and your entire household for a thousand generations? (Without an enclosure-creating *eruv*, the above act would constitute "carrying" in the public domain, a major no-no on the Sabbath.)

You see, the annoying but undeniable truth of the matter is that so very much of that mighty and unsurpassed rabbinic rationality – in its various versions from the pre-talmudic period all the way down to the pilpulistic study methods in the yeshivas of today – has always been pressed, willy-nilly, into the service of the most incorrigible *irrationality*.

The rabbis may well be wicked logicians – but just look to what ends they're *using* those logical powers! The point of departure in each and every one of the cases adduced above, as well as hundreds of others, is clearly as *irrational* and *impractical* as can possibly be; the *method* of dealing with each case is the only logical element here. Rabbinic rationality, then, is merely a *tool*, an instrument by which to carry out commands and achieve objectives that are – at least according to *our* contemporary perspectives – irremediably irrational. The dizzying feats of logic displayed on every page of the Talmud and its juristical offshoots essentially function as a bridge: a bridge connecting unaccountable motivations (such as the commandment "Thou shalt not sow thy vineyard with two kinds of seed" – Deuteronomy 22:9) to inscrutable goals (fleshing out the hundreds of sub-regulations required to facilitate the *observance* of this commandment). Or perhaps a better analogy would be the humble sandwich, where the two slices of bread on bottom and top represent the supremely illogical underlying premise and no less illogical ultimate aim of a given talmudic pursuit, while the reasoned arguments of the rabbis in between are the edible cement that holds these two slices together – like the yummy, cream-filled center of an Oreo cookie.

What?! God *forbid*, an Oreo cookie! Oreo cookies contain dangerously high concentrations (translation: a few molecules) of animal shortening, obviously derived from…animals – animals that were either inexplicably blacklisted as "unkosher" in the Pentateuch to begin with, or were not ritually slaughtered in the approved manner, or whose flesh was mixed at some point with dairy products, or who are tainted by all three of these unaccountable shortcomings combined. (Oops: this just in! It seems that – according to my friend Yael, who actually makes it her business to stay abreast of such matters – the Nabisco company has now *replaced* its animal shortening with *vegetable* shortening, and has received in return for this sacrifice the much-coveted Kosher stamp of approval. Another major trans-national corporation knuckles under to the Jewish Lobby.)

Anyway, I've made my point, yes? Despite the genuinely logical "interlude" leading from impetus to objective described above, the truly *essential* components of talmudic and overall Judaic discourse and practice – the original commandment and its successful implementation – *simply make no sense* (let alone hold out any appeal) to the modern, rational mind.

At this moment, you are hollering bloody murder at the volume in your hands: "Ob*jec*tion!!" Let me be presumptuous and formulate your objection for you: you're thinking, "Hey, now just *hold* on there, pardner! Up until now in this febrile philippic of yours, you have seemingly canvassed the whole gamut of Jewish observance from high to low and from alpha to omega, in search of the weirdest, wildest, zaniest, *freakiest* ordinances and customs available, on the books and off. Of *course* Judaism will appear irrational in today's terms when you deliberately arrange for such a selective presentation. What you virtually ignored throughout this whole nasty diatribe are all the manifold *mitzvahs*, all the precepts and prescriptions and proscriptions and principles spread across the pages of Judeo-classical literature, which are and always have been the very *epitome* of rationality (no less in terms of their motivations and objectives than in terms of the arguments utilized to get them from the former to the latter) and that are geared solely to the practical betterment of the individual and of human society. Heck: in many cases, Judaism *invented* these seminal theological, ethical and juridical concepts, and generously bestowed them upon the rest of mankind! Check out the *Ten Commandments*, for starters, why don't you?!"

I hear ya. The Ten Commandments – from "Honor thy Father and thy Mother" right through "Thou shalt not Steal" and "Thou shalt not Murder" and all the way down to "Thou shalt not Bear False Witness" or "Covet thy Neighbor's Ass" – are indeed only the tip of the iceberg. The Torah, Talmud and fathomless ocean of legal literature spawned by these two texts, are all stuffed like a Thanksgiving turkey with every kind of regulation, recommendation, exhortation and interdiction you can possibly imagine involving people's relations with other people (most of the statutes I detailed up till now have involved the individual's relationship with *God*). These tenets and laws – unlike those we have surveyed thus far – are quite down to earth, admirably efficient, eminently pragmatic, evince a deep understanding of human nature, are chock full of both lofty sagacity and unparalleled "street smarts," and purpose to make the world a kinder, gentler, fairer, more pleasant and civilized place in which to live.

The Bible and rabbinic literature devote immense amounts of well-used space to such basic human-rights and communal-interest issues as protection of the weak; charity and social welfare; justice and impartial courts; prevention of bribery and corruption; ethics in business; public safety; marital and familial happiness; proper conduct in war; education and the raising of children; fair treatment of laborers; health, hospitality and humility; generosity and the systematic forgiveness of debt; solicitation for strangers and the fair treatment of foreigners; edicts banning slander and provisions prohibiting gossip; rules against bearing a grudge or taking revenge; kindness to animals; the bases of good government; the responsibilities of friendship; the good old Golden Rule (as formulated by Hillel himself); and everything from taking all necessary pains to "return thy brother's straying ox or sheep unto thy brother" (Deuteronomy 22:1); to doing the same for the lost property of your adversary (Exodus 23:4); and up to and including the flat-out prohibition against turning a blind eye and "passing by the ass of he that hates thee staggering under its load – rather, thou shalt surely assist him in releasing his ass's burden" (Exodus 23:5). Yup, it's all in there, these and many score more subjects of the same pragmatic and palatable sort, each one worked out in exquisite detail and codified into miles and miles of practical clauses, to be learned, preserved and – what's more to the point – largely *ob*served by generation after generation of Jews throughout history.

Was it path-breaking stuff? Much of it, yes – especially the realization that lofty moral notions need to be strapped down to mounds of mundane legislation in order to be properly and pervasively implemented in society. Moreover, I don't doubt for a minute that "Jewish genius" or Jewish compassion – or, from a more metaphysical point of view, the special Jewish relationship with God – was indeed responsible for introducing not a few of those fundamental ethical notions *themselves* for the first time into humanity's universe of discourse (no less a paragon of moral conduct than Honest Abe himself effused: "The Bible is the best gift God has given to man; but for it, we could not know right from wrong!"). Some credit us with the introduction of the idea of progress and linear time, others with the development of the notion of resistance to authority, and still others with the creation of the concept of free-will and even revolution. And to the extent that monotheism is necessarily and from all perspectives a good thing – a premise taken for granted, for some reason, by authors across the board (with apologies to Berdichevsky, Chernichovsky and Gore Vidal) – we Jews can certainly take the lion's share of credit for bringing *that* blessing, as well, to some three quarters of the population of the planet. Overall, the "legacy of Israel" to Occidental culture is positive, profound, polymorphous and incalculable. Tolstoy didn't call us "the creators of true civilization" for nothing.

"Give me a 'J'!" ("*J*!") "Give me an 'E'!" ("*E*!") "Give me a 'W'!"... Whoa, *whoa* – put your pom-poms down. Let's deal with this issue soberly, shall we? It's one thing to recognize our weighty contribution to modern culture and civilization – quite another to go off half-cocked like a long parade of modern partisans of the Jewish cause and claim that we basically invented the *very notion* of morality, and created the best mechanism anywhere for its implementation in human relations. Purveyors of this perennial patting of ourselves on the back have an avid supporter (with a twist) in the nineteenth-century German philosopher Friedrich Nietzsche. Read this:

> All that has been done on earth against "the noble," "the powerful," "the masters," "the rulers," fades into nothing compared with what the *Jews* have done against them; the Jews, that priestly people, who in opposing their enemies and conquerors were ultimately satisfied with nothing less than a radical revaluation of their enemies' values...It was the Jews who, with awe-inspiring consistency, dared to invert the aristocratic value-equation (good = noble = powerful = beautiful = happy = beloved of God) and to hang on to this inversion with their teeth, the teeth of the most abysmal hatred (the hatred arising from impotence), saying, "The wretched alone are the good; the poor, impotent, lowly, alone are good; the suffering, deprived, sick, ugly alone are pious, alone are blessed by God – and you, the powerful and noble, are on the contrary the evil, the cruel, the lustful, the insatiable, the godless to all eternity."

A follow-up to Nietzsche's extensive treatment in *Beyond Good and Evil* of what he famously dubbed "Slave Morality" (invented by our ancestors in Egypt during heated intellectual exchanges whilst shlepping pyramid stones), the above passage from the same author's *On the Genealogy of Morals* can best be understood if we remember that Nietzsche – like so many other thinkers of the late 1800s – was heavily under the spell of Darwin, and especially the Darwinian notion of "Survival of the Fittest." Evolution into ever-improving versions of the human species (extrapolated Nietzsche from the

Darwinian thesis) occurs via process of elimination: the strong and well-adapted vanquish – or just outlive – the weak and misfitted; those thus "naturally selected" mate with each other and produce even mightier offspring; and eventually we arrive at the *Übermensch* – the Superman, the Master Race, the purpose and pinnacle of all human existence, indeed, of all creation.

Sounds like a plan! Only just as all those rough ridin', chest-thumpin', Achilles-meets-John-Galt-meets-Dolph-Lundgren vital warrior types were busy charging across the countryside, grunting and hunting and frolicking and bathing their chiseled muscles in pure-water streams, picking off your occasional ninety-pound weakling for target practice and leaning over their equine shanks to scoop up and bless with their superior DNA whatever buxom blondes they could find and carry off – just as all this merry and manly natural selection was proceeding apace to the zestful soundtrack of "Ride of the Valkyries"...in come these pathetic, sniveling, wimpy, sparrow-chested, bespectacled Jewish weasels and spoil all the fun and progress with their incessant and self-righteous whining about (to be read in a really petulant, goody-two-shoes tone of voice) "Oppress not the *widow*, nor the *orphan*; molest not the *stranger*, nor the *poor*" (Zechariah 7:10); and "Deliver the *feeble* and the *downtrodden* when they cry out, and redeem their souls from *violence* and *persecution*!" (Psalms 72:12); and "Be eyes to the *blind*, and feet to the *lame*, and a father to the *needy*" (Job 29:15); and "Thou shalt not abuse the *toiler*, nor the *destitute* and *impoverished*, whether a fellow countryman or a foreigner!" (Deuteronomy 24:14). Under this new Jewish affirmative-action system, the weak and poorly adjusted mate as often, if not more so, than the strong and splendidly adjusted, and the species, far from improving, may even regress. Say *Auf Wiedersehen*! to the *Übermensch* – say *Willkommen*! to the *Untermensch*, or to what Nietzsche liked to call the "last man," the personification of mediocrity and cockroach-type survivability.

To hear Nietzsche and – on the opposite side of the same coin – the many modern champions of Judaism tell it, until the ancient Hebrews descended upon and enlightened (Nietzsche would say emasculated) the savage peoples of the primitive oecumene with their newfound system of morality, the prevailing ethical norms and values of the ancient world could more or less be summed up by Arnold Schwartzneggar in Conan the Barbarian's answer to his master's classic question: "Conan, what is best in life?"

Conan: "To crush enemies; to see them driven before you; and to listen to the lamentation of the women."

Before the Jews showed up – so this theory would have us believe – life anywhere you went was basically nasty, brutish and short (and the orthodonture *sucked*). No one had any scruples or was ever nice; they all ran around day-in and day-out drawing and quartering one another and making off with each other's wives; it was just one long Hutu-Tutsi incubus of a Mardis Gras orgy-massacre.

Needless to say, this portrayal is far from accurate. Although I wouldn't recommend time-travel vacationing in the Middle Bronze Age without some really wicked health coverage, nevertheless not a few cultures, religions and civilizations contemporaneous with and even antedating the Israelite advent have left ample evidence of intricately constructed moral and legal systems designed – among other things – specifically to shelter the defenseless from the depredations of the mighty. One thinks immediately of the Babylonian Code of Hammurabi, circa 2500 BCE, the preamble and epilogue to which sum up the motivation for its enactment: "so that the strong should not harm the weak…to protect the widow and the orphan, to establish justice throughout the land, to settle disputes and heal injuries…" One is put in mind also of the formulaic "ideal biography" found engraved on so many upper-class tombstones in ancient Egypt – centuries before the Theophany at Sinai – to wit: "I spoke the truth, acted in good faith and judged fairly, rescuing, with all my power, the weak from the strong, giving bread to the hungry and clothing to the poor…" Or how about that truly magnanimous and earliest-ever "declaration of human rights" known as the "Cyrus Cylinder," etched in cuneiform by the greatest of Persian world conquerors in the sixth century BCE, and currently sitting pretty in the British Museum with all that other purloined art. And while we're on the subject, Iranian Zoroastrianism should not be overlooked, with its epic, dualist battle between Good and Evil, in the context of which humans are the dedicated *fravashis* or foot-soldiers fighting on the side of the good god Ahura Mazda and the light. One thinks, as well, of the moralistic "Way of the Ancient Kings" of pre-Ch'in China, revered and to some extent revived by Confucius and his cohorts; nor can we even ignore many aspects of traditional Greek and Indian civilization.

So I'm really sorry to disappoint you, but – with all due respect to Adolph Hitler's backhanded compliment: "The Jews have inflicted two wounds on mankind: circumcision on its body, and conscience on its soul" – the truth of the matter is that we can claim neither the patent nor the monopoly on a large number of the purely ethical ideas ensconced in Jewish law. And concomitantly, it must be admitted that this moral-rational aspect of Judaism, as incredibly impressive and undeniably effective as it has often been, is most definitively *not* the aspect of our faith which *uniquely* characterizes it, which sets it apart today as specifically "Jewish" (it is the *irrational* component – all the weird rituals and customs, several of which we caricatured earlier on – which shoulder *that* responsibility). Say what you will, but I know of no major religion or culture in the modern world where murder is *not* prohibited or probity in business *not* enjoined. And *everybody* encourages – and many enforce – the giving of charity and the promotion of social welfare. You don't have to be Jewish to inherit or adhere to a decent moral-ethical system.

Nor, I daresay, do all the legislative gifts we *did* come bearing to the world necessarily represent what most of us today would view as an advance in matters moral. Like, try this here on for size: "If a man lie with another man as one does with a woman, they have both committed an abomination, and shall surely be put to death" (Leviticus 20:13). Execute homosexuals – enlightened enough for you?

Fairness and accuracy require a momentary digression. The Talmud sets up so many practically unfullfillable conditions for the carrying out of death sentences in general, that Rabbi Elazar ben Azariah can declare: "A Supreme Court that puts to death even one person in seventy years is termed tyrannical" (Makkot 1:10). In the particular case of the homosexual act, for instance, in order actually to enforce the ultimate (or any) penalty, you would need – among a host of other prohibitive prerequisites – at least two competent witnesses standing right next to the perpetrators just prior to the deed, who must admonish the eager paramours repeatedly, as well as obtain explicit testimony from both participants to the effect that (1) they (the homosexuals) are aware that the act they are about to commit is a flagrant violation of Torah law; (2) they are aware that the act they are about to commit in fact constitutes a *capital* crime according to that same scriptural source; (3) they are aware of the specific *method* of execution – stoning – that they will be forced to undergo if convicted (a thought that has been known to depress the libido); and (4) despite their complete awareness of all of the above, they plan to go ahead and perform this "abomination" of theirs anyway. Both witnesses must subsequently perceive no less than the *locus coitus* itself, and observe actual penetration with their own four eyes.

Thus does the Talmud make short work of the condemnation and punishment of homosexuals recorded in and required by the Torah, rendering it entirely impracticable. But none of this in any way changes the fact that this law is *on the books*, on the "Good" Book, the one that we teach to our children and read publicly every Saturday in the synagogue, indelibly inscribed there by the finger of the very Divine Entity we praise in prayer on that same occasion in that same venue.

And while we're talking about problematic prescriptions, how about this biblical version of von Clausewitz:

> When thou drawest nigh unto a city to fight against it, call upon it to surrender…if it does not surrender to you, but would make war against you, then shalt thou besiege it. And when the Lord thy God delivereth the city into thy hand, thou shalt slaughter every male therein with the edge of the sword; but the women, and children, and cattle, and all that is in the city, you shall take with you as booty…and if thou seest among the captives a beautiful woman, and hast a desire toward her and wouldst have her as thy wife; then shalt thou bring her home to thy house, and she shall shave her head and pare her nails; and she shall put off the raiment of her captivity, and shall remain in thy house, and shall cry over her father

> and mother a full month: and after that thou shalt go in unto her, and be her husband, and she shall be thy wife. And it shall be, if thou have no delight in her, then thou shalt set her free to go where she will, and shall not sell her for money – thou shalt not treat her as a slave, because thou hast humbled her. (Deuteronomy 20:12-14; 21:10-14)

Talk about crushing enemies and listening to the lamentation of the women! Actually, as is clear from even a cursory glance at the above text, this whole procedure represents what was without doubt a remarkably "progressive" attempt in its time to alleviate the unspeakable suffering of ancient female POWs (just read Euripides' devastating account of the fall of Troy, to get some idea about *that* predicament). And yet the level of morality reflected in these verses is obviously *still* not up to our standards. We are not big fans today, last time I checked, of slaying all the men and hauling off their wives as booty in time of war, whether or not we let them do their nails. And that brings me to my next point, which concerns Ringo Starr.

When I was a kid, my Mom drummed it into my head that Ringo Starr was the greatest percussionist who had ever lived (she also had me convinced that he was Jewish – which I believed primarily because of his nose. I later obtained a snapshot of his baptism certificate). I grew up accepting as gospel truth that no one could *ever* pound them tin cans like Ringo, not in a million years – they had simply broke the mold. My Mom still clings tenaciously to this belief. I, on the other hand, was privileged as I cruised through teenagerhood to have my eardrums bashed in by the likes of Keith Moon, Carl Palmer (of Emerson, Lake and…), Led Zeppelin's John Bonham and the amazing and versatile Neil Peart (Rush), and gradually my faith in mother's catechism began to falter. Now that I am a man, I have put away childish things. I know that there are lots of better drummers out there than Ringo. Oh, sure, these other maestros were raised on the Beatles just like the rest of us, and many enthusiastically admit their debt to the style, techniques and innovations of Richard Starkey (Ringo's real name). But they took what he had to offer, incorporated what they liked (and *improved* on it), discarded what they didn't, and then *moved on*. That's what makes them such great drummers!

Like rock-n-roll, like human moral development. Did Judaism originate or at least give a new and more powerful form to a whole spectrum of rational and ethical concepts? You betcha. Has a steady stream of societies, religions and ideologies since that time imbibed from this overflowing source, selecting, modifying, integrating, combining with attractive and useful finds from other rich cultural mines, culling the best of many worlds in order to synthesize them all into a whole that aspires to be greater than the sum of its parts? No doubt about it. That's what we affectionately refer to as Western Civilization. But let's simplify the matter. If Judaism has so much to offer, then hey: separate out what you personally see as its wheat from what you personally see as its chaff (a sort of "fillet of Judaism," if you will, sans the bones and other yukky stuff). Then do the same for all the other systems you encounter, add a healthy dash of *your* particular personality and outlook, *et voila*: your very own individual ethical hodge-podge. That's the rational, modern, truly *moral* thing to do, now isn't it?

And were you to venture that perhaps Judaism is a package deal, designed so that it will only work with all its parts intact, I could only respond by saying that it sure beats me what possible connection avoiding cheeseburgers could conceivably have to making this a better world, or for that matter what possible connection it could conceivably have *to anything*. Would the more moral and rational side of the Judaic system collapse if we were to just remove this really nasty little dietary clause? (You remember my Methodist girlfriend Sue? Her family members were some of the nicest, most decent, caring, principled, moral and upstanding people I have ever met in my life – and they ate *shrimp* by the bucketful!)

Now: are there upwards of nine hundred and thirty-six *thousand* Jewish fundamentalist spin doctors running around today who have made entire careers out of deftly defusing such annoying doubts and dilemmas and demonstrating with the greatest aplomb how – if only we approach these matters from the "proper" perspective – Judaic principles and precepts turn out to be (surprise, surprise) the most enlightened and moral principles and precepts to be found anywhere on the planet? Of course there are. Disturbed by Darwin, galled by Galileo, non-plussed by Newton, troubled by issues of God and evil? No need to fret. These ubiquitous PR men of Providence, who are invariably hip to the "Theory of Everything," will be right on over to vacuum your brain out of your ear with the help of every specious justification and fallacious rationalization cooked up over the centuries by the cowardly mind of man. I grant you, none of our Jewish propagandists has risen to the dizzying heights scaled by a contemporary defender of the *Islamic* faith – one Dr. Abdullah Sakr of Illinois – who, in his recently re-issued blockbuster book, *Pork: Possible Reasons for its Prohibition* (Lombard, 1998), undertakes to explain why his religion, like ours, forbids the ingestion of swine products:

> The hog is a unique animal. The boar does not mind seeing his sow mate with another boar in front of him. This habit is unique in that other animals cannot tolerate it. To speak for the boar, one may say that the boar is, in effect, saying: "Let my sow mate with other boars! Who cares, as long as they (his sow and the other boars) agree among themselves and are enjoying sex among themselves." Thus, the sow has permission to mate with as many boars as she wants and in front of her own boar without any shame of either. In such a situation the sow behaves as the worst prostitute while the boar acts as her pimp, allowing his female to mate with others even in front of his eyes and without much concern. We have seen that the hormone diethylstilbestoral, injected into calves, was passed on to humans who ate their meat and thus increased the ratio of homosexuality in man. Therefore, eating the flesh of the hog may affect the personality character of the individual by increasing immorality, including homosexuality, lesbianism, adultery, prostitution, streakers [!], looting, killing, stabbing, shooting, snipring [sic], strangling, robbing, stockpiling of arms, and the like. The free mixing of the sexes that one sees in non-Muslim societies is really a dreadful thing to observe. There is no concept of ethics or morality, but their

> concept is only sex enjoyment and free sex interchange...As for vegetarians, on the other hand, experiments were conducted on children in Maryland, USA. They were given a daily diet of carbohydrates and sweets without animal proteins. The children turned out to be hypersensitive, intolerant, aggressive and hyperactive. This may partially explain the persecution of Muslims in India today by the strict Hindu vegans there... (pp. 18-19)

Of course, our Jewish apologists are far more sophisticated than Dr. Sakr. For instance, here is how they prove that the six days of creation described in the Bible "actually did contain the billions of years of the emergence of the cosmos, even while the days *remained twenty-four-hour days*." Einstein is called to the colors: at velocities approaching the speed of light, time slows down, taught the not-so-dumb patent clerk from Ulm. Our indefatigable champions of *creatio ex nihilo* duly extrapolate: the expansion of the universe in the Big Bang from the original infinitesimal mass-energy point to the present-day vast circumference of space, occurred at such breakneck speed that billions of years of development fit in to exactly six days. Pretty impressive, huh? Get these guys a Nobel Prize!

Two thousand years before the discovery of relativity, the rabbis of the Talmud were already hard at work "apologizing." Case in point: King David, the Bible tells us (2 Sam. 11-12), saw a married woman – one Bathsheba – bathing buck-naked on a Jerusalem roof, the glistening droplets of mountain-spring water cascading like so many precious gems over the hills and valleys of her callipygian contours; he sent for her, seduced her and impregnated her, while her husband Uriah – one of David's most loyal and steadfast servants, who loved his sovereign like nobody's business – was off at war risking his life on David's behalf.

Talmud: "What are you – on drugs?"

David then *rewarded* Uriah for all those years of unswerving devotion by sending him *back* to the front carrying *his own death warrant* in his hands, signed and sealed by the King himself, which instructed the commander of the Hebrew forces to (and I quote) "place Uriah in the first line where the fighting is fiercest, then withdraw your forces from around him, so that he be smitten and killed" (2 Samuel 11:14).

Talmud: "Yeah – *right.*"

No, really. In fact, the Prophet Nathan (2 Sam. 12:1-10) subsequently brought a direct message from no less venerable a source than *Almighty God Himself* excoriating King David for committing this horrible sin!!

Talmud: "Almighty…*who*?"

Here is the actual talmudic text (Shabbat 55b):

> Rabbi Samuel son of Nahmani said in the name of Rabbi Jonathan: Whoever says that David sinned [in the matter of Bathsheba] is in manifest error, for it is written (1 Sam. 18:14): "The Lord was with David." Is it conceivable that David would sin while the Lord was with him?!…[What really happened was that] every soldier who went out to fight in the wars of David wrote a temporary bill of divorce for his wife (so that were he to fall in battle without witnesses to his demise she would be allowed to remarry).

Get it? Bathsheba was, technically speaking, "on the market" when David ravished her; no adultery here!

Ok, fine. Let's say. But what about the murder of her poor husband – sorry, I mean her poor *late* husband – Uriah?

"Oh, *that*," says the Talmud, and deftly refers us to 2 Sam. 11, where David, having been informed that Bathsheba is "with child" as a result of their assignation, quickly summons Uriah back from the front and instructs him to "go down to your house and bathe your feet," in the hopes that he will engage in some hot and heavy conjugal relations with the Mrs. and thereby cover their tracks (ah, the heady days before DNA testing!). But the noble Uriah will not hear of it:

> The Ark and Israel and Judah are on the battlefield at Succoth, and my master Joab and your majesty's men are camped in the

> open; how can I go home and eat and drink and sleep with my wife? By your life, I will not do this.

"Ah hah!" cry the talmudic rabbis (Shabbat 56a). "Defy the King's authority, will you? That's a capital offense! Uriah clearly *deserved* to die." (Should these guys be somebody's campaign manager, or what?)

The omnipresent vindicators of orthodox doctrine do not, of course, confine their efforts to the realms of science or sexual morality: they will be happy to evaporate discomforting dilemmas for you in a whole hoard of existential disciplines, so that you can achieve true inner tranquility and walk around with a stupid smile on your face while drooling on your shoes. Is there, for instance, any antagonism between the traditional Judaic approach to the status of women and the modern struggle for women's liberation otherwise known as feminism? Should a self-respecting woman today be bothered by the first words of God to a female, as recorded in the beginning of the Bible: "Your passion shall be toward your husband, and he shall rule over you" (Genesis 3:16)? Should she be offended by the prescribed prayer Jewish men have been accustomed to utter for millennia, hard upon awakening: "Blessed art Thou, O Lord our God, King of the Universe, for not making me a woman"? How about the prohibition against her singing in the presence of men (no such proscription exists vice-versa), the mandatory covering of her hair from the day she is married until death do us part, her complete disqualification as a witness in Jewish courts, the fact that she is debarred from active participation in some fifty percent of the religion's rituals – should any of *this* give the modern woman pause?

Nah. She just doesn't *understand*. In truth, you can be a fully observant Jewish woman *and* a fiery feminist…all at the same time! There's no *contradiction* here, God forbid! Indeed, if only properly comprehended, Judeo-classical sources clearly place women on a rung far *higher* than that occupied by men, who constitute the unquestionably inferior party in this enlightened system, and who have to perform all those silly rituals and time-consuming ceremonies solely in order to make up for their relative spiritual inadequacy.

Many years ago as an American tourist in Jerusalem, I went to buy myself a pair of phylacteries – thus designated in English from the Greek *phylakterion* meaning "amulet" – those black leather cubes-on-straps containing parchment inked with verses from Exodus and Deuteronomy, which are tied around the forehead and weak arm during morning prayers and otherwise known as *tefillin* (from the Hebrew *tefila* or supplication). I was accompanied on this pious excursion by a young woman whom I had recently met named Shari, and together we entered the store of the *sofer st.a.m* (the first word means "scribe," the second is an acronym for *sefarim* – scrolls, *tefillin* – phylacteries, and *mezuzot* – mezuzahs. This fellow is a Jack of all sacred inscriptions). The *sofer* laid out my options for me: there was this perfectly kosher and entirely respectable $100 pair he could let me have, or – if I were really serious about my *tefillin* – he could cancel all appointments and spend the remainder of the afternoon working me up a super-deluxe $400 set.

I was candy. I certainly didn't want my prayers to be ignored by the Power That Be due to insufficiently fancy phylacteries, and what was far more important: *the girl was standing right there.* I had no choice but to yank out my wad and peel off four crisp Franklins, half the money I had brought with me to the country.

We walked around the neighborhood for a few hours, and when we returned to pick up the goods, Shari asked the *sofer* out of curiosity why it was that *she* couldn't wear *tefillin.* The *sofer* asked us to pull up a chair, began swaying and tugging at his beard, and delivered himself of a long soliloquy, the upshot of which was that *tefillin* are (ready?)...a punishment. That's right: phylacteries are nothing more and nothing less than an amaranthine, fathers-ate-sour-grapes-so-sons'-teeth-are-set-on-edge, Original-Sin-type penalty-cum-penance for the worship of the Golden Calf in the wilderness over three thousand years ago. And since the Midrash (rabbinic stories, legends and interpretations of the Torah text) states that the *women* of that ancient desert generation did not participate with the men in that particularly heinous abomination, therefore (concluded the *sofer* with a flourish) ladies are fortunate enough to be exempt from this burdensome and humiliating penitential commandment. Thank your lucky stars, Shari!

Impressed by how fast he was on his feet, it was nevertheless all I could do not to string up that *sofer* by his own black straps: I had just shelled out four hundred bucks – for a *punishment*?! Had I only known beforehand, I would have definitely purchased the no-frills pair. (Lord – You *know* that's going on Your tab.)

In case they come across an individual with a bona fide brain in his head who doesn't buy into any of this unconscionable claptrap, the professional exonerators of the Holy One, blessed be He, inevitably resort to one final, as it were, "rational" argument for why we should adhere to the tenets and directives of Judaism. It goes like this: you really ought to be a committed, observant, practicing Jew because…*God said so.*

In accepting this assertion, we would be following the exemplary behavior of our sandy ancestors, who greeted the Lord's offer of a covenant at Sinai with the simple commitment: "*Na'aseh ve-nishma*" – "We will do, and we will hear" (Exodus 24:7). Interprets the Talmud: do what God tells you first – ask questions later.

Now, as is obvious to one and all, this claim relies before anything else on the assumption that God does indeed exist, and that He is specifically the God of *Jewish* historiography – you know, the one who handed down the Torah through Moses to the recently released slaves on their way to the Promised Land. Whereas the learned propagandists can prove this to be the case in a New York minute, slow-witted ignoramuses like myself cannot.

But that's not what bothers me about this claim. Let's accept as a given – whether on faith or under the influence of some truly convincing apologetic logic – that God definitely does exist, and that He's *exactly* the God that the Jewish sources (and only the Jewish sources) say He is. Fine. In that case……um……**so what**? I still don't get it: why on earth should I obey Him?

You're confused: "Because He's *God*, dingbat" (you point out). "He's the indisputable Boss, the Commander in Chief, the Head Honcho, the Big Cheese. He's the Ultimate Supreme Overlord – *by definition*!"

Oh – I see the problem. It's all clear to me now. You were obviously hiding out somewhere in central Antarctica teaching penguins how to play mahjong during the sixties. That must be how you managed to miss all those groovy dudes with the Hendrix Hairdos and the six-mile-wide bell-bottoms sporting that absolute greatest t-shirt of all time, upon which were emblazoned the simple but revolutionary words:

Yeah, I guess you must have hibernated through that. You see, maybe once upon a time you could have convinced people – people who had never experienced or even heard about the inexpressible joys and breathe-the-air *amazingness* of that singular phenomenon called freedom – maybe you could have convinced such deprived souls sometime in the distant past that authority figures should be obeyed **because they are authority figures**. Not anymore. The new and most marvelous imperative for decades now, even for centuries, is to question, to challenge, even to *defy* authority – and the Greater, Higher and more Absolute the Authority…*the more that authority needs challenging*!

True: our faithful guide through sand and spirit, Moses son of Amram, is honored no less than seven times in the first chapter of the Book of Joshua with the post-mortem accolade: "*servant* of God." Yet even *he* was not half the Lord's lackey they say he was. At least three times, the Bible shows Moses defying a direct divine order, and remonstrating with the Lord – *who invariably backs down* – for daring to issue it in the first place. As, for instance, in this here:

> The Lord spoke unto Moses and Aaron, saying, "Stand back from this community, so that I may annihilate them in an instant!" But Moses and Aaron fell on their faces and said:

> "O God, Source of the spirits of all flesh! When one man sins, will You be wrathful with the entire community?!" (Numbers 16:20-21)

Or this:

> The Lord said to Moses: "I see that this is a stiff-necked people. Now, stand down from Me so that My anger may blaze forth against them, and I may eradicate them utterly, and I will make of thee [Moses] a great nation"...
>
> ...And the Lord [after three verses of scolding from Moses] *renounced* the punishment He had planned to bring upon His people. (Exodus 32:9-14)

Or this:

> The Lord said to Moses: "I will smite this people with pestilence and destroy them, and will make of you [Moses] a nation greater and mightier than they...
>
> ...And God said [seven verses of Mosaic tongue-lashing later]: "I have pardoned according to thy word." (Numbers 14:11-20)

(Appalled by the Lord's short fuse? Try working with a large group of Jews on a common project sometime, and see if *you* don't start fantasizing about a hundred and one uses for a neutron bomb.) And how about the following impressive bit of Mosaic brassiness:

> Moses went back to the Lord and said: "Alas, this people is guilty of a great sin in making for themselves a god of gold. Now, if You will forgive their sin, well and good; but if not, than *erase me from Your book which You have written.* (Exodus 32:32)

The Talmud goes even further. It describes Moses "knocking words against the Height," grabbing God by the seat of His pants, and actually urging the Master of the Universe on one occasion to stop "acting like a woman." The Lord is shown, for His part, sheepishly thanking Moses for "instructing Me well," altering scriptural diction – nay, scriptural *principles* – at Moses' demand, even expressing gratitude to the desert prophet for "giving Me a new lease on life" (see Berachot 32a and Numbers Rabbah 19). Moses and God, the Bible stresses, "spoke face to face, as a man speaketh to his friend" (Exodus 33:11).

It is significant that the Bible also takes pains to inform us that "the man Moses was exceedingly humble, more so than any other person on earth" (Numbers 12:3). Don't you see? All that unparalleled humility – and he *still* didn't knuckle under to the Lord's authority! Shall you and I, then, be *haughty* enough to lay claim to *more meekness than Moses*? It would be downright *presumptuous* on our parts to defy the Lord any *less* than he did! And while we're at it, check out our father Abraham who, despite his own abject humility ("I am but dust and ashes") rails at the One God he is credited with discovering: "Shall the Judge of all the land not do justice?!" (Genesis 18:23-33).

It was Abraham's grandson Jacob, however, who set the seal on this subject by pulling no punches with the Lord – literally: they had a boxing match (Genesis 32:29) – and thereby acquired for us our national name, the most majestic, noble, valiant, and exhilarating honorific in the entire history of world literature: **Isra-el – "He who fights God**." We Jews are theomachists: no cow-towing to the Creator for us.

In short: this groveling, truculent, sycophantic argument based on authority worship – as if everything from the Magna Carta down to Abolition never even took place – really sets my kettle a steamin'. God would take me out of Egypt, would He, with a mighty hand and an outstretched arm, so that I might be "a slave unto Me, and not a slave unto My slaves"? I'll tell You what: *don't do me any favors*! I am nobody's slave.

"Hail, Spartacus!" you jeer. "Kirk Douglas couldn't have said it better! But surely you are familiar with the famous interpretation of the verse describing the Ten Commandments – 'The tablets were the work of God, and the writing His writing, *engraved* upon the tablets'

(Exodus 32:16) – bidding us to tweak a vowel here and a consonant there and read not 'engraved (*kharut*) upon the tablets,' but 'freedom (*kherut*) upon the tablets'?"

Yes, I've heard that Midrash. "Bondage to the Highest," mocked William James, "is seen as identical with true liberty." *The law will set you free*. Well, you know what? There's truth to that. It is undeniably the case that without limits, without structure, without at least some semblance of discipline, nearly everyone will become a slave – to his passions, to his addictions, to just plain laziness (ask any smoker you know if she is "free" to smoke, or any obese person you know if he is "free" to fill his belly). In this sense, the law does indeed facilitate freedom. But whose law? And why necessarily *God's* law? Maybe there's a better normative structure around for the taking – or for the making! Besides, only when the law can be changed by its adherents (if, for instance, it no longer serves the cause of freedom in their eyes) may its adherents be said to be truly liberated. In the eyes of believers, God's law *cannot* be changed, period – say what you will.

"Very well," you hit back. "What about the fact that He *created* you? Isn't *that* sufficient reason to submit to God's sway?"

Um…*no*. Where's the connection – between creation and total and everlasting obligation, I mean? Do you remember that *Star Trek* where they beamed aboard this satellite-robot named NOMAD that hovered in mid-air and would always obey William Shatner's orders because (as it had mistakenly concluded) "you – are – the – Kirk; you – are – the – *Creator*." Do you remember that episode? Then would you tell me something, please: DO I FREAKING *LOOK* LIKE R2D2 TO YOU?! Is *that* why you think I should do whatever my "Creator" tells me? Because I'm some kind of clanking tin-can automaton? Jeez, man. You have *got* to be kidding.

The Talmud avers that there are three participants in the creation of a human child: the mother, the father, and the Holy One, blessed be He. Now, does that mean that – just because she was involved in the "creative" process – you should *always* listen to your mother? (Well, the answer to *that* question is: "yes," but that's not the point.) Why should creature necessarily be enthralled to creator – whether the latter is spelled with an upper or a lower case "C"?

"Because, you unbearable fool," you plough forward, increasingly frustrated by such unheard-of contumacy – "*as* your Creator, and the Author of all that exists, God is obviously omniscient, sees the big picture, and knows what's best for you. It therefore behooves you to comply with His commands."

Oh, please – behoove me no behooves! I mean, it goes without saying, doesn't it, that few aspects of life are more precious and beautiful – are more supremely *alive* – than that adventurous Magical Mystery Tour known as *independence and uncertainty*. I'll make my own mistakes, thank you – and I'll take the consequences! That, over living a "paint-by-the-numbers" existence any day (yes: even if the painting in question is a Da Vinci). Imagine Frank Sinatra singing: "I did it…*His* waaaaaaay." Doesn't have quite the same ring, now does it?

"Well," you venture, disgusted and getting ready to call in the Inquisition, "perhaps you would consider 'nullifying your will in favor of His will' (as the Talmud formulates it) because…you *love* Him."

Hmmm. Let's accept for the sake of argument that we are all truly head over heels in love with the Creator (it's not like we have a choice in the matter – we've been commanded: "Thou shalt love the Lord thy God with all thy heart, with all thy soul and with all thy might" [Deuteronomy 6:5]…and that's an *order*, private!). "And so," says you, "obey Him – because you *love* Him!"

Sigh. The Russians have a name for people (well, men) who conduct themselves in this uxorious manner: *podkablukom*, which literally means: "under his wife's stiletto heel." English speakers have a name for such types, too: dishrag. Would you please *give me a break*? Who, for crying out loud, actually advocates that you should do everything you are told, *just because you are in love with the one who's doing the telling*?

That's it – now you're pissed off. "Very well, you recalcitrant, overweening, too-big-for-your-britches Epicurean infidel. How 'bout you just fall in line with the Guy upstairs because He's the *biggest, baddest, meanest, roughest, toughest entity in the entire universe*, and you had better knuckle under to His holy hegemony or else He's gonna whup your tail smack into the middle of…"

Yeah, yeah. I was waiting for that. Always the last resort of every doctrinaire ideologue: coercion. Let me tell you a little story.

I had the somewhat dubious privilege as a child to attend the Lamberton Public Elementary School in Philadelphia. It's true, I was unceremoniously booted out of this institution of lower learning in the second grade for subversive and un-American activity (I'm not kidding – but that's a story for another time). Nevertheless, the campus was more or less adjacent to my house, and so for the next several years I used to sneak back into class every so often, to hang out wit my homies. Anyway, on the occasion of one of these atavistic visits, the fifth grade social studies teacher, Mrs. Artin, in what was – I must say – a surprisingly enterprising display of both pedagogical initiative and ecumenical pluralism, had managed to assemble together all at once in our homeroom a rabbi, a priest and a Protestant minister. These representatives of their respective confessions had been commandeered, so it turned out, for the purpose of exposing us to the salient texts of their competing faiths. You can imagine the plethora of golf-course jokes engendered among us kids by this singular panoply of diverse divines standing with their backs to the blackboard, but after we had calmed down, they began their presentations.

The Very Reverend kicked off with – believe it or not – Luther's *Ninety Five Theses*, and he was soon yanked off the stage by a vigilant (and Catholic) Mrs. Artin. The Padre then weighed in with "Our Lord's Prayer," which went over rather well, especially since four-fifths of my predominantly Italian and Irish class reverently recited it by heart together with him. Finally, it was Rabbi Plinker's turn (whose name has been slightly altered to protect the…rabbinic).

Now, Rabbi Plinker, well – let's just say, the Vilna Gaon he was not. He was one of those rabbis, you know, who had studied at the Seminary for seven years, and he's still working on: "The congregation will please rise; the congregation will please be seated. The congregation will please rise…" Anyway, the right rabbi had brought with him – appropriately enough – the *Shema Yisrael* or "Hear O Israel" prayer for our edification, the most significant Jewish supplication on the books. He handed out the text, and together we read, *inter alia*, the following sentences:

> Beware, lest you go astray, and you worship other gods and prostrate yourselves before them. For then will the Lord's anger be kindled against you, and He shall shut up the heavens and there will be no rain, and the land will cease to yield its fruit, etc., etc. (Deuteronomy 11:16-17)

Now, not coming from a religious family, to put it mildly, I sure didn't know very much about Judaism at ten years of age, but ignorance never having constituted a barrier to pontification on my part, I raised my hand, and initiated the interrogation:

"So now, let me see if I've got this right, Rrrrabbi. According to what we've just read in this here prayer – which you yourself stated is the most important of its kind in the entire Jewish religion – the *reason* that we have to do what God says, and serve Him exclusively, is because if we *do not* do these things…um…He's gonna kick our butt."

"Well, well," responded Rabbi Plinker, a bit taken aback but still sporting that condescending clerical tone. "You certainly do have a straightforward way of putting things, young man – 'kick our butt,' indeed! – howbeit, yes, I think we can fairly say that your statement sums up the position outlined in the passage in question, yes…"

So I'm like: "I see. And I wonder…could you *tell* me, Rabbi: what's the worst possible thing God could do to us – you know – in retaliation for our insubordination to these various ordinances? (I'm embellishing: I didn't know the word "various" in fifth grade.) What's the *worst thing* He could do?"

The rabbi stroked his goatee, went pensive for a moment. Then his eyes lit up, and he exclaimed: "My dear boy – He's *God.* He can do *anything*. Why, He could…*destroy the world*!"

Now I had him. "A-*ha*!" I bellowed (silly rabbi) – "*No He couldn't*!" You see, I had read my Child's Bible and watched endless episodes of "Captain Noah" just like the next kid, and I knew just as well as anybody that the Lord had placed one massive, Mississippi-arch-like, razzle-dazzle rainbow in the firmament *après la deluge*, as a sign and a witness and a solemn commitment that He would never – and I mean *never* – destroy the entire world again: "I have set My bow in the clouds, and it shall be for a token of a covenant between Me and the earth…that I will never again smite every living thing, as I have now done" (Genesis 9:12 and 8:21).

So now Rabbi Plinker is getting a little flustered, and he starts in with – you know – "Ahem, mmmmmmm, yes…right…of *course*. That is...uh…a very astute observation young man. Now, if we could just move on to…"

Yeah, right. Like I was gonna let him off the hook now, just as I was closing in for the kill: "Hooooold on!" I thundered. "Just *one* more little question, Rrrabbi" – this, accompanied by my best Clarence Darrow smile. "I read last month in *Newsweek* where the Soviet Union has stockpiled enough nuclear warheads in its arsenals to blow up the entire world *seven times over*. Now if – as you maintain – the reason we are supposed to obey God is because of the severity of the punishment He might mete out to us human beings if we *don't* do what He says; and if – as we have just established – God's ability to punish us is heavily *restricted* by His own eternally binding pledge never to destroy the world again, whereas *Russia* fully enjoys the same catastrophic capability to raze the planet, but is entirely *unhindered* by any such self-limiting oaths or self-restraining covenants…then what you are *telling* me, Rrrrabbi, is that we the people of this good Earth should be rendering our allegiance and tendering our obedience, not, indeed, to God – *but to Leonid Brezhnev*!"

Know what his answer was? He had me thrown out of class, and I was subsequently denied ingress to the Lamberton campus, this time for Communist and Atheist agitation.

Chapter Thirteen

Let's recap, shall we? What we have tried to do so far is show that – *pace* apologists of every stripe and color – Ofer, the still sandal-wearing Hebrew Hare Krishna from the LA airport, is even more right than he knew: Judaism makes *absolutely no sense* for this day and age – not its norms, not its mores, not its theology. There is no genuinely logical justification for adhering in our progressive era to the laws and concepts set out in the Torah and Talmud. As a program for life in the modern world, the Judaic code, in package form or even piecemeal, is simply not the rational or practical choice – anybody who tells you different is trying to sell you something (unlike the present author, you see, who has *already* sold you something, and whom you can therefore trust implicitly).

By making this statement about Judaism – and by spending all those pages trying to demonstrate its veracity – I realize that I may, in the case of many readers, be preaching to the extremely convinced. But I wanted to do my darndest to make sure that by this point in our relationship, you and I had more or less achieved what is known in Hebrew as a *yishur kav*: a "straightening of the lines." In Israeli army boot camp they teach you what is no doubt rather obvious to anyone with a military mind (or a mind at all): that before you (the infantry) charge them (the enemy), you simply *must* see to it that all members of your unit "*yishru kav*," have lined up on the same horizontal axis – otherwise, when you switch your Galil rifle to "automatic" and empty out an entire magazine in 3.7 seconds like Rabbi Rambo, you'll spray your own pals with bullets from behind, which is a bit of a downer.

Anyway, in this particular operation, I get to play commander and you, for your part, get to hear me bark orders: "*liyasher kav*! – straighten that line! (you slimy worms!) – prepare to charge!" Do you have to obey those orders? Do you have to toe that line? (Did you *read* the paragraph on "authority" a few pages back?) Obviously not. If you and I aren't on the same wavelength by now regarding at least *some* of the problems traditional Judaism presents to the modern, rational, pragmatic mindset, that's just fine. I'll be happy to shoot you in the back of the head.

You may have noticed that this is not exactly the first time I have mentioned the Israeli army, and you may perhaps have concluded by now that this is because I am a Militarist Zionist Imperialist Colonialist Warmonger. That would be correct, but there is a slightly more prosaic – if related – explanation for this theme's eternal recurrence. You see, I am (thank God, *tfu tfu tfu*) still an able-bodied young fellow, and like all the other able-bodied young fellows in this country, I am not seldom called up to serve for several weeks at a time in the Army Reserve Corps (glossary: according to the Israeli Defense Forces, "young" means under fifty-three, "able-bodied" means you don't have a foot growing out of your head, and "not seldom" means about once every five months – especially of late, what with the "situation" and all). When you spend one week out of every six bivouacked instead of bedded down, similes and anecdotes hailing from the military milieu come somewhat naturally. Here's another one.

Having not so long ago received and reluctantly responded to an "Order no. 8" – an "extraordinary" call-up for emergency purposes – I found myself, for the umpteenth time, at some miserable, muddy, border-bunker type establishment, way out there in the middle of northeastern yekhup. It was midnight, and there we were, me and my buddy Boaz the Blond Beast, biding our time in the *budka* (a dinky little circular watch-tower at the furthest extremity of the outpost, somewhat resembling an upside-down shuttlecock). Boaz is a kibbutznik from the upper Galilee, currently doing his masters in microbiology at Tel-Aviv University, and we have been friends in the framework of the reserves for a couple of years now. He's the strong, silent type (opposites attract), with emphasis on the strong. One of the many stories told about Boaz in our division is that some years ago, on patrol in southern Lebanon, he got separated from his company, and was suddenly set upon by three Hizbollah fighters bearing down on him in a flat-bed Ford, Kalachnikovs blazing like the Clanton brothers at the OK Corral. Unperturbed, Boaz aimed his M-16-mounted *gharnat* missile at the soon-to-be-ashes vehicle and passengers, pulled the trigger and…nothing. The whole contraption had jammed stuck, and Boaz could fire neither missile nor sub-machine gun. Whereas normal people under such circumstances would begin rapidly making peace with their Maker or lose control of their bodily functions or both, what Boaz did was to charge into a hail of bullets – two of which he caught – and kill all three gunmen by bonking them consecutively over the head with the weighted end of the inert missile. In short, we're glad he's on our side.

Anyway, there we were, just the two of us, hunkered down under all of our less than state-of-the-art gear, staring listlessly out at the hostile black and plucking raw seeds off of sunflower heads. At about one o'clock, Boaz broke his characteristic silence to comment on some graffiti scratched into the ceiling of the *budka* and signed "Yaron, '73" (Yaron was posted here around the time of the Yom Kippur War. If he survived it, he is probably a grandpa by now). He had carved the following words into the metal, which comprise a rather famous verse from the book of Psalms: "Some call on chariots, others call on horses, but we call on the name of the Lord our God" (Psalms 20:8).

"Personally, I'm an atheist," mused Boaz, in response to this terse literary stimulus. "But I was *born* Jewish."

Poor Boaz. What he no doubt thought had been a perfectly innocent, offhand remark, was in point of fact a fatal error, one which he was going to continue paying for throughout the whole remainder of our night-long watch. By three in the morning – having learned the true meaning of the phrase "captive audience" – Boaz was wishing he had stayed in southern Lebanon with the Hizbollah. By five o'clock, he had removed his flak-jacket and was waving his flashlight wildly back and forth over his head in the hopes that a Syrian sniper would put him out of his misery. In what follows, I will have more pity on the reader than I did upon my comrade-in-arms, and make you endure only a severely abridged version of the interminable *budka* lecture. But endure you must: because certain things have simply *got* to be set straight, once and for all.

We have spent much time and effort in the preceding pages discoursing upon the irrationality of Judaism. There is, however, one thing out there in this big wide world even *more* irrational than Judaism. And that thing is…being Jewish.

Huh? Is there a difference? Most folks certainly don't seem to think so. Boaz, for instance, says he's an adherent of atheism, and since he believes atheism to be unalterably opposed to the tenets of Judaism, he figures he isn't Jewish anymore. Wow – what a whopper of a mix-up between apples and oranges *that* is!

In order to get our minds around what makes "being Jewish" even more irrational than all the norms and notions we've been discussing so far under the rubric of "Judaism" – and, for that matter, in order to grasp what makes "being Jewish" a category twenty times more mystifying and illogical than "being Christian" or "being Muslim" or "being an atheist" or "being a socialist" – we must begin by nailing down some highly essential but widely ignored distinctions.

The first and most important difference between being Jewish, on the one hand, and Judaism, on the other, is this: the former state exists, whereas the latter institution simply doesn't. Yup: you heard me. And if we want to understand anything at all about this whole, humongous, mind-boggling business we're about to delve into – including, perhaps, the exceedingly fundamental issue of *who and what we are* – we had better do ourselves one very big favor right this minute and indelibly burn the following incontrovertible fact onto the write-only CD-ROM of our cerebrums:

THERE IS NO SUCH THING AS JUDAISM.

That's right. This is not a word game, or some cute little semantic ploy – it is at the very heart of everything we Jews are and always have been about.

Would you care to field a wild guess how many times the term "Judaism" – in Hebrew: *Yahadut* – appears in the Torah, the Prophets, the Writings, the Talmud, the Midrash, the Geonic commentaries, the masterpieces of the medieval philosophers, the mystical works of Kabbalah – in short, in the entirety of Judeo-classical literature? Go on – take a stab: whadya think? Maybe a total of... nine hundred and ninety-four times? Perhaps...two thousand three hundred and seventy-five times? No? *Six million seven hundred and forty-two thousand, nine hundred and fifty-eight times*? Sorry. You are slightly off. The correct answer would be: zero. Zilch, nihil, nada, naught, nothing, cipher, zip. This term appears *absolutely nowhere* in our sources – and for good reason.

The usage "Judaism" – with its modern suffix "ism" (Hebrew: *ut*, in *yahadut*), denoting an ideology, doctrine or system – clearly gives the impression that what "Jews" are, is a *group of people who adhere to a common faith or set of beliefs and practices* that together may be designated "Judaism" – just as Christians are people who follow the doctrine known as "Christianity" (involving belief in Jesus as the "Christ" or anointed savior), Muslims are those who confess "Islam" (entailing *islam* or "submission" to Allah) and Buddhists are those who pursue the Eightfold Path to Enlightenment of Siddhartha Gautama Sakya, a.k.a. the Buddha. And indeed, the label "Judaism" was invented out of the blue in the modern period more or less in **deliberate imitation** of the above religious traditions, as if to say: "Hey – just as you people all constitute 'faith communities,' so *we Jews, too*, constitute a 'faith community.'" (Yes! We're not such freaks after all!)

Nothing – but *nothing* – could be further from the truth.

Let's begin with the simple philological fact that unlike the other denominational derivations enumerated above, *Jews aren't called Jews because they practice Judaism.* Rather, quite the opposite is the case: the regrettable neologism "Judaism" was derived – and that, as we said, only in the last few centuries – from the ancient word "Jew" (Hebrew: *Yehudi*), which itself goes all the way back to the Bible. Now, if "Judaism" is just a latter-day derivative of the word "Jew," then what does the word "Jew" mean?

That's simple. Jacob had a dozen sons – the eponymous progenitors of the Twelve Tribes of Israel – and the fourth of these sons was named Judah (*Yehudah*). Upon arrival in Canaan after the Exodus from Egypt (so we are told by the biblical narrative), the various Hebrew tribes conquered and took up residence in their allotted territories, with the powerful clan of Judah settling a large swath of land in the mountainous area south of Jerusalem. Now that the sometime wandering Israelites had more or less decided to park it in their old-new homestead, *tribal* consciousness – a natural product of nomadic life, where land is transitory and people are constant – began to peter out, and made way for *territorial* consciousness – a natural product of sedentary life, where people are transitory and land is constant. Thus, the name "Judah" or *Yehudah* came over the centuries to refer to the *province* inhabited by the tribe of that name as much as, if not more than, to the tribe itself.

Meanwhile, a scion of the house of Judah who slung a mean sling-shot, plucked a wicked harp, composed a righteous psalm, and never even *contemplated* committing murder and adultery – this son of Jesse united the squabbling and occasionally even skirmishing tribes under his charismatic leadership at Hebron in about the year 1000 BCE, took the mountain stronghold of Jerusalem, and established a far-flung Hebrew empire that he eventually bequeathed to his son Solomon. When Solomon died, however, *his* son Rehoboam managed in one fell swoop to antagonize and alienate the ten northernmost tribes, by reacting to their plea for alleviation of his father's harsh fiscal policies with the not entirely diplomatic rejoinder: "Hey: my *pinky* is thicker than my father's loins!" (where "loins" is…um…a euphemism). "*He* only flogged you with whips," continued Rehobaom. "*I* will flog you with *scorpions*" (1 Kings 12:10). The shocked and offended northern tribes seceded, and David's realm was rent in twain: the Kingdom of Israel, in the north, and the Kingdom of...*Judah*, in the south (with some nearby Benjaminites mixed in).

Two centuries went by, and in the year 722 BCE the northern Kingdom of Israel – having bet on the wrong regional superpower (Egypt) – was utterly sacked by Sargon, Emperor of Assyria, and much of its population transferred the-Lord-only-knows-where eastward, to become the famous "Ten Lost Tribes of Israel." All that was now left of the ostensible seed of Abraham and Sarah in the Promised Land were *the inhabitants of the Kingdom of Judah*, or quite simply: *HaYehudim* – "the Judeans" (as the prophet Jeremiah and the restorer-reformer Nehemiah consistently refer to them).

And what language did these "Judeans" speak? Good question. The word "Hebrew" (*Ivrit*), in the sense of the national tongue, appears exactly nowhere in the Bible. The medium of communication employed by our biblical ancestors was known in those ancient times as *Yehudit* – "Judean." As, for example, in 2 Kings 18:26, where the emissaries of the advancing Assyrian monarch are transmitting their master's demands for some serious groveling by shouting over the Jerusalem wall to the representatives of King Hezekiah, and these last – afraid to lose face in front of their own populace when they eventually knuckle under to those demands – beg the messengers:

> Speak, we pray thee, in the Aramean language, for we understand it; and speak not in *Yehudit*, for you are within earshot of our people gathered here on the wall.

(Bootlickers!) So now what we have is a mildly mountainous "Land of Judah," populated by a hardy remnant of patriotic "Judeans," who are busily flapping their gums in the lilting language of "Judean." Fine.

About one hundred fifty years later – in 586 BCE – Judean policy makers, too, put their eggs in the losing Egyptian basket, and as a result, Nebuchadnezzar the Babylonian brought upon the Kingdom of Judah what Sargon the Assyrian had earlier brought upon the Kingdom of Israel: devastation and mass deportation eastward (as it is written: "I will remove Judah also out of My sight, as

I have removed Israel" – 2 Kings 23:27). And it is there, ladies and gentlemen – there where we sat down and wept, by the rivers of the Babylonian-Persian Exile – that we are finally privileged to meet him, our first individual "Jew": "*Ve ish* Yehudi *haya be-shushan habira, u-shemo Mordechai…*" – "And there was a certain *Judean* man in Shushan the capital, by the name of Mordechai…" (Esther 2:5).

It is, indeed, natural enough that we should encounter the earliest single fellow to be called by the text a "*Yehudi*" or "Judean" (shortened in English to "Jew") specifically in the Diaspora. I say this because when good old, palm-pumping Mordechai – the lovely Queen Esther's cousin – would introduce himself at Persian palace parties ("Hi! How ya doin'? Mordechai the *Yehudi* at your service!") all he was really doing by modifying his name with that unassuming epithet was explaining why he and his partner in conversation had never gone to summer camp together, or watched the same cartoons as kids: *Mordechai wasn't from these parts.*

> Goshtasp: "Oh, yeah? Where're ya from, Mordechai?"
> Mordechai: "I'm from *Judea*."
> Goshtasp: "Really – how exotic. Get much rain there?"
> Parvoneh: "Oooh, Mithra, *look* – there goes that dreamboat new courtier, Mordechai *the Judean*!"

…And that, honored reader, is the simple story of how we got our name (a story that works whether Mordechai was a first or – as some scholars believe – a fourth generation exile, and whether his character is genuinely historical or some kind of composite or myth). "Mordechai the Jew" meant then what "Peter the Pennsylvanian" means now – nothing more.

To sum up: from the terminology's inception and down through its several vicissitudes until we arrive at Mordechai himself, "*Yehudi*" was never anything other than a tribal-territorial designation. When the Bible describes Mordechai, Esther and the entire exilic community in Persia as "*Yehudim*," the intent (as with Jeremiah and Nehemiah) is certainly *not* "people who believe in one God, eat only kosher food, loll around on Saturday, refuse to wear linsey-woolsey, and go bats in the belfry around Passover time." True, it is quite easy to see how such qualities eventually came to be *associated* with the term "*Yehudim*." In the same fashion, after all, we have been privileged in modern times to watch ourselves become an addition to the *English* dictionary: "Whadya mean, thirty bucks? Are you tryin' to *Jew* me down?!" (Dig it: we're a *verb*!)

But just as not all Jews today will overcharge you (*heh-heh* [wink]), so not all Jews (*Yehudim*) way back when kept the commandments of the Torah or bought into its theology. Indeed, *most* of the biblical "Judeans" spent a good deal of their several centuries-long history worshipping – *not* the God of their forefathers, Abraham, Isaac and Jacob – but a whole host of other local and regional pagan deities ("The number of your gods is as the number of your cities, O Judah!" – Jeremiah 2:28). They were especially keen on a certain Canaanite rain and fertility boss named Baal. The prophets, in taking them to task for this odious betrayal, would rail (in almost so many words): "Hey – how come you *Judeans* are worshipping that good-for-nothing, to-the-manure-born, phony pagan pseudo-divinity?" Worshipping Baal, you see, made them…*Jews who worshipped Baal.* (Which is why, by the way, the name of the worldwide missionary organization known as "Jews for Jesus" is not, technically speaking, a contradiction in terms – a fact that should in no way discourage you from physically assaulting these devious sons-of-bitches if they ever get within a kilometer of your kids.)

So once again, for emphasis: all the biblical text means by "*Yehudim*" is people who hail from the land of Yehudah – Judea. The title "Jew" was originally (and still is!) a geographical and national – not a "religious" – appellation. And that is why, for example, the following SAT exercise simply doesn't work:

"Jew": Judea :: "Christian": __________(Christiana?); "Muslim": __________(Muslimland?); "Buddhist": __________(Buddhistan?)

None of these three latter designations (Christian, Muslim, Buddhist) is etymologically or in any other way connected to a particular land or nation. The designation "Jew," on the other hand, is not only *connected* to the land and tribe of Judah – *that's all it means.*

In the same vein: do you know anyone who speaks "Christian"? How 'bout "Muslim"? "Buddhish"? Languages are rarely named after religions, for a lot of obvious reasons. We name them after *peoples and regions*. And that is why, while Christians never spoke "Christian," Muslims never spoke "Muslim," Buddhists never spoke "Buddhish" and Zoroastrians never spoke "Zoroastrian," our ancestors could and *did* speak "Judean."

The "Jews" are – to this very day, and according to their own time-honored regulations and specifications – most definitively *not* adherents of a faith (we already mentioned this in passing, way back in part one). They are members of a confederation or a super-clan – a clan that once lived (and part of which lives again) *in a certain country*. Their individual and collective identity as "*Yehudi*" and "*Yehudim*" respectively, is in no way, shape or form dependent upon how they act or what they believe!

Still not buying it? Still stuck on the fact that everybody always told you that you were a member of a "religion" (itself a term and notion *entirely foreign* to our sources)? Think what I'm saying was maybe true "back then," but not anymore? OK, then tell me this: what happens if a Christian gets up one fine morning in the year 2001, goes out on his veranda, cups his hands to his mouth and declares loudly (and sincerely): "Hear ye, hear ye! This very morning I realized, that I just don't credit one iota of this business about Jesus being the Son of God and dying on the cross for the sake of my salvation – that's a large load of flapdoodle. And don't even get me *started* on the virginity of the Mother Mary…"

Question for you: is this guy still a Christian? Answer: *not by a long shot he isn't* (go ask your parish priest). At the precise instant he changed his mind, this gentleman ceased – *by definition* – to be a Christian, because a "Christian" means nothing else but a *believer in Christ*. Christianity is a religion, a belief system, and according to its own unequivocal doctrine, if you stop believing – you obviously stop being a member (and if you start again, you're back in). Capish?

What about a Muslim? The central creed of Islam – the *shahada* or "affirmation" – goes like this: "I testify that there is no God but Allah, and that Muhammad is his prophet." Now suppose some young sport raised in a Muslim home walks outside of an evening in Afghanistan or Yemen or Mauritania, and proclaims from the heart at the top of his lungs: "I testify that there are – oh – about four hundred and seventy six *thousand* other gods besides Allah; and as for Muhammad, well, he was nothing but an illiterate, camel-driving charlatan" (this doesn't happen all that much). Is this outspoken jasper still a Muslim, ya think? Not on your life. Not according to Islam. He's *instant infidel.*

We could go on in this vein, but let's get to the *Yid.* Ready? A Jew wearing an "I love Yasser Arafat" T-shirt with a huge cross dangling around his neck and an "Aryan Nations" logo tattooed to his left arm, drives his Harley Davidson through the doors and down the aisle of the neighborhood synagogue in the middle of Yom Kippur services, hops up onto the stage in his knee-high leather boots and – after wolfing down five ham-and-cheese sandwiches (without a blessing) in front of the hundreds of horrified worshippers – cleans his camshaft with the rabbi's *tallis*, punts a *siddur* through the stain-glass window, douses the Torah scroll with kerosene and lights it on fire, tosses a live grenade into the holy ark, slugs the sexton, pummels the president, rapes the rebbetzin, cuts the cantor's head off and sucks his blood out through the narrow end of the *shofar* and caps off this entire grizzly performance with a stream of bellowed blasphemies that would make the directors of the movie *The Exorcist* faint.

So who wants to guess: is this extremely rude fellow still a Jew? *Hmmm*? You bet your bagel-and-lox, he is! (Jewish law is unanimous on the subject.) Is this because we Jews are more tolerant of dissent or deviation than other folks? Hardly. Our sacrilegious, one-man pogrom-on-wheels remains Jewish – will *always* remain Jewish, no matter what he thinks, feels, believes, says, does or doesn't do – for the simple reason that "being Jewish" is not at all like "being Christian" or "being Muslim." It is a lot more like "being one of the Goldblatt kids."

If you are one of the Goldblatt kids, you and your parents can do pretty much anything y'all can think of to try and alter this state of affairs: you can renounce them in court, they can disown you in their will, you can join a whole new family complete with coat-of-arms named von-Hohenshtinkleheim, they can take a space shuttle to

Mars and never see your face again – but *nothing* you or they could ever do can change the simple, ontological fact that you are (like it or not) one of the Goldblatt kids. The only way to cease being one of the Goldblatt kids is…to cease being. In the same fashion, and for the same basic reasons, you simply *cannot stop being Jewish* – **ever**. (Help!! There's *no way out of heeeerrre*!!)

When Boaz said that he had been born Jewish but was now an atheist, he had seriously tangled up his categories. Christianity, Islam, Buddhism, Shintoism, Hinduism, fascism, pacifism, atheism, anti-vivisectionism? These are religions or philosophies or systems or ideologies. Judaism? *Ain't no such animal* (we have employed the term up till now for the sake of convenience, and the better ultimately to blot out the memory of its spurious syllables from the reader's lexicon – forevermore!). As for the *Jewish People* (alias the "Children of Israel"), well: that's a big tribe, is what that is, a veritable Hebrew horde, a massive, dispersed, matzah-masticating mafia. It is what the West refers to since Rousseau, Diderot, Herder and Fichte as a "nation" – from the Latin *natio*, meaning "to give birth," i.e., a group claiming descent from common progenitors. From the biblical book of Exodus onward, Jewish sources have consistently designated our cooperative entity an "*Am*" – a Semitic word denoting "uncle" (and allied to "with") and connoting "a bunch of birth-related people." We have thus always been literally "a *natio*-n" in our own eyes – as in the famous, exuberant cry: *Am Yisrael Chai*! ("The *Nation* of Israel lives!") We Jews were "*natio*nal-ists," for good or for ill, *long* before this notion's modern European vogue (more on this later).

An illustrative story told by my mother: she was in fifth grade at H. C. Lea public elementary school in Philadelphia. During a free period one day, she and two of her classmates, Louis Barnazian and Frank Androli, were sitting around, idly looking through the dictionary (we have a word for kids who spend recess this way, Ma). Mom chanced upon the word "Armenian," pointed to Louis, and said, "That's you!" She then flipped through the pages again and found the word "Italian," pointed at Frank, and said, "That's you!" Whereupon Louis snatched the dictionary, flipped through the pages, came upon the word "Jew," pointed at my mother triumphantly and said "And that's *you*!" My mother was all set to argue that they were mixing apples and oranges (after all, *she* hadn't identified them as *Christians*) – but she was struck by what had occurred: those ten-year-old boys had our number!

The House of Jacob is, then – or at least has always deemed itself – one vast extended family, glued together over four adventurous millennia by a whole slew of factors, only *one* of which consists of belief in and obedience to that timeless national constitution known as the Torah (and *this* factor – as we have just shown – does *not* in any way affect affiliation). Boaz is an atheist. At the same time, he is *not one wit less Jewish* than your local rabbi – and if you don't believe me, go ask him (the rabbi, I mean). Boaz is a *Jewish atheist* – a point he finally conceded at around six forty-five in the morning (of course, by then he would have confessed to being a bestial necrophiliac).

"Objection! *Objection*!!" That's you – counsel for the defense of clumsy classification and unreasonable taxonomy – leaping to your feet (oh, don't go getting all offended, I'm jes' joshin' wid ya!). You have a *kasha* (Yiddishized talmudic Aramaic for: a difficulty to raise, a challenge to present, a refutation of my thesis). You savor the moment, licking your chops, poised to pounce: "What about......... conversion?"

Oucchhh!

Excellent *kasha*. After all, folks of all stripes have been "converting to Judaism" for as long as anyone can remember, beginning with Ruth the Moabitess (ancestress of King David), moving through the forebears of Rabbi Akiba and other notable talmudic figures, and reaching all the way down to Rod Carew the Home Run Jew. Now if – as we have been claiming – being Jewish is in truth like "being one of the Goldblatt kids," if it's mostly a matter of consanguinity (real or imagined) coupled with a common *patria*, then how is it possible that you can *become* a Jew? Moreover, if one's identity as a Jew is not based on or dependent upon one's beliefs, then how can *switching* your beliefs *make* you a Jew? This whole conversion option seems to militate heavily for the rehabilitation of that word, the reputation of which we have so mightily endeavored to sully: "Judaism."

Well, now – don't go counting up your winnings just yet, OK pardner? Let's look at this issue a bit up closer-like. For starters: suppose you have this Christian evangelist with a big "John 3:16" sign hanging around his neck, a Muslim preacher selling Koran tapes, some Hare Krishnas be-bopping to their tambourines, and a bunch of Lubavitcher (Chabad) Hassidim complete with "Mitzvah Tank," blasting their slightly less aesthetically pleasing version of the Mormon Tabernacle Boys Choir – all standing together on the corner of Fifty-Second and Broadway, hawking their spiritual wares. Suddenly, a Chinese guy walks by. Now, what's everybody going to do?

Well, the evangelist is going to chug over and expose our Asian friend to the way, the truth and the light of the Gospel; the Muslim preacher will unquestionably walk right up and relate to him how Muhammad brought God's *latest* revelation to mankind – which just happens to supersede that being preached by the evangelist; and one of the Hare Krishnas is bound to bound over and go into contortions about the fantabulous virtues of Vishnu. How 'bout the Hassidim? What are *they* going to say to our Oriental passerby? They are going to say: "Hi. Nice day, isn't it. Know any decent Chinese restaurants in the area – preferably glatt kosher?"

The Jew just isn't interested. He doesn't proselytize, he doesn't missionize, he doesn't actively recruit membership (actually, the Lubavitchers are specifically *not* the best example I could have adduced of this apathetic insouciance – they've gone a tad ballistic over the past several decades, addressing not a few campaigns to gentiles as well – but even they harbor no real zeal to *convert* non-Jews). This is *not* because Jews are not solicitous of the spiritual welfare of others, or are "exclusivists" who think they're better than – or need no help from – everyone else. Rather, it is because of that same old serious category mix-up we've been talking about.

Dig it: say you are a member of this association, the whole or primary *raison d'être* of which is that its members believe they have been vouchsafed a set of significant spiritual and cosmic truths about the universe and how one ought to live in it. Lovely. Such a group will (unless one of its central tenets is out-and-out selfishness) naturally strive to spread this blessed message, this universally applicable categorical imperative, to as many other uninitiated souls as possible.

So how come the Jews don't do this? I'll tell you why (and this may involve the annihilation of some pretty widespread and well-entrenched assumptions, so keep that mind open!): because although we Judeans unquestionably believed for most of our history (and many of us still believe) that we have been vouchsafed one lollapalooza of a set of spiritual and cosmic truths concerning the universe and how one ought to live in it…*that is not now and never has been our whole or even primary raison d'être*! Unlike the many "religion-based" communities dotting the face of the globe, we Jews neither have nor need a "reason to exist" – anymore than the Goldblatt family (or your family) has or needs a reason to exist! And we don't try to convert "outsiders" for *exactly* the same reason that the Goldblatts don't go around every day and try to increase *their* numbers by persuading everybody and their grandmother to join the Goldblatt nuclear household. Because why would anyone *do* such a thing? To go out and "spread Judaism" is as ridiculous and meaningless a project as to go out and "spread Goldblattism"!

And by the way: this reticence goes both ways. As we bang on the keys, the newspapers are filling up with all types of hype about the upcoming Durban Racism Conference in South Africa, at which – so it would appear – participants hailing from the many far-flung regions of the globe plan selflessly and altruistically to ignore all the indescribable miseries and injustices characterizing the lands they represent, the better to focus without distraction on the singular crimes of the State of Israel (now *there's* an original concept!). And this time, as last time, Zionism will no doubt be proclaimed the pinnacle of Racism and the Root Of All Evil based primarily on the infamous "Law of Return," which clause was designed – in the wake of that mildly racist episode known as the Holocaust – to give preference to Jews who wish to immigrate to Israel. This, of course, makes us guilty of "racial discrimination."

Now, I'm not going to waste your time with the well-known fact that some decades ago in the mid 1980s, and later again in the mid 1990s, Israel spent billions of dollars and countless man-and woman-hours for the sole and express purpose of bringing home to the motherland tens of thousands of Jews from Ethiopia. Neither will I dray your kop in the matter of the immigration policies of almost all of the countries who will vote against us, policies that – in comparison – make ours look like Abraham's legendary tent, with flaps flung wide open to the four winds. Nor will I even mention the fact that the only people besides Jews who have ever expressed any genuine desire to immigrate to Israel in any appreciable numbers have invariably tacked on to this wish the avowed intention of permanently erasing my country from the face of the planet earth. (Remember that promise I made in the introduction about no politics? Screw it.)

Let's ignore all of that, and make reference instead to the straightforward conception underlying the nation-state in general, and the Israeli Law of Return in particular. And that notion is this: in the same way that the Goldblatts don't go around every day *trying* to increase their numbers by persuading strangers to join their nuclear household, they also – just as naturally and just as understandably – wouldn't *allow* such a thing to happen if the impetus came from the *outside*. I mean, say some stranger knocked on the front door of your house, waltzed in, plopped down on the couch, put his feet up and declared: "Hi. I'm moving in to your house and joining your family. Would you mind turning the music down – as in *now*? Oh – and I like my eggs scrambled."

What do you suppose your reaction would be to this insolent interloper? I'll bet I wouldn't be allowed to print it. Well now: *we Jews are a family, and we happen to have only one very tiny little itsy-bitsy national home, and guess what: you are* damn right *we are going to regulate who – if anyone – joins that family or takes up residence in that home*, the more so since (as I promised not to mention) the only people who really want to do so are rather fiercely bent on *evicting us*. Ain't racism ugly?

Back to our train of thought: You were attempting to utilize the institution of conversion to refute my "no Judaism" thesis, and I was trying to counterattack by explaining how Jews don't actively *pursue* converts. "That's all well and good," say you. "But you've skirted the issue again. Despite all the above, people still *do* convert. It's the fact that it *can* be done – not the question whether it is sought or encouraged – which is germane here. And when one converts to Judaism (you heard me: *Judaism*) one is first and foremost adopting a *new faith* and a new set of laws for living."

OK, OK, you're right. Conversion these days – and for centuries – has been inextricably tied up with learning, professing and promising to practice the precepts and injunctions found in the Torah and Talmud. But is that what Jewish conversion is *really* all about? Is that what is *essential* to conversion in the Jewish context, what underlies it, what it truly *means*? Let's see.

What is the Hebrew word for "conversion"? Right. That word would be: *giyur*. And for "convert"? Here the word, related to the first, is *ger*, a biblical term originally denoting "stranger" or "foreigner" (as in the etymology provided for the name of Moses' firstborn son: "[I'll call him] *Ger-shom*, because I am a stranger, a *ger*, in a strange land," Exodus 2:22). We're not quite done etymologizing: where, in its turn, does the word *ger* come from? You betcha! From the Hebrew root-verb *gar*, which means "to dwell, to sojourn" (and, without going into all the Semitics, probably even "to migrate, to immigrate"). The precursor of what we currently call a "convert" was the biblical *ger ha-gar betochechem*, the "stranger who comes to dwell among you" (see, e.g., Exodus 12:49).

Now, why do I bother you with all this? Because "conversion" in the biblical context is – like the essence of the Israelite entity itself – fundamentally a *geographical-tribal* phenomenon. When you *mitgayer* – conventionally translated today as "convert" – what you are *really* doing is not so much adopting a new set of beliefs (although later on this did become, as we said, an indispensable aspect of the *giyur* process). What you are really doing, on the most fundamental level, is *moving into the neighborhood*, is joining the block association and the local PTA, is saying: "I bind my destiny to yours: if Nasrallah's missiles fall on your country, they might hit my house just as easily as yours; if there is a campaign on to murder people solely because they are members of your tribe, then they will see in me no less a target than in you; I will sow together with you shoulder to shoulder, and if the harvest is plentiful, I will reap the benefits in equal measure, and if not, we will starve together. I am one of you guys now."

This was, in fact, the act and attitude of Ruth, the prototypical convert of Jewish historiography, when – out of devotion to and affection for her bereaved mother-in-law Naomi – she made the famous commitment: "Whither thou goest, I will go; and where thou lodgest, I will lodge; thy people shall be my people, and thy God, my God; where thou diest, I will die, and there will I be buried. Thus and more may the Lord do to me, if aught but death come between thee and me" (Ruth 1:16-17). Ruth *joins her fate to ours* – and she does so, not out of conviction or principle (Naomi's God will be her God – primarily because He is *Naomi's* God) but out of sheer, inextinguishable, preferential love (a fact strangely ignored by later jurists, who often fault conversions undertaken solely for the sake of marriage).

And even though, as the period of exile wore on, the previously negligible "ideological" element in conversion chipped away at the originally geographical and tribal nature of this process, and ultimately managed to usurp the lead role – its victory was to a large extent illusory. For underneath the surface, the primal character of Jewish conversion still hums confidently, informing every facet of this institution. Let me give you one example of this ongoing influence.

Remember how badly Joaquin Phoenix wanted to make it with his sister Connie Nielsen (*shwing*!) in *Gladiator*? Incest, alas, was frowned upon even in Rome (and Commodus was no Caligula). *Ach* – what frustration! And all so unnecessary. There was, after all, a simple solution to the libidinous emperor's priapic predicament: convert to "Judaism" – he and his sister both! Then they could get married and roll in the hay till their heart's content.

What? *What*? You mean the Torah forgot to include a clause against incest?! Hardly. What's going on here is far more interesting, at least for our purposes: you see, once Commodus and Lucilla convert, they are *no longer brother and sister*. Yes, you heard me: somewhere in between the first and final dunks in the *mikveh* (the conversion immersion pool), a convert loses all of his or her previous family ties, becoming a "son or daughter of Abraham and Sarah." So she's all yours, Commodus-Melamedus – let 'er rip! (Well, all right – not quite.

Even though permitted according to the letter of the law, the rabbis placed a special, exceptional ban on this practice, lest we get a seedy Nevada-like rep – see the talmudic tractate of Yevamot, page 22a.)

Or let's pretend you are an Eskimo from Khatanga in northern Russia, and by a quirk of fate you end up working at a Chabad-Lubavitch matzah factory in Brooklyn, you and your two adolescent children: Yuputak and Gort. You yourself are already too old to be very impressionable, but as for the kids, they are dazzled by the new and different lifestyle they see around them – not to mention that music! – and in a fit of teenage rebellion, they convert to "Judaism" without so much as asking your permission. A few weeks later, in a freak accident, you succumb to massive matzah fume inhalation, and kick the bucket intestate. Now, according to *halakha* – that is, Jewish law – what happens to all your savings from working in the matzah bakery? You might assume that Yuputak and Gort would automatically inherit the dough, but then…you'd be **dead wrong**. Yuputak and Gort are *not your kids anymore* – stopped being so the moment they converted – and they wouldn't be your kids even if *you* had converted, as well! (Here, too, however, although according to the letter of the law the youngsters don't automatically inherit, the rabbis of the Talmud stepped in and layed down a special provision allowing them to do just that.)

Now, none of this would be the case if there existed such a thing in the entire universe as "conversion to Judaism" – you could then change your "faith," while fully maintaining your family ties. But there *is* no such thing as "Judaism," nor is there any such thing as "conversion" to it. What there *is*, is a Jewish tribe, a Jewish people, a Jewish household writ large – and you can in fact join it (it's a sort of "adoption"), but by definition, when you do so, you are somehow "switching families." You are passing through an almost enchanted barrier – enchanted, because while there is nothing particularly weird or "magical" about adopting a new set of beliefs or ideas, there *is* something that partakes of the unnatural, of the miraculous, in adopting a new family. And the magic would seem to work both ways: you emerge on the other side of this bewitched barrier having gained *and* lost a set of "hereditary" relationships.

Let me bring this argument to a close by making one thing perfectly clear. I do not intend by any of the above statements to strip or disembowel the overall Jewish experience of what common parlance dubs its "religious" side, nor do I intend to empty that experience of positive content, God forbid. What I *have* been attempting to do is establish what to my mind is an absolutely vital distinction and sort of symbiotic dichotomy – often ignored – between two intertwined but nonetheless differentiated components of the Jewish "thing" in history: the Jewish People, on the one hand, and the Jewish People's founding and enduring constitution (the Torah) on the other. And while Saadya Gaon unquestionably hit the nail on the head when he declared: "Our nation would not be a nation but for its Torah," nevertheless, *violation* of this national constitution, in thought or in deed, cannot and does not entail a revocation of citizenship. A Jew is – *not* as a Jew does – but simply…as a Jew is.

Chapter Fourteen

So fine: there is indeed a Jewish People in this world, and membership in it is not contingent upon any particular amount of pentateuchal piety. So what? Well, like I was saying (before I was so rudely interrupted by my own twenty page-long digression geared to bolstering that assertion): this aspect of the Jewish phenomenon is even more baffling, more inscrutable and more impractical than the bizarre enactments and crazy comportment detailed at the beginning of our section. Even more than the ideology and practice of "Judaism," "*being* Jewish" is completely and totally *innnnn-saaaaaaaaane*.

Do you need to ask what I'm talking about? I mean, while there may be certain "practical" advantages to being Jewish – better dentistry, matzah-ball soup, your occasional insider trading deal – I think we can safely agree that these "pros" are more than offset by, you know, pogroms, inquisitions, slavery, blood libels, expulsions, massacres and all the other pleasantries that have punctuated our collective career throughout history to date. I'm definitely not one to dwell on anti-Semitism, but I think it's pretty safe to say we've never been well liked (at this writing, while innocent Jewish men, women and children are murdered by gunmen and suicide bombers almost every single day here in Israel – and we, for our part, barely bark in response, let alone bite – the "international community" led by Europe [!] organizes to condemn us and impose sanctions. It boggles the mind. It makes you feel special). The Russians say: "*Yesli vkranye nyet vadi, znachet vuipili Zhidi* – If there is no water in the tap, that's because the Jews have drunk it – *ah yesli vkranye yest vada, podli Zhid nasal tuda* – whereas if there *is* water in the tap, the stinking Yids have pissed in it!" The Arabs say: "*Lo la al-Yahud, lam yakhnaz al-laham* – If it weren't for the Jews, meat wouldn't spoil" (are you hearing this? We are responsible for *meat going bad*). T. S. Eliot versified: "The rat is underneath the piles, the Jew is underneath the lot." And we just sigh and say: "*Shver tzu zein a Yid* – It's tough to be a Jew." Always has been.

And the rabbis of the Talmud knew this, already two thousand years ago. According to their instructions, here is what we are supposed to respond to a prospective proselyte who comes to us seeking to convert:

> WHAT DID YOU SAY? YOU WANT TO *WHAT*?? ARE YOU OUT OF YOUR *FREAKING SKULL*?! DID YOU BANG YOUR *HEAD* ON SOMETHING? BERYL, BRING THIS GUY A GLASS OF WATER, MAYBE THE HEAT GOT TO HIM. WOULD YOU LIKE TO LIE DOWN, SIR?

Well, that's not the exact formulation. The exact formulation is:

> If a non-Jew comes to convert, we ask him: "What possible reason could you have to convert? Do you not know that the People of Israel today are wretched, hounded, exiled, and in a constant state of suffering? You must be aware of how this nation is more downtrodden, persecuted and oppressed than any other people on earth, how all manner of calamities and afflictions come our way, how we bury our own children and our children's children, are slaughtered because of the laws of circumcision and immersion, and massacred all the day because of the manifold other commandments." (Yevamot 47a, Gerim 1:2)

Which, translated into modern English, means:

> *HAVE YOU GONE STARK RAVING MAD*?! ARE YOU ON ANY HALLUCINOGENIC DRUGS?! WOULD YOU CONSIDER THE RELATIVELY SAFER OPTION OF *MAKING A PASS AT OSAMA BIN LADEN'S WIFE*?

Every time I travel internationally, I remember how unbelievably dumb it is to be Jewish. Because that's when I have to take my Israeli passport onto a jumbo-jet. You just know that when they hijack the plane, the terrorist – whatever particular cause or faction he or she happens to represent – is going be coming down the aisle collecting passports: "Passport, please. France? *Merci Beaucoup*, *Monsieur*. Passport, please. Australia? Much obliged, Mate. Passport, please. Mozambique? *Turumbu-utuwa*, *Watasi*. Passport, please. Israel? *Blaaam*! Passport, please…"

Nor is it impractical to be a member of Our Gang solely because – as Tom Lehrer put it so eloquently – "everybody hates the Jews." We've got other disadvantages, as well: like size, for instance (even the Pentateuch admits this sad fact: "For you are the *smallest* of all the peoples"; Deuteronomy 7:7). Complaints regarding *this* particular matter should be addressed and postmarked directly to He Who Hangs Out On High And Makes All The Big Decisions, given that we have in writing His explicit promise to Abraham (and I quote): "I will make your descendants as numerous as the stars in the heaven and the sands on the sea-shore" (Genesis 22:17). Now, I just got back this morning from a full week of tank maneuvers in the Negev desert (yes, reserve duty again) and I currently have more sand *in my shorts* than there are Jews on this planet. As for the stars, well, this promise must have been made while the Lord was out clubbing on a cloudy Manhattan night.

But when I say that membership in the Jewish People is even more impractical and irrational in our times than observing the commandments of "Judaism," I refer not just to the dangers, difficulties and disadvantages involved in such membership. I refer, even more directly, to the all-out *senselessness* of identifying with and feeling loyalty to a bunch of people – most of whom one has never even met, indeed, *will* never meet – based upon the sole criterion of a conceivable common descent, of a partially possible propinquity, of some degree or another of what's commonly known as historical "kinship." Now *that* is nuts.

Oh, it might be logically argued that we feel a natural connection with those who share certain religious or cultural norms with us. If I am not allowed to smoke on the Sabbath, and you are not allowed to smoke on the Sabbath – we can get together on the Sabbath and commiserate (or smoke). If we both share the exclusive common literary heritage of, say, active Talmud or Midrash study, then we certainly have a compelling reason to gravitate particularly to one another. Even if all we have in common is a weekly craving for Nova lox, an argument could still be made for hanging out, sympathizing, and stuffing our faces in unison.

But what if we have *none* of these things in common? Like for instance: about fifteen years ago, that eschatological eventuality on behalf of which so many of us demonstrated practically every Sunday throughout the entire seventies and eighties finally came to pass *en masse*: the Iron Curtain came crashing down, and maybe a third of Soviet Jewry – close to a million people – found its way home to Israel. Now, the Russian immigrants are (to generalize grossly) some of the most fascinating and fortitudinous people I have ever met. But as for having anything in common with them – you can forget it. Religion? The opiate of the masses: most of them don't know anything about it, don't want anything to do with it. And in terms of the cultural side of things, well, let's just say that as a Western Jew born and bred in the good old US of A, I am *still* trying to find *one* common character trait, one mutual predilection or joint pursuit that could possibly forge the basis for collective bonding between formerly Soviet and formerly American (or indigenous Israeli) Jews. So far: abject failure. These people are from the moon. Their idea of a fun time is taking the whole family down to the beach sometime after midnight in the dead of bitterest, biting-est, if-liquid-nitrogen-had-teeth-they-would-chatter winter, where everybody takes turns emptying a bottle of Smirnoff and ruminating on golf-ball-size chunks of raw garlic, after which Pushkin is read, clothing is shed, and Mom,

Dad and offspring are all off on a three mile swim out into shark-infested, sub-zero temperature waters. (Whoopee!)

And then there is sitting – an activity the rest of the world takes for granted. The Russian will not just "sit" anywhere (what do you take him for?). Most surfaces simply won't do: stone, marble, wood, metal, grass, earth – quite unsittable (try running a summer camp on the outskirts of Odessa sometime, where it takes literally half an hour and threats of KGB intervention to implement the simple directive: "OK, kids, let's all sit in a circle!"). In every conceivable department of daily life – sports, leisure, health, gender relations, manners, superstitions, rites of passage, work ethic, attire, decor, cuisine, literature, music (if you play under three instruments, they revoke your Russian nationality), not to mention that extra-terrestrial language of theirs – in all of these areas and more, a Grand Canyon-size cultural chasm separates us proud products of the Free World from these outlandish ex-Commie-Pinkos.

And yet.

And yet somehow – somehow – without rhyme and without reason and without one shared cultural characteristic or joint intellectual interest to tie us together and merge our distinctive destinies – somehow still: they are ours and we are theirs. Indelibly. Indissolubly. And we all know it, and *they* all know it, know it down inside, in the recesses, don't even have to ask. That's why – isn't it? – we spent all those Sunday afternoons out there in front of the UN, or the Soviet Embassy in DC, or on the Ben Franklin Parkway in Philly (or wherever y'all demonstrated in Chicago, Miami, LA and the various other provincial backwaters) chanting *SVA-BO-DA, SVA-BO-DA*, chaining ourselves to embassy fences and shooting fire-crackers up tutus at the Bolshoi Ballet, making secret trips to the "Evil Empire" and successfully petitioning our congresspeople to *starve Russia* if it's damned dictatorial government didn't agree to "Let Our People Go" post haste ("*our* people" – whom we'd never even met, whom the vast majority of us *would* never even meet, and with whom we had *nothing whatsoever* in common!).

And when they finally came; when they began arriving, in their hundreds, and then in their thousands, emerging exhausted, exhilarated, bewildered, beautiful, pouring out from the cabins of planes that were landing almost *every twenty minutes* day-in and day-out, month after month for close to a year; when that happened, you see, *we* went down; went down, is what we did, in *our* hundreds, and then in *our* thousands, went down to Ben-Gurion airport and *wept* – you got me? We wept, and hugged, and kissed, and danced, and we carried the communist luggage of complete and total strangers whose tongue was as foreign to us as Swahili is to a Cambodian.

Beruchim haba'im ha-bayta! ("Welcome home!")

Ni nada askarblyat shlyapu mayei zhenui! ("I'll teach you to insult my wife's hat!")

True, it took only about a week until we were cheating them blind ("Step right up and view a *fully-stocked supermarket* – only twenty shekels entry fee!") and accusing them of stealing all our menial jobs *and* hogging all the prestigious university positions. But none of that changes the fact.

When I was around nineteen – not a particularly pious period of my life, to put it mildly – I descended once late at night down to this very badly lit, really almost pitch-dark, low level subway track in New York City, to catch a Brooklyn-bound train. I was in town for a freestyle Frisbee tournament held on Central Park's Great Lawn, and I definitely looked the part: Bermuda shorts, "War is Unhealthy for Plants and Other Living Things" t-shirt with sleeves ripped off *de rigueur*, hyper-shoulder length tresses cascading out of Grateful Dead bandana, unshaven, barefoot (it was my "shoes impede communion with mother earth" stage), and indulging in the inhalation of that type of cigarette in which one may with impunity indulge in the abandoned bowels of the Manhattan subway system. I shuffled my way along the deserted platform of this soundless, lightless nether-station until I banged into a bench, and slumped down. A train soon came, but it wasn't mine, and the strobe effect caused by its rapid passing abruptly illuminated the face of a petite young hassidic woman sitting all alone on the bench directly opposite mine, not five feet away. Properly covered from head-to-toe, her bone-white face with its turquoise eyes and pronounced veins encircled by a tightly drawn kerchief, she was perched there frozen, clutching her bag. She saw me, too (in all my glory) – and her eyes instantly registered fear.

Now, it might have been the marijuana, but – and try not to laugh *too* hard, OK? We're getting into some really embarrassing, super-personal and perhaps not entirely un-flaky territory here – I was simply unable to stop myself from leaning forward and trying to communicate with her (I *did* retain enough composure not to fall to my knees, which had been my original impulse). You see, the sight of this lone, petrified Jewess appearing and disappearing between Bronx-bound flashes, looking for all the world (so I imagined) like our great-great grandmothers must have, as newlyweds in the *shtetl*, her features so fragile, her eyes so frightened, her skin so porcelain pale – had suddenly sent me back to an old Lamed Shapiro story I had once read, entitled "White *Challah*." All I remembered of the story was the last scene, in which the Cossack anti-hero, participating in an "unofficial" pogrom somewhere out in the Pale of Settlement, bends down over the hassidic woman he has just beaten, raped and strangled to death, and – obsessed as he has always been since childhood with the snowy hue of Jewish female flesh, which is associated in his fevered mind with the white *challah* these same women bake on Fridays – takes a large bite out of his victim's soft shoulder, and savors the taste until the end of the tale.

With that image swimming around in my addled cerebrum, then, I leaned forward and addressed the following heartfelt soliloquy to My Modest Lady of the E-train's tremulous silhouette: "What? You – afraid of me? *Of me*? Why, for God's sake…don't you know? *Could it possibly be that you do not know* – that I would die for you? That I would gladly *sacrifice my life* to pull you out of harm's way? That…that if they came, those vodka-swigging savages, on their horses, those vicious, feral beasts, with their bloodshot eyes, those drunken peasant butchers, those flaxen-haired, jack-booted, mustachioed cannibals – that if they came charging through your village, to soil, to despoil and to slaughter – that I would protect you, that I would be a shield unto you, that I would go find young Jabotinsky and his friends and we would form a circle around you and keep you safe from them, from their ravaging hands, from their lupine teeth, that we would…"

Poor creature took off as fast as her black-stockinged legs would carry her, down the platform, up the stairs and out of reach of one more Manhattan subway psychopath (she'll be taking cabs from now on). Now, look: it is news to no one by this point that your humble author is a raving loon – and at the time I was, you will be kind enough to recall, a nineteen-year-old loon under the influence of some super-prime Aloha bud – but still: *where in the hell did I get that from*? Who put that in my brain? (And on the off chance that I'm not as loony as all that – that I'm not entirely alone in this matter – who put that in *our* brain?) After all, could there possibly be, anywhere on this planet, two human beings whose lives and outlooks are more diametrically opposed and more thoroughly alien to one another than those of this ultra-Orthodox paragon of regimented purity, traditional values and introverted virtue hailing from the utterly unmodified Middle Ages – on the one hand – and the drugged, dissipated and debauched Frisbee freak flopped in front of her in all his "anything goes" progressiveness, recognizing no rules, bound by no restrictions, and either unaware of or unalterably opposed to almost every aspect of this lady's lifestyle and worldview? And I would *die* for her? Give up my *life*?

What in the name of Sir James Dalrymple is *going on* here?

Maybe I'm not making myself clear. You see, I can certainly understand why, for example, Christians feel a sense of group camaraderie, why they might even be willing to sacrifice themselves to save one another (say, in Diocletian's lion's den, or today in the southern Sudan). This makes a great deal of straightforward, rational sense to me: because Christians believe the same things (overall), stand for the same values, aim at the same momentous goals. But the Jews? Ha! Even if one *could* make a convincing case for some sort of ultimate "Mission of Israel," "Light unto the Nations," "*Tikkun Olam*" (Reformation of the World) or just plain messianic Jewish "goal" in history – and those who would do so need first of all to get past the formidable essays of the almighty Ahad HaAm – no two Jews would *ever* agree anymore about what that utopian objective should in fact be (just ask, oh, Leon Trotsky and Alan Greenspan). What basis, then, do we Jews – who are currently bereft of anything even resembling a consensus regarding individual ideals of daily behavior, let alone any long term collective aims – what motivation could we possibly have for caring so damn deeply about one another?

Why did I spend all those Sunday afternoons in high school – not at football practice, like the other kids – but marching hither and thither and yon in order to secure the release from "refusenikdom" of this thoroughly unknown quantity on the other side of the planet that went by the name of Anatoly Sharansky? (To be fair, the reason I wasn't at football practice was because, as my grandmother used to put it, only a dyed-in-the-wool, *doch getribene goy* would use his head as a battering ram, and also because…well…I was cut during the first day of tryouts.) Weren't there enough folks suffering from a wide variety of ailments and injustices in my immediate surroundings, in my own neighborhood, in my city, in my country, at least in my *hemisphere*, people with whom I could more easily identify, who spoke my language, listened to my music, watched my movies, understood my references, and would sit on practically any surface available without giving it a second thought? Then *who the hell* is this Sharansky dude, and why in God's name am I wasting my precious Sundays on him? Why – in the same vein – did Theodor Herzl work himself *literally to death* in order to save millions of people, with the overwhelming majority of whom he – as an avid and avowed atheist and secularist, as a thoroughly Westernized Viennese *fin de siècle* dandy – shared not even a *single* article of faith or common pursuit in life (the man was never even personally subjected to anti-Semitism)?

And if you answer, almost on fire in your fed-up-edness, that – dammit – "while Herzl may have had little in common with the *Ostjuden* of the Tzarist tundra, and while you [meaning me] may share very little with Sharansky (or with the Yemenite, Moroccan, and Iraqi Jews in your neighborhood, not to mention the Kurds who live across the way and feast on fried calf brains every evening) – while all this may be true, nevertheless: *we all share a common history*, or at least a thematically similar set of historical experiences!"

If you resort to this rebuttal, then I will immediately riposte as follows: **Who's "we," white man**? What do you mean, *we* all share a common history? I don't know about you, pal, but as for me, well, shucks: *I just wasn't there*. I wasn't around for all that stuff, way back then when things were rotten (in Kishinev, at Trent, on the slopes of Gamla or the beaches of Portugal) nor even for when they were good (at...uhhhh...I'll get back to you). *I am not those people who experienced those things*. I do not know them from Adam, and I probably wouldn't get along with them very well if I did. So if what you're telling me is that I should shlep around a giant placard that says "Free Ida Nudel!" solely because way back when in the reign of Catherine the Great, Ida's great-great-great-great-grandfather and my great-great-great-great-grandfather got a great-great-great-great deal together on an ox in Bialystok, or were simultaneously run over by the same droshky in Plonsk – then we're back where we started from, and I'll ask you again: who in heaven's name is my great[4] grandfather to me, and *why in hell should I give a rat's rump about him and the people he hung out with*, or let my life be in any way influenced by their exploits, trials and tribulations?

Who? *Why*? Permit me to answer my own question. The operative, politically incorrect and therefore much maligned concept here is – as we noted above – *kinship*. "A little more than kin," opens Hamlet, "and less than kind." This happens to be a little more than a pun (in Shakespeare's time "kind" rhymed with "pinned"). The two words are full-blooded etymological siblings: "kind" merely means "behaving as one would toward one's *kin*." And the latter term, in its turn, is derived from the Greek-Latin root "*gen*" – as in generate, genesis, genes – and thus denotes a group of people linked together by descent from a common pro*gen*itor. Kinship it is – purported or genuine or a little of both – which *alone* is capable of tying me, as a Jew, twice. It ties me "vertically" or temporally, to those never-seen and all-too-culturally-and-ideologically foreign Jews of yore who *did* in fact share "as one person" (at least in certain eras) a common history and fate; and kinship *thereby* also ties me "horizontally" or spatially, to members of my hereditary clan in the here-and-now, wherever in the whole wide world they may be found, whatever the level of their observance of or indifference to Torah law, and whichever language they may speak or surfaces they may agree to sit upon. Kiss me: I'm a Jewish "essentialist" (we all are).

We Jews are a family (have I mentioned this?), and I daresay you relate to family members – wherever they may be holed up, whatever they may be involved in, and whether or not you've met them to date or will *ever* meet them – with at least a few CCs more than the standard dosage of solicitousness earmarked in your heart for the average fellow on the street. ("Hello? Hi! This is your third cousin Benny's sister-in-law Meredith's niece Jennifer's Great Uncle Lenny – how ya doin'?! *That's right*: Len Feldstein, house lawyer for the NRA – you recognized the name! Listen, I'm sorry to call so late, but word is you might have some interesting information to share about a certain merger in the offing…") "Kinship," then, is the *only* reason I marched for Sharansky.

Suppose you had a best friend, a bosom buddy, who not only spent much of his childhood by your side, but who always had your back and on one occasion even risked his life to save yours. Then, when you were both in your late teens, the poor guy (let's call him Harry) got hit by a bus – *yisgadal ve yiskadash*. Seventy years later you are this doddering *alter cocker*, but a filthy rich one. One day you meet a bum on the street, a miserable, strung out junkie, and for whatever reason the two of you strike up a conversation, and would you believe it? It turns out that before he died, good ole Harry had had a one-night stand and got a girl pregnant, and the gutter-bound vagrant you are now talking to is none other than your long lost bosom buddy's grandson! Upon discovering this fact, you proceed to:

(a) give him fifty cents as you would any other beggar and continue on your way to the shareholders' meeting;
(b) scoop him up into your limo and spend a considerable amount of time and money getting him back on his feet and then some.

I'm going to assume that you answered "b" (if not, then please send me the telephone numbers of your current closest friends, I'd like a word with them). The question is, why? I mean, sure, you feel duty-bound – indeed, you probably feel privileged – to honor your old friend's memory, as it were, to return the favor. But why in this manner? In what way does improving the life of this homeless mendicant achieve that goal? Well, you might answer, this sorry sap of a man is sort of like an extension of your erstwhile pal; or, you might say, that's what your childhood friend would have wanted you to do for his offspring. But wait: in what way is this bum an "extension" of Harry? Harry never met him, exerted no influence on his upbringing. And by the same token, why should Harry care a whit about the welfare of a grandchild he has never met (and, as ill-luck would have it, will never meet)? For that matter, why should any of us give a hoot about what happens to our great-great-grandchildren, none of whom we will ever meet? We don't know them, will never spend time with them or learn to love them for the particular people that they are. More than this: suppose you eat a lot of cabbage and do a lot of aerobics and end up living long enough to eat Thanksgiving dinners and have Memorial Day barbecues with these fifth generation descendants of yours, and as it turns out, they don't resemble you in the least and their personalities are not even to your liking. What reason is there in this case for you to give any more of a flying fadoodle about them than you do about anybody else? The answer to all of these questions is, of course, the same answer: *blood.* DNA, genes, lineage, pedigree, extraction, heredity, consanguinity, kinship. Kinship, dear reader, is the only reason you would help out Harry's grandson.

Aye, but don't you see? There's the rub! Because what could possibly be more irrational *in the world* than this particular motivation? Kinship? *Kinship*?! Just because the sniveling little poli-sci prof who systematically usurps my parking space every day at the university *happens* to be descended (maybe), as I just *happen* to be also (maybe), from the great primeval Sarah-Womb – because of this and this alone, I came here to this crazy country and made common cause with his thieving butt, indeed, regularly risk my skin for him when in uniform (and he returns the favor)? *Hello*? As criteria for group loyalty go, the fact of similarly structured DNA (a fact, I am told, that they have recently more or less proven in the Jewish case) is about as senseless a touchstone as they come. Common ideals, common aspirations, common theology, common behavior, common social class, common region of residence, even a common predilection for Boar's

Head knockwurst – all of these I can understand as logical bases for communal identity and consolidation, for the justification of associational allegiance. But a common womb, *four thousand years back*? Descent from similar familial "stock"? What's *that* got to do with… anything? In what way does it constitute a rational criterion for preferring some people over others? In what way can it be characterized as anything other than pure, unadulterated racism?

And yet that womb is – as I have been struggling so hard to demonstrate – the primary motivation for Jewish coherence and cooperation in this day and age (and, I would argue, historically as well – even when slightly more ideological unanimity reigned among us).

What's more, we Jews are rather unique in this regard. There aren't too many bona fide tribal confederations left in the world. They've mostly been dismembered or swallowed up over the course of history by far more *rationally defensible* geographical-, religious-, ideological- and economic-based associations – which is one reason why gentiles today have such a hard time understanding what they see as Jewish "exclusivism." It just makes no sense – indeed, appears standoffish, chauvinistic and racist – to anyone who doesn't have a tribe or mega-family, especially if they count themselves members of more or less *ideologically-based* ***inclusive*** *communities* (Christianity, Islam, Hare Krishna, Communism, the EU, even America). The Jewish People, then, represents in our day and age the prototypical example and international poster-child of what certain anthropologists – displaying that well-known penchant of theirs for the romantic – refer to as an "**Irrational Solidarity Group.**"

Chapter Fifteen

And so, the prosecution rests. Ofer's prosecution, that is. I have sincerely endeavored in the preceding to bolster and elucidate his fast and furiously phrased Arrivals Lounge thesis – no less on the button for its heated extemporaneousness – to wit: that the Jewish reality in history (and the more so today) is composed of (1) a largely irrational and impractical constitution (biblical-talmudic law and theology), which is (2) busy governing (or not governing) a largely irrational and impractical solidarity group (the Jews).

Why in hell, asks Ofer, should I be a part of *that*?

I'll confess this to you. While arguing on Ofer's behalf over the last hundred or so pages, I have on more than one occasion despaired of being able effectively to counter the claims I myself have been heaping up in his name – primarily because *I believe every bleeding word of it*. The fear has accosted me that I would be justly accused – as Maimonides once was by his famous critic Abraham ben David of the Posquieres – of *matkhil bedavar veh lo yode'a lehashlimo*, starting something that I didn't know how to finish. What encouraged me to keep going at such trying times was, more than anything else, the awareness of the following auspicious paradox. Here I am (said I to myself), a guy who does indeed hold all of those opinions and harbor all of those sentiments regarding the irrationality and practical inadvisability of involvement in "Judaism" and the Jewish People in our day and age…

…ve af al pi khen – and yet.

And yet here I am. Here I am in the newly formed and fiercely struggling Jewish State, until death do us part (I sure hope mine comes first). Here, with my nation, with my people, smack in the middle of their hard-won renaissance, plumb in the thick of their confusions and clarities, their comedies and catastrophes. Here I am, for that matter, doing no small amount of that voodoo that we do so well, that we've been doing with such pertinacity for so many centuries: making *matzahs*, building *sukkahs*, lighting *menorahs*, avoiding shellfish, declaiming *kiddush*, shaving with the Eva Braun, wrapping those deluxe, four-hundred dollar punishment phylacteries around my arm so tightly that my hand turns blue and topping off the entire semi-pious package with nothing less than a *yarmulka* (which – by a weird quirk of poetic justice and symbiosis – is at one and the same time both the *cause* and the *camouflage* of this imperceptibly expanding bald-spot on the top of my head). Here I am, an incorrigibly independent and abrasively critical fellow raised on the likes of Bertrand Russell and Rosa Luxemborg (and John Lennon), who agrees with every single thing that Ofer said and then some – **and yet**: somewhere along the line, I managed to reach the *diametrically opposing conclusion* based upon the same damned data! Ofer left; I joined up. There must be a reason for this, I told myself – and that gave me courage.

And so the defense calls its first witness…

Chapter Sixteen

Judaism" and Jewish nationalism are indeed two of the most irrational and impractical pursuits anyone could possibly think of. The apologists lied when they told you otherwise, when they performed so many feats of acrobatic chicanery to show you how logical and pragmatic it all is, how it really does make so very much sense, even for us today. But throughout their many and strenuous efforts toward this end, the apologists themselves have always been motivated by – and have therefore consistently communicated to their reading and listening public – a far more monstrous, far more odious, far more pernicious and ruinous lie, a lie that packs greater destructive capability per cubic centimeter than a two-hundred-and-fifty-megaton hydrogen bomb, I think perhaps the single most poisonous and lethal lie ever told to anyone anywhere at any time. And that lie is…

…that making sense is the most important thing.

Oh, and it's not the apologists' fault – they've been duped, like all the rest of us. The entire Western world lives this lie, a lie compounded in recent centuries with every additional generation that grows up. The long climb of the apparently irresistible perspective known as "Reason" to the apogee of the human value heap began in ancient times (especially among the Greeks), gathered steam in the Middle Ages (especially among the Muslims), and reached the pinnacle of omnipotent, unchallengeable dictatorship in Europe hard on the heels of the fourteenth-to-seventeenth-century Renaissance. Since that time, the supreme reign of rationality in the theory (if not always the practice) of Occidental society has occasionally had its detractors and even virulent opponents (especially among the Romantics), but – as they say in Greek – "*gornisht helfen*": no theory, no philosophy, no thinker and no movement has to date succeeded in dislodging the bolted-down posteriori of the all-mighty Emperor of Epistemology from his geometrically constructed throne.

Reason rules the roost.

I do not mean to say, of course, that since Newton and Descartes, we all walk around like Mr. Spock (the *real* science officer of the Enterprise – not that milky android twit they replaced him with) measuring everything we see and do by the pure, mathematical criteria of logic. What I do mean to say is that most all of the mega-trends noticeable in the world in recent decades and centuries – in the fields of science, technology, philosophy, politics, commerce, industry, law, education, even religion – have served to "rationalize" human life in ninety thousand different ways. Let me try to explain what I'm talking about by tackling the last and least obvious of the categories just enumerated – least obvious, that is, in terms of its perceived susceptibility to rationalization. I mean religion itself.

Once upon a time there was this God, you see, with whom we human beings could *truly identify*, because we were reputedly created in His spitting image (Genesis 1:27). For not only did that mean that we were like Him – a chip off the old Rock (of Salvation), as it were – but also, obviously and no less significantly, it meant that *He was like us*. We were the Deity writ small, and *He was us writ large*. The God of the Bible was most emphatically and unabashedly possessed of all the juiciest characteristics, propensities, aspirations, needs, emotions, quirks, idiosyncrasies and yes, even many of the weaknesses and shortcomings that are found in – *that run the lives of* – human beings. Oh, He was happy (Psalms 104:31) and He was sad (Gen. 6:6) and He laughed (Ps. 2:4) and He cried (Isaiah 16:9) and His soul was grieved (Judges 10:16) and He got mad (Isa. 60:10) and He became angry (Deuteronomy 32:21) and He waxed furious (Exodus 4:14) and He went apoplectic (Numbers 16:21) and *great balls o' fire*! (Deut. 4:24) and He calmed down (Num. 25:14) and He waned weary (Malachi 2:17) and He took a nap (Gen. 2:2) and He was merciful (Ex. 34:6) and He was unmerciful (Jeremiah 13:14) and He was jealous (Deut. 5:9) and He was zealous (Deut. 5:9) and He boasted (Isa. 44:6) and He saber-rattled (Jeremiah 49:28) and He gloated (Amos 2:9) and He made mistakes (Gen. 6:6) and He worried (Gen. 11:6) and He loved (preferentially – Deut. 23:6) and He hated (Mal. 1:3) and He took vengeance (Deut. 32:41) and He forgave (Ex. 34:7) and He was compassionate (Ex. 20:6) and He changed His mind (Ex. 32:14) and He enjoyed the sweet savor of a good calf roast (Leviticus 2:12) and He *did not* enjoy the sweet savor of a good calf roast (Hosea 9:4) and He took constitutionals in the late afternoon (Gen. 3:8) and He lost arguments (Num. 16:22) and He lost wrestling matches (Gen. 32:29) and He started out demanding fifty righteous men in order to spare the city of Sodom, and Abraham jewed him down to ten (Gen. 18:26).

WHERE IS THAT GOD?

I miss Him, that dynamic Divinity. What has become of Him – that most feeling of Fathers, that flexible, emotional, *imperfect* Deity? Where did He get to, that *human* God?

Where did He get to? I'll tell you where: He's been *kidnapped*. That's right. Held for ransom. And while I don't know exactly *where* He has been taken, if you're interested, I'll tell you who the kidnappers are. Let's hop a red-eye to Athens.

The Greek gods were a roaring good time. Take Zeus, for instance. Zeus was the single greatest skirt-chaser the world has ever seen. He makes Casanova look like a castrated monk. Goddesses, demigoddesses, nymphs, nereids, sirens, mermaids, mortal girls, married, unmarried, virginal, divorced, widowed, male, dead – he wasn't that particular. If you caught Zeus' eye, your jig was up. This was true not just because when Zeus got really excited – on the verge of climax – he would often turn into a thunderbolt and incinerate you (just ask the ashes of his poor paramour Semele); nor only because he sometimes liked to do it disguised as a swan, in the aftermath of which you would be forced to lay a large egg (just ask Helen of Troy's mother, Leda, thus named because she exclaimed: "By Jove – I've leda large egg!"); nor were you in trouble solely because Zeus used to get the munchies big-time after carnal intimacy and might decide to have you for dinner over a sweet Chianti (as he did with Metis, Athena's mom). No. The main reason it was bad news to be raped by Zeus was named Hera – his anile battle-axe termagant of a sister/wife – who invariably assumed that you had obviously been asking for it, you brazen hussy, and devoted the rest of her extremely lengthy immortal existence to making your every moment on this earth an excruciating nightmare from Hades. It is for this reason that many ladies, fleeing across the verdurous fields of pastoral Arcady from a low-flying, priapismic Zeus, preferred turning themselves permanently into various inanimate objects (fauna were decidedly *not* a Zeus-deterrent) to getting it on with "the king of the gods."

One clever mermaid named Thetis found an easier way to extricate herself. Both Zeus *and* his brother Poseidon had the hots for this salty little sea-nymph, but she paid off Prometheus to coax a convenient prophecy out of the Delphi Oracle, according to which any son of hers would grow up to outshine his father. Well, neither divine sibling was having any of *that*, so Zeus arranged to get the fishy femme fatale hooked up with the adventurous mortal Peleus (who would in time father by her no less a paladin than brave Achilles himself). All the gods attended their wedding, except Eris ("strife"), whom they had fatefully overlooked. To avenge this slight, Eris crashed the party, throwing into the midst of the assembled Olympian guests a golden apple, upon which were inscribed the words "for the fairest."

"Oh, that'll be for me," says Hera nonchalantly, like it's obvious. "Pick that up, Zeus honey."

"Not so fast, you old hag," says Athena (she had meanwhile popped out of her father's forehead). "It says 'for the fairest,' not 'for the furriest.' I'll be wanting that aureate orb."

"Athena darling," injects Aphrodite. "Put your disgusting face back behind your Medusa-head shield, like Daddy always told you to, so the nice people can eat. Hermes, you fleet-footed godkin: *fetch me that apple.*"

"You are *not* my sister," Athena hisses back. "In fact, I hadn't noticed it before, but you bear a rather striking resemblance to your *real* parentage: Uranus' severed scrotum!"

In the end, Zeus transported all three squabbling divas to Mt. Ida, where Paris – the handsomest hunk in all of Anatolia and son of Priam, King of Troy – was languidly shepherding his sheep. He was to judge the beauty contest. Each goddess offered him a bribe: Hera dangled rule over Asia before his greedy eyes; Athena tendered wisdom and military might; but Aphrodite knew her man. She held out Helen (of the egg), the hottest chick on earth.

"Here she comes...*Miss* Olympia!" – Aphrodite was instantly awarded the golden apple, and Paris went off to seduce Helen (who happened to be quite married already, to Menelaus of Sparta, brother of Agamemnon, King of Greece, which minor point the little trollop promptly forgot the second she laid eyes on the Prince of Troy). Her adulterous face launched a thousand Greek ships – across to Ilium to get her back – the Trojan War got underway, and the rest is history.

Why do I tell you all this? Because if you in any way enjoyed reading the above story, don't thank Plato. In his most famous Dialogue, the "Republic," the Father of Philosophy and zealous Boswell of Socrates maps out the educational curriculum for his Stalinist-McCarthyist utopia. In order to raise a generation of rationally thinking and properly obedient children who will always play nice with their fellow citizens in his perfectly planned Nowhere Land.

> WE MUST BEGIN, IT SEEMS, BY A CENSORSHIP OVER OUR STORY-MAKERS.
>
> Censorship – *nice.* What sorts of stories were you thinking of banning, Socrates?
>
> THOSE OF HESIOD, HOMER AND THE OTHER POETS.
>
> *Damn*: that's pretty near the entirety of your culture's classical literary canon – and you propose to remove *all* these works from the core curriculum?

THE BEST SOLUTION WOULD BE TO BURY THEM IN SILENCE, AND IF THERE WAS SOME NECESSITY FOR RELATING THEM, ONLY A VERY SMALL AUDIENCE SHOULD BE ADMITTED UNDER PLEDGE OF SECRECY AND AFTER SACRIFICING, NOT A PIG, BUT SOME HUGE AND UNPROCURABLE ANIMAL, TO THE END THAT AS FEW PEOPLE AS POSSIBLE SHOULD HAVE HEARD THESE TALES.

May I suggest a Blue Whale for each paragraph of the *Iliad*? Why are you doing this, Socrates? I thought you were "Mr. Free Speech."

WE MUST NOT ADMIT THAT GODS WAR WITH GODS AND PLOT AGAINST ONE ANOTHER AND CONTEND, AND STILL LESS MUST WE MAKE BATTLES OF GODS AND GIANTS THE SUBJECTS OF STORIES AND EMBROIDERIES FOR OUR YOUNG...AND HERA'S FETTERINGS BY HER SON AND THE HURLING OUT OF HEAVEN OF HEPHAESTUS BY HIS FATHER AND THE BATTLES OF GODS IN HOMER'S VERSE ARE THINGS WE MUST NOT ADMIT INTO OUR CITY...BECAUSE IF THERE IS ANY LIKELIHOOD OF OUR PERSUADING THE CHILDREN THAT NO CITIZEN IN THE PAST EVER QUARRELED WITH HIS FELLOW CITIZEN AND THAT THE VERY IDEA OF QUARRELING IS AN IMPIETY, THEN WE MUST COMPEL THE POETS TO KEEP CLOSE TO THIS IN THEIR COMPOSITIONS.

Oh, I get it: lie to your kids and keep them ignorant, so they are docile and obsequious and don't make trouble for your philosopher-king. Hell, Socrates: of all people, I never pegged *you* for an apologist. How the mighty have fallen!

YOU'RE RIGHT. I AM NOT WORTHY TO CONTINUE CONVERSING WITH A LOGICIAN OF YOUR STATURE. I AM GOING TO GO HOME AND DRINK SOME HEMLOCK.

To be fair, Socrates-cum-Plato thinks *Homer* is the liar, and he doesn't want his eugenically produced *über*-children exposed to such silly and corrupting mythological fabrications. Nor is he done enumerating the things that authors may not say about the gods. He goes on to prohibit, *inter alia*, the description of divinities as able to change their form (no more Zeus-goosing for Leda), or to change, *period* – in any fashion. His reasoning on this score is as follows: (1) "change" necessarily entails moving from one state or condition to another; (2) a god's *current* state or condition is obviously perfect (what do you mean, "why?" Because he's a *god*, dodo!); thus, (3) a god can only change for the worse; and, (4) you'd have to be a complete *retard* to do *that*.

Now watch how Plato's student Aristotle picks up the ball and runs with it, and on top of Socrates' syllogism, builds his own. Aristotle posits that (1) anything corporeal or tangible must change – must at least undergo "generation and decay"; (2) God (Aristotle prefers the singular) does *not* change, as Plato has already proven; thus, (3) God is clearly *in*corporeal and *in*tangible. But do we know of any substance that is clearly incorporeal and intangible, asks Aristotle? Only one, responds he: *thought*. In other words, God must be...thought.

That's cool. Now, what would God – that is, Thought with a capital T – spend His time thinking about? Would He think about many *different* things, or about the same thing? Well, switching subjects of cognition would involve *change*, and we already know that God can't change, right? So He must consistently contemplate only one and the *same* thing, for all eternity.

And what might that thing be, that He consistently contemplates? Well, reasons Aristotle: He could either be thinking of Himself, or of something else, *n'est ce pas*? Now, no one in his or her right mind would deliberately ponder an inferior subject when there is a superior one around to meditate upon, and since God is obviously and by definition superior to any other subject there is, He must spend the entirety of eternity... *thinking about Himself*.

And what did we say "Himself" was? That's right: Thought. And thus does the great Aristotle, with an initial push from Plato, arrive at the ultimate conclusion that God is *Intellectus Intelligens Intellectum* – "Thought Thinking about Thought," an entity that is not only uninvolved in the universe, but is entirely unaware of that universe's existence, given that He focuses His thoughts in perpetuity on only one single subject: on *thinking*. On thinking, that is, about Himself.

Now, if I may be allowed to interpose a word here, I'd just like to say at this juncture that

> YOU INSUFFERABLE ATHENIAN *IDIOTS*!!! CAN'T YOU SEE THAT YOU HAVE REDUCED THE DIVINE TO A HEEDLESS, HEARTLESS, OBLIVIOUS, IMPOTENT *GEOMETRY PROBLEM*?! DON'T YOU REALIZE THAT YOU HAVE SPENT YOUR ENTIRE LIVES STRIVING TO MAKE THE GODS OR GOD FIT INTO YOUR MATHEMATICALLY EVOLVED RULES OF IMPECCABLE RATIONALITY AND YOUR FROZEN, IMMUTABLE LAWS OF NINETY DEGREE-ANGLE LOGIC, AND YOU HAVE FORGOTTEN THROUGHOUT ALL THIS CALCULATED COGITATION THE SIMPLE AND ESSENTIAL POINT THAT *WHAT MAKES THEM GODS, OR HIM GOD, IN THE FIRST PLACE,* THE VERY *DEFINITION OF THE DIVINE*, IS THAT **THEY ARE, OR HE IS,** ***NOT SUBJECT TO THE RESTRAINTS OF LOGIC AND RATIONALITY THAT YOU HAVE SO LABORIOUSLY CONSTRUCTED***!!! GOD *IS* GOD, YOU UNREHABILITATED *MORONS*, **FOR THE SOLE AND INDISPENSIBLE REASON THAT HE IS** ***UNQUANTIFIABLE, UNPREDICTABLE, UNLIMITABLE, IMMEASURABLE AND NOT MATHEMATICALLY PERFECT***!!! THAT IS, IN THE FIRST AND LAST ANALYSIS, WHAT THE TERM "GOD" *MEANS*, AND DAMMIT: **THOU SHALT NOT TAKE THE NAME OF THE LORD THY GOD** ***IN VAIN***!!!

Sorry. Let me calm down and explain. It is really very simple. Aristotle claims – elsewhere, in a different context – that God is of infinite extension. He's endless, that high-flying Narcissistic Brooder. Aristotle proves this (you guessed it) with a syllogism that goes like this: (1) the "spheres" (basically, the universe) keep on spinning around forever; (2) whatever is causing them to spin must therefore be possessed of infinitely enduring power; (3) anything possessed of infinitely enduring power must necessarily be of infinite size; (4) since God is the Prime Spinner (a.k.a. the Unmoved Mover), then God is clearly...of infinite size. QED

If Aristotle were not six feet under fertilizing Chalcidic daffodils, I would ask him the following question: "Tell me, O illustrious son of Nicomachus: Can God do *anything*?"

HMMMM – WELL, *OBVIOUSLY* HE CAN, FRIEND. HE'S GOD.

I see. So, now: if God wanted to, could He turn himself into a little green toad the size of your thumb, or into a toll-bridge or an aspirin tablet or a quasar or the Fonz – and then *still* make the universe keep on "spinning" forever? Could He be both omnipotent and, say...short, fat, bald and cross-eyed, all at the same time – *if He so desired*? Well, whadya think? *Could He*?

I...I...

And could He also, by the same token, laugh, or cry, or change His location, or His mind, or be corporeal and finite, or pick up mermaids at an underwater bar, or be a guest-host on Saturday Night Live or have a BLT on rye hold the mustard?!

BUT...BUT...

Don't you *understand*, you pompous, peripatetic old *coot*, that it is the unique hallmark, singular prerogative and *very essence* of the Divine, that – if it exists at all – it is *above and beyond* all these logical constraints and limitations...by very virtue of *being what it is*? Otherwise – if you insist on describing and therefore circumscribing God by means of the same "natural law" with which you characterize and restrict everything else, then what would make Him different in any qualitative way from the rest of existence, and why would He warrant the designation "divine"? And just *who the hell are you*, anyway, and *who the hell is logic*, to restrict God, to tell God what He can and cannot be, what He can and cannot do?! Don't you see that trying to make God conform to and abide by human notions of rational science or syllogistic "sense" is to elevate the most flagrant and foolish contradiction imaginable to the very crest of your philosophical system?

WOW. I NEVER THOUGHT OF THAT. MY ENTIRE LIFE HAS BEEN A WASTE. I'LL GET THE HEMLOCK.

In truth, Aristotle would have denied my first statement right off the bat. He didn't think that God could do anything. He (like Plato and Pythagoras before him) thought that *math* could do anything. Aristotle thought that God *was* math – and (what is more to the point) that math was God.

The great masters of Greek philosophy turned on their own mythological and religious heritage with a ferocious, astringent vengeance. They systematically eviscerated, deracinated and ripped out any semblance of personality from the heretofore wildly colorful Olympian pantheon, leaving nothing but a few sterile equations in its place. They killed their gods more than two thousand years before Nietzsche's madman proclaimed his own Deity DOA in *The Gay Science.*

Now watch this: enter Origen, Augustine, Abelard, Aquinas; enter Jahm, Al-Ghazali, Ibn Sina, Ibn Rushd; enter Philo, Saadya, Maimonides, Ibn Shaprut. Take a bow, gentlemen. Honored reader: say hello to the fine-feathered medieval fellers who are about to import what was without a doubt the premiere, most effective, most lethal *anti-divine methodology and ideology* in the entire ancient world, and – are you ready for this? – apply it, within the context of their own religions, *to the Divine*! (Look how well that can of Raid Insecticide worked on those cockroaches, Betty – let's feed it to Ralph, our two-year old!)

Greek philosophy had been seeping into the Middle Eastern monotheistic water table ever since Aristotle's energetic pupil, Alexander the Great, brought it here in his baggage train around the year 335 BCE. The Talmud is already aware of, and even to no small extent influenced by, Hellenistic terminology and ideas (who's up for a subterranean, solar-powered Jacuzzi?). But still, most of classical philosophy was "Greek to them" until the works of the major players were translated into Syriac, Arabic, Persian and Hebrew in the early Middle Ages. Then it was that our first-string theologians of Christianity, Islam and Judaism contracted Greco-mania. They just couldn't lap up the new and improved logical techniques fast enough. These were, after all, the science and rationality of their day – and science and rationality, as we well know, are the Holy of

Holies. Greek approaches to just about everything were all the rage, and they eventually became the final criteria against which the veracity and even the value of any belief or institution were measured. In our particular case, hundreds of Hellenistic speculations were reproduced – often verbatim, without modification of so much as a jot or tittle – as Jewish gospel truths, as "Torah from Sinai." The Maccabees, it seems, had fought in vain.

And that is how it came about that the Greeks (with some fifth column assistance from our own well-meaning savants) kidnapped the romantic, immanent, passionate, caring, *human* God of the Bible, and replaced Him with an imposter: a "rational" God subject to "natural law," a mathematical machine, a dry and lifeless set of formulas: transcendent, impersonal, unknowable and unlovable, unchanging, imperturbable, symmetrical, inhuman and – of course – **perfect**. And it is to *this* cross-the-board de-anthropomorphization, to this Platonic, Aristotelian, Stoic and yes, *Epicurean* **dehumanization of the Deity**, that Maimonides insists – in what has become his thoroughly mainstream "Thirteen Principles of Faith" – that we all pledge allegiance every single day in prayer. *Timeo Danaos et dona ferentes* – "I fear Greeks, even when they come bearing gifts." Thus did Laocoon, priest of the city, warn his fellow men of Troy against dragging that Wooden Horse through the municipal gates. The Trojans should have listened. *So should the Jews.*

I had a friend once who was perfect. Really. The guy simply did everything right. He ate well and exercised, shunned strong drink and abstained from tobacco, drugs and firearms (well, not firearms, he was a commando), he dressed appropriately, paid his bills on time, gave his seat up to the elderly and always bussed his own table at cafes. His talents were legion, his muscles were big, and he exuded a quiet confidence: this was a man to be trusted. He was considerate, respectful, responsible, attentive and scrupulously honest. If he had been female, I would have married him.

Except that one day, we were discussing a hypothetical situation while charging up a Jerusalem mountain during the forty-five minute, uphill-all-the-way, "I wish I were dead and decomposing or better yet had never been born" run he used to make me join him in three times a week. The issue was abortion, but that (believe it or not) was not the problematic aspect – neither of us was on record as being against the procedure in principle. The sticky part came when I brought up the following case in between gasps and wheezes:

"Say you have this twelve-year-old-girl who has fallen desperately in love with an older boy from high-school, and he takes advantage of her innocent adoration, and pressures her to sleep with him. Although she resolves to resist, as they lie in bed together and he looks lovingly into her eyes, whispers anything that will work into her ears, and manipulates various erogenous zones all at the same time – she finally caves in, and gives him the only thing he really wanted from her in the first place. He gets off, gets up, leaves and never speaks to her again. She finds out three weeks later that she's pregnant. So whadya think – abortion?"

"Did she have sex-ed in school?"

"Well, yes. She knew the basic lay of the biological land, but all of that went out the window in the heat of the moment. So, *nu* – abortion?"

"She should have known better, don't you think?"

"Uh – yeah. She should have. But she didn't. *Abortion*?!"

"Well, it seems to me she was extremely irresponsible."

"She was extremely *twelve*, you jerk – and head over heels in love! She got carried away! A-BOR-TION?!"

"She should have thought about *that* before she jumped into the sack with that shameless sleaze in the first place – now shouldn't she? No: I'm afraid she'll just have to live with the consequences of her actions. Now pick up the pace, slacker!"

Regardless of what I may think about the abortion issue itself, I made a very important discovery that day: perfection is *not* a quality you want in a judge. My jogging partner was massively ill-equipped to understand or empathize with the extenuating circumstances surrounding irresponsible, impulsive, immoral or just plain stupid behavior – because he himself would *never* have been guilty of the same. He was on unfamiliar ground, poor thing.

So no: perfection is most decidedly *not* a quality you want in a judge, nor in a parent, nor in a teacher, nor in a spouse (in a *mohel* – a ritual circumciser – yes), nor in a friend, nor in a novel's protagonist…

…nor in a God.

Oh, most of believing world Jewry never carried the aforementioned scholastic makeover of the Deity's character all the way to its logical conclusion: God remains for most theistic Jews to this day "the Merciful and Compassionate" Father, whose tear ducts are flooded by the slightest supplication, who can be bribed and buttered up and whose hand can even occasionally be forced, and who plays constant musical chairs between the justice and the mercy seats (a sea change – of position and attitude – if there ever was one!). Still, the Schoolmen did their work well: we are far more estranged from, and far less able to identify with (let alone *bargain* or *wrestle* with), the Jewish God than ever before in our long history. Our relationship with Him has grown exceedingly distant, as He has dropped His original *imitatio hominis* and grown in abstraction and transcendence (and as we – so we are told – have concomitantly declined in every conceivable way). Witness the simple historical-philological fact that we once used to be on a first-name basis with Him (the Tetragrammaton: Y-H-W-H, which we don't even remember how to pronounce today, and wouldn't be allowed to if we did); then we dropped down a rung to the employment of a sort of respectful sobriquet: *Adonai* (meaning: "My Lord[s]"); and finally, in recent centuries, we have increasingly opted for a *substitute for that substitute*, a deliberately unfamiliar title that evokes "roadblock" far more than it does "access": *HaShem* ("The Name").

God and His Children, thrice removed (how close do we generally assume kids are to their father, when they consistently address him as "Sir"?). And all this, because these medieval, logic-frenzied luminaries were so hell-bent on rationalizing and demythologizing – and thereby neutralizing and devitalizing – a Deity who was once so chock-full of personality, passion and verve. What our Greek masters had done to their gods, *so did we to the Lord our God*. We "cleaned Him up," we took away His humanness. We hid His face from us.

Chapter Seventeen

If you're wondering how we got here, to what looks like a theological discussion, well – we didn't. I have attempted a short survey of the gradual "rationalization of religion" process, but only as an instance of (and precursor to) the far more encompassing phenomenon of the *rationalization of human life in general* that has characterized and distinguished the modern period. Once post-medieval Europe began to emerge from the "long night" of rain-making, superstition, taboo and ballyhoo that was, well, *all of history* up to that point, things finally began to get a little neater and more orderly around here. Science soon came to represent much more than merely the unrivalled helpmeet of humankind, providing new gadgets, medicines, conceptions and the like. It became, in a very real sense, the *metaphor and paradigm* for large parts of life. This does not just mean – as we saw with Nietzsche's use of Darwin – that particular theories and discoveries in various scientific sub-fields were readily transposed and applied to diverse aspects of the human condition. Rather, it means that *the entire mindset and methodology* subsumed under the freshly sanctified heading of "science" began to inform and ultimately to dominate countless areas of *non-scientific* mortal endeavor. For the first time in history, human beings set out to *live logically*, to live "sensibly," to go about the business of being human in a decidedly more rational, more *practical* manner than did our hypnotized and mesmerized predecessors who – thanks to their incorrigible irrationality – did everything the hard way.

Taking its cue from that epitome of all logical procedures known as the Scientific Method – described by the eighteenth-century French thinker Étienne Bonnot de Condillac as "a new method of philosophizing, applicable to *all* areas of human enterprise" – modern society grabbed itself a Crocodile Dundee-size Occam's Razor and started vigorously shaving away all that excess, unnecessary, hand-me-down frippery. Tagged for disposal were the myriad unavailing and ridiculous notions (supernatural, metaphysical, mystical, mythological) that had comprised the lion's share of the traditional world-view, along with the mammoth accumulation of absurd customs and inefficient behaviors that had long played loyal handmaiden to such fantastic nonsense. Any idea, convention or institution that failed to make obeisance to the newly apotheosized criterion of rationality, or was unable satisfactorily to demonstrate its *empirical* worth and its *utilitarian* value, had to go. Like capitalist entrepreneurs privatizing a state-owned concern, we streamlined, optimized and downsized. We cut away all those layers upon layers of superfluous chicken-fat, and began running life and society like an efficient and lucrative business. We stripped existence bare, down to its sensible essentials: convenience, security, expedience, gratification...and convenience.

Speaking of stripping, there is perhaps no more salient and conspicuous illustration of this denudatory trend than the field of fashion. Tell me: do you ever find yourself at the Louvre gazing at paintings of noblemen from the Elizabethan period or the Court of Louis XIV (What? You *don't* frequent the Louvre? *Quel scandale*!!) and wondering: When is this dude gonna look in the mirror and say, "I am wearing green tights, puffy bloomers, a long cape, high-heeled shoes with silver buckles, a six inch ruff around my neck, my face is powdered, my cheeks are rouged, and I have on a long, curly-haired wig topped off by a pointy hat with a plume in it...*am I the world's biggest ass, or what?*" Not to mention the ladies, who wore hoop skirts requiring their own zip codes and corsets drawn just tightly enough to cut off ninety percent of the oxygen to their brains, lest they demand equal rights.

Well, we've since "rationalized" couture, that's for sure. The present author is – as he writes these lines – all spruced up in his Sunday best: a tank-top and a pair of shorts. Granted, not everyone can scale the heights of shlubbdom like I can, but still: compared to days gone by, we now dress largely for comfort and convenience. We've stripped away all that weird, wasteful, unnecessary and annoying bedizenment.

This paring away of the pointless, this shaking off of the nonessential, of the complicating, of the cumbersome, manifests itself in almost every area of human enterprise today. The notion that we should run our lives rationally – that we should control our reckless hearts with our reasonable heads and subject all our conventions, traditions and legends to the merciless scalpel of the logical and practical – is by now such a commonplace, is so deeply ingrained and so pervasively influential in our society and culture, that it has almost assumed the status of axiom. Ofer's challenge to both the doctrines of "Judaism" and the institution of Jewish identity is based largely if not entirely upon this very same axiom.

There is even a Jewish way of putting this ubiquitous, wretched cliché, taken from latter-day hassidic literature. It goes like this: if you put your *Mo'ach* (brain) before your *Lev* (heart), then you are a *MeLech* – a king. But if you put your *Lev* (heart) before your *Mo'ach* (brain), then you are a *LeMech* – a clown. In what little time remains to us in these proceedings, then, we will set before ourselves only one preeminent and crucial objective: to dethrone the king…

…and crown the clown.

With this objective in mind we shall now endeavor to host the bout of "heart versus head" in three main arenas: the arena of the *self*, the arena of the *world*, and the arena of the *good*. In each of these heavily interrelated contests, we will first talk sense, then nonsense. The reader will decide which talk is worthwhile, and which talk is cheap; which leads to life, and which leads nowhere good. And so, without further ado, we hereby put on our thinking caps and attempt to prove rationally…

…how rationalism will be the death of us.

Chapter Eighteen

A. THE SELF

We begin by pointing out what should be as obvious to anyone as an elephant in a *sukkah*: that everything we human beings instinctively believe ourselves to be – conscious, feeling, willful, free, alive – partakes of an outlook as indisputably *irrational* and as irremediably *nonsensical* as a flying pig or a sixteen-sided triangle. Neither sentience, nor emotion, nor volition, nor liberty, nor even indeed that fantastic agglomeration of marvels we allude to when we breathe the word "life" – none of these phenomena are *in any way possible* within the bounds of purely logical or strictly scientific discourse. We'll try to show this now, while standing on one foot.

Let's start the way one invariably should: with a definition of terms. I don't mean a precise dictionary or etymological definition. What we need is rather an agreed upon, common sense conception of what most people intend when they say certain things. Thus far, we've been batting around a number of usages without bothering to nail down their meanings, premier among them the words "rational" and "logical." Now, these adjectives are admittedly understood in a wide variety of ways, depending on the context in which they are employed and on who is doing the understanding. Ultimately, however, all the many different interpretations of both terms emanate from an underlying notion familiar to and assumed by us all (which is why you will probably find yourself repeating the word "duh" rather often during the next few paragraphs).

Logic is first and foremost a system of thinking that is rigidly dependent upon the *derivation of a new proposition from a previous proposition or set of propositions* (duh). This is not news to anyone: logic relies upon the notion that "things follow," that they follow from *other* things. Now, in order for such a cognitional system to function and be intellectually valid for the universe it describes, all phenomena comprising that universe must be linked to and arise from *other* phenomena, and they must be linked to them and arise from them in a *consistent* manner: identical stimuli under identical conditions must produce identical responses (duh). Were this ever to cease being the case – or were it ever to be shown not to have *been* the case in the first place – on that very day logic in general, as well as its mother, mathematics, and its favorite son, the scientific method, would all go "*poof*!" and disappear.

Suppose we are playing pool, and you take your cue stick and use it to propel the white ball, which is at "W" place, toward the five ball, which is at "X" location, and you do so with "Y" force, and it strikes the five ball on spot "Z" of its convex surface, and the five ball promptly rolls into the corner pocket. Nice shot! Now, imagine – for the sake of argument – that when you immediately take up your cue stick again, the conditions prevailing around the billiard table are *in every way, shape and form* equivalent to those just prior to your most recent, successful attempt: no new weather fronts converging on the region, no electric storms or nuclear meltdowns anywhere in the general vicinity, cue stick powdered with the identical quantity and distribution of chalk as before, no molecule shifting, however negligible, in the white or five balls or green felt covering of the table due to the impact or friction of your previous stroke – in short: all environmental circumstances are one hundred percent the same as they were before. You step right up and (hypothetically, now) replace the cue ball *exactly* where it had previously been at place "W"; put the five ball down *precisely* at the identical location "X"; strike that white ball with *just the same* amount of force "Y"; which proceeds to collide with the five ball on *bingo* the same spot "Z." OK? Only this time, the upshot of all this skillful and fastidious activity is that the five ball rolls itself – not into the corner pocket, as previously – but rather right as rain and straight as an arrow directly into the…*side* pocket.

Some balls, eh? Were it possible for what we just described actually to take place, then all logical thought, all scientific calculation, all syllogistic demonstration, indeed: the entire epistemological structure of human knowledge maintenance and acquisition, would come crashing down like a ton of bricks. All detectives would be out of business overnight. All researchers would be forced to take up flute playing. All confirmations or refutations of hypotheses would instantly become acts of the most abject silliness. Because every single "logical" procedure ever invented – observation, induction, deduction, reduction, computation, inference – depends for its legitimacy on the axiomatic assumption of a *rigorously consistent relationship between cause and effect*. Take that relationship away – even on just *one* occasion or in *one* context – allow for more than a single possible effect to result from one and the same cause, and logic (as Mr. Spock famously said in the Harry Mudd episode) "becomes a tweeting bird." Such that even were we to make the claim (as did, for instance, David Hume and Immanuel Kant) that phenomena exist in our universe or in ourselves that are not necessarily bound by the laws of causality, we would at the very least have to admit that such phenomena were not rational. Indeed, we would be forced to classify them as *ir*rational, metalogical, and even "supernatural."

What we essentially mean, then, when we say that something is "logical" – or that it is "rational" or "sensible" or "reasonable" (nuances aside, these are all interchangeable terms that necessarily lean on logic) – is that that thing may be conceived of in a framework ruled absolutely and unconditionally by the *principle of universal causality*. Indeed, this definition of ours is in a certain sense so obvious as to be a tautology (a needless repetition of the same idea *posing* as a definition). Because if you really think about it, **logic *is* cause and effect** – nothing more and nothing less. And consequently, the two absolutely indispensable prerequisites of the purely logical conception of existence are that (1) no effect can occur without a cause, and (2) the same cause will *always* bring about the same effect. Do we have a *yishur kav* – a cognitive "alignment" – on this general point? Excellent. May you live long and prosper.

The rationality-based reign of causality therefore presupposes that nothing that inhabits the cosmos can act without being acted upon. Nor can anything anywhere in the universe act in a way not *directly dictated and fully choreographed* by the forces that act upon it. The laws of logic thus necessarily entail the notion that all action of any kind in the world is really just *re*action, and that absolutely *nothing* in existence can possibly act "freely," "independently," "of its own accord" or "on its own initiative" – not to any degree whatsoever.

This conclusion is far from new. It was reached by the Greek philosopher Epicurus some twenty-three hundred years ago. Epicurus had studied the theories of his predecessors Democritus and Leucippus, who taught that "everything in existence, including gods and men, consists solely of atoms of solid matter moving through space" (a formulation that – with a few minor adjustments – would still be acceptable to most physicists today). All change, and every incident that ever takes place in the organic as well as the inorganic world – extrapolated Epicurus – is ultimately explicable in terms of the "spatial relations and interactions of atoms among themselves."

Now, if you think of all those quadrillions of atoms or smaller particles making up the many and varied things in our world as the billiard balls gracing our pool table, you begin to understand why Epicurus could proclaim, way back in the fourth century BCE, that: "Given the shape, speed and direction of the atoms at any single moment in time, all later states of the universe and everything in it would naturally follow." Had we a sufficiently souped-up computer-cum-monitor able to register *all* the conditions prevailing on the pool table as you cue up to strike – sizes, shapes, densities and distribution of balls; friction factor of felt surface; resiliency of bumpers; level of static electricity in air; amount of chalk on pool cue; force and direction of shot, etc. – said calculating machine would be able to predict the exact position of every single ball ten seconds later, when the action ensuing in the wake of your shot dies down. It could easily prophesy the future! In any overall cause-and-effect scenario, if all the circumstances of a closed system are known at a particular "freeze frame" of time, then all the circumstances that will obtain at *any other* freeze frame of time in that system are *also* conceivably calculable – because (as we said) only *one* possible set of effects can result from the set of causes that preceded it. It's one big fat foregone conclusion. If you fully know what is, you can fully know what will be!

Two millennia after Epicurus, the French mathematician Pierre Simon Marquis de Laplace finally took up the scientific-determinist thread:

> We ought to regard the present state of the universe as the effect of its antecedent state, and the cause of the state that is to follow. An intelligence, who for a given instant should be acquainted with all the forces by which nature is animated and with the several positions of the entities composing it, if further his intellect were vast enough to submit those data to analysis, would be able to include in one and the same formula the movements of the largest bodies in the universe as well as those of the lightest atom. Nothing would be uncertain for him: the future as well as the past would be present to his eyes.

Just as the fifteenth-century Protestant theologian John Calvin had based his own uncompromising doctrine of Predestinarianism on an amplification of the well known Christological conception of Original Sin – according to which all future generations are born in a state of iniquity due to a transgression committed way back when in the Garden of Eden – so preeminent logicians from Epicurus to Laplace and beyond have based *their* portrayal of a *thoroughly mechanistic and predestined universe* on the rationally indisputable fact that any current situation or occurrence is the *inevitable outcome* of a series of events going all the way back to the Big Bang. Given the unbreakable sequence of cause and effect, the entirety of existence *simply cannot be anything else* but a vast, grinding, pneumatic engine, its innumerable cogs and gears moving in a manner already fixed from the very beginning of time and forevermore! Never forget this, dear reader: if logic is a valid tool for understanding the universe around us, then *existence is perforce a machine* – no ifs, ands or buts.

Now, dear reader, be so kind as to answer me this: do you perchance consider *yourself* to be a part of existence? I mean, do you figure that you and everything that makes you up constitute one or more of the elements inhabiting the universe? I'll take your silence as a "yes." Now, let's play syllogism again, that most fundamental and undisputed of all logical operations: if (a) according to the rationalist outlook, all of existence is perforce governed by the principle of cause and effect; and if (b) you and all of your component parts are card-carrying members in good standing of existence; then (c) *you and all of your component parts are inevitably governed by the principle of cause and effect.*

And this, in its turn, necessarily means that all of the elements that go into composing "you" invariably do whatever they happen to do for the same scientific reasons and according to the same physical rules that govern the balls on a pool table, or any other particles of matter in existence: they have been *induced* to act thus. Like everything else in the cosmos, you are and can be nothing more than a *stimulus-response mechanism.* Obviously, none of the components that make up the entirety of you takes any "decisions," possesses any "initiative," has a "will" of its own – anymore than the balls on a pool table roll around hither and thither out of *their* own volition. Nothing this hapless, gumption-less, rag-doll machine called "you" ever does, no physical or mental movement that it ever makes, occurs without being either "pushed" or "pulled." And therefore: if human life as we have traditionally perceived and imagined it is defined primarily in reference to all those intangible institutions known as "thought," "feeling," "desire," "will," "love," "creativity" and "independence" – then my condolences to you, dear reader. Because from any "reasonable" or "sensible" perspective, you are as dead as a doornail.

Did you ever meet a doornail that just up and decided to zoom across the room – with no inducement, propulsion or transportation provided by anyone – just because it *felt* like it, or because the hinges looked less rusty at the other entrance, or because the nail just felt it needed a change? I didn't think so. But doornails – as we have said – are dead. They are inorganic and inanimate. How can we extrapolate from such objects to what are usually conceived to be live, organic, animate beings like ourselves?

Simple: because in rationality-based reality, *no such distinction*, no such breakdown between "passive" and "active" matter, between "reactive" and "autonomous" mechanisms, between "living" and "dead" tissue can possibly exist or hold true. Let's look at your begonia. Why does it turn to the sun? You think maybe because it "wants" to? Because it "decides" to? Because it figures a nice tan would help it attract more bees? I'm sure you don't want me to start delving into that entirely mechanistic, fully push-and-pull-based process involving nothing more than molecules forcibly exchanging ions with other molecules known as photosynthesis. Don't *make* me remind you of that nightmare called eighth-grade biology! The point is this: could the begonia have decided *not* to be heliotropic – for a day? Could it have chosen to "defy" the demands of photosynthesis, rudely turn its back and, as it were, "moon" the sun? Does the plant have consciousness? Is it willful? Is it free? Or is it – as we would invariably expect of any entity *made up solely of physical matter* and *partaking of existence* – in every way, shape and form nothing but a cause-and-effect-propelled machine?

Is it the slightly different *arrangement* of the same dead atoms making for more carbon molecules in a begonia than in a doornail that's confusing us? Is it the supple feel or verdant look of plant matter, and the no less mechanistic operations known as "growth" or "reproduction" – is *that* what has always thrown us off, making us attribute some different, some "vital" character to this purely stimulus-response-driven chain of events known as a "plant"? Is *that* what makes us hold onto the unbelievably silly distinction commonly drawn between a plant and – say – a chair, or an avalanche, or a truck, or a penny, or a rubber ducky, or a stalagmite, or a vending machine, or a quasar, all of which "do" things for the very same reason as the plant, and for that reason alone: because their molecules are being moved around by *other* molecules, just like the balls on a pool table? Otherwise what *other* ridiculous fiction could it be that makes us cling so stubbornly to the arbitrary, preposterous and completely illogical notion that so-called "organic" things are somehow qualitatively different or more "alive" than so-called "inorganic" things? From a truly rigorous, rational and scientific perspective, the word "alive" is one hundred percent meaningless.

Let's move rapidly up the food chain, and talk about your dog Biff. He's alive enough, now isn't he? And cute as a button! Why just last week, Biff…OK, spare me. So your ostensible "dog," composed of so-called "organic" matter (which follows *precisely* the same laws of causation as so-called "*in*organic" matter), this "dog," because the particles composing it move a wee bit faster than those of the begonia in response to being pushed around by various stimuli – because of this you've decided that *its* motion is somehow "volitional," that Biff is a loyal, loving, independent, spontaneous, initiative-taking organism – your "best friend"! – and not just a bunch of temporarily bonded molecules being shoved around by other molecules in the vicinity. No way – *not my Biffy*! Why, he's every bit as alive as *I* am!

Magna est veritas: you're certainly right about that, dear reader. According to every possible **logical and rational** take on the matter, *you* are not one wit more "alive" – despite any and all illusions to the contrary – than your dog, or his fleas, or your begonia, or a doornail…or the vending machine at your office. Indeed, all of these things possess the *same exact degree* of "vitality," of will and power and initiative and autonomy and passion and sentience and spontaneity and feelings: *zero*. You, me and the dog are all mechanisms, are automatons, no less than anything else in the world. Animal, vegetable and mineral, they all move *because they are moved*. Come on: let's see you deny that we are all associations of particles that are pushed around by other particles in an endless chain of causation. Go ahead – *make my day*.

THE GROUP OF ATOMS FORMERLY KNOWN AS "YOU": Shut up, shut *up*, that's blasphemy! Do you deny that we human beings have a mind, a heart, a *soul*, for Chrissake?! I don't know about you, but *I* for one am the proud owner of *all* of those things, and they are what make me willful, human...*alive*!

THE GROUP OF ATOMS FORMERLY KNOWN AS "ME": Oh, really, you obstinate advocate of unreason and irrationality? In possession of a "soul," are you? How adorable! And what – pray tell – does *that* nonsensical word indicate, in a matter-composed, logical universe? How can you speak of this "soul," from a *rationalist* point of view? What is a soul made of? Does it have substance, extension, resistance? And where is it, this "soul" of yours, in that messy, molecular scheme of things known as "your" body? Is it in your "breast"? In your brain? In your pineal gland? Is it in your *left knee*? Stop using words that have no meaning just out of convention, solely because you like the sound of them, or because they make you feel good – stop this instant! Such nebulous terms obfuscate far more than they clarify. If you're going to be rigorously rational about this – then *be* so!

And besides: suppose I were to humor you and grant for the sake of argument that your "soul" (or your "mind") exists, even as some kind of "non-corporeal" entity. Well, need I remind you for the fiftieth time that according to logic, the indelible property characterizing – and immutable law governing – everything that exists is the unbroken chain of cause and effect? If that "soul" of yours exists, as you say it does, and if it may be conceived of and discussed in a *rational, logical* framework, then it is of necessity a predetermined, mechanistic, subjugated, pushed-around *piece of trash*.

We could go on in this vein, dear reader, but you see where we're headed. We are headed toward the final conclusion that cannot *but* be reached by the rational or logical mindset (if followed consistently), and there are a good many names for slightly varying versions of this conclusion: Determinism, Materialism, Pyrrhonism, Behaviorism, Epicureanism, Spinozism, Charvaka, Epiphenomenalism. They all boil down, in our connection, to the conception described so pithily by the seventeenth-century English philosopher Thomas Hobbes: "All that exists is body, and all that occurs is motion." It of course followed from this postulate, that – as Hobbes himself put it – "a person is as predictable as a pendulum clock." And this scientific version of strict Calvinist determinism is based upon the same reductionist analysis that today makes the human being a genetic, glandular and electro-chemical machine in the biologist's eyes, nothing more than a complex diagram of afferent and efferent nerves. Thoughts, feelings, memories, hopes, love, hate, life itself, are nothing but the purposeless and predictable interplay of little bits and pieces of heedless floating stuff, a set of reactions between sub-atomic particles that are themselves in reality (according to the latest physics rage) just a bunch of endlessly vibrating strings. Happiness and sadness, empathy and ennui, bravery and cowardice, mystery and fantasy – all are ultimately explicable in terms of cause and effect-based chemistry and physics. In the nineteenth century, the British scientist Lord William Kelvin summed up the same determinist and quintessentially rationalist idea when he wrote: "I cannot imagine *anything* of which I cannot construct a mechanical model." Kelvin and Calvin – and Calvin and Hobbes!

Pop Quiz:

In the War of 1812 between the United States and Great Britain, what was *really* going on?

a. For the first and last time, an event besides the weather was taking place in Canada.
b. A bunch of limey sore losers were trying to regain their self-esteem by infringing upon the legitimate rights of American frontiersmen to plunder Indian land.
c. Particles were moving around.

In Gottfried's *Tristan and Isolde,* when the "chaste and lovely lady" discovered that her new boyfriend was her uncle's murderer and made haste to avenge this deed upon Tristan while he lay buck-naked in the bathtub, what was *really* going on?

a. The ground was being prepared for the "chaste and lovely lady" to become the "lovely lady."
b. The ground was being prepared for world-class conductor Daniel Barenboim to make a complete ass of himself

by attempting to force the Israel Philharmonic to play Wagner in front of an audience of concentration camp survivors every Monday and Thursday.

c. Particles were moving around.

In *Star Trek: The Next Generation,* when the producers ushered the famous stage-actor Jean Luc Picard onto the bridge of the Enterprise and allowed him to sit in the chair previously occupied by Captain Kirk, what was *really* going on?

a. Shakespeare fans around the world breathed a massive sigh of relief.
b. The Klingon plot to take over the Federation by installing the single blandest object in the known universe as captain of a crucial starship was entering its final stages.
c. Gene Rodenberry's body was swallowed by a black hole as a final act of mercy to the great man.
d. Particles were moving around.

The Nobel Prize-winning founder of "Behaviorism" and persistent advocate of "stroking and tickling" experiments, Dr. John Watson; top name on the anti-vivisectionist's black-list, Dr. B. F. Skinner (author of the book: *Beyond Freedom and Dignity*); that interwar salon of super-ripe logical positivism known as the Vienna Circle – these and hundreds of other mathematicians, chemists, physicists, biologists, physicians, cosmologists and philosophers throughout the modern period have been sufficiently possessed of the strength of their logical convictions to tell it like it is: *and it is mechanical.* And if perchance you are the sensitive type, and the empty feeling of utter purposelessness engendered by this supremely rational position depresses you to such an extent that you feel the urge to head on over to the window and jump – let me save you the effort. Because the inescapable upshot of all of modern science and rational philosophy is, as we pointed out above, *that you are already dead.* Jumping won't change a thing.

And you know, one really has to hand it to 'em, all these latter-day logical thinkers. I mean: Bra-*vo*, guys – **braaa-*vo***!! Here you were, this truly awesome expression of humanist self-assertion, an unprecedented collection of strong and independent minds bent on making nature your willing servant and all events occurring in nature subject to your calculation and control. Here you were, resolved to conquer the earth and subdue it. What, therefore, could be more humiliating and preposterous, what could be more twisted and ironic, than how you ended up: not as victors and masters, but rather as *prisoners, victims and slaves of the very calculations that your will to world domination required.* You pathetic saps! For hundreds of years, you have allowed logic to lead you around by the nose, and taught all the rest of us to do pretty much the same. Through your immense cerebral achievements you incomparable losers have succeeded in reversing Descartes' most famous declaration, so that it now reads: "I think – therefore *I am not.*" You uber-eggheads have actually managed to *cogitate yourselves out of existence.* Way to go, guys! Hats off to you. That takes real talent.

Are they fazed by my criticism? Listen to world-renowned physicist and Nobel laureate, Professor Steven Weinberg:

> The opponents of reductionism are appalled by what they feel to be the bleakness of modern science. To whatever extent they and their world can be reduced to a matter of particles and fields and the interactions thereof, they feel diminished by that knowledge...I would not try to answer these critics with a pep talk about the beauties of modern science. The reductionist worldview *is* chilling and impersonal. It has to be accepted as it is, not because we like it, but because that is the way the world works. (From his Bar-Mitzvah speech, 12.4.53)

Now, what this "reductionist, chilling and impersonal," logical-scientific worldview cannot in any way conceive or stomach – indeed, what would instantly reduce the entire edifice of philosophical rationality and scientific reason to a smoldering heap of unrecognizable rubble (and force Weinberg to return his prize) – is simply this: **the discovery of something that acts, without being *induced* to act exactly thus.** If there exists – anywhere in this universe of ours – even *one* thing that is not mechanically impelled to do what it does in the cause-and-effect manner of the vending machine or the photo-synthetic plant; if there is an entity that in actuality has before it at any point in time *more than one option*, that can choose a path that was not "mapped out" for it from the beginning of time by the domino effect of eternal causality; if the cosmos contains anywhere in its cavernous expanses a being that is not shackled to the all-pervasive chain gang of stimulus-response, that can *decide* of its own *free will* to act, without being irresistibly pulled or irresistibly pushed in one or another pre-destined direction; if such a creature exists, then science is superfluous, rationality is ridiculous, and logic is a laugh riot (or at least they are all of them demoted to "second string" criteria for understanding what's *really* going on in the world). And as luck would have it, there *is* an outstanding candidate for the position of such a wild and willful creature: take a bow, dear reader – it is you.

You see, if it exists at all, then your "soul" (or psyche, or sentience, or personality, or consciousness, or mind, or self – call it what you will) might just be the valiant knight that bravely slays the dragon of materialistic determinism, single-handedly saves the entire universe and proclaims liberty to all the inhabitants thereof! It may possibly be the ten-pound sledgehammer that smashes the shackles of the causal chain gang, and gives the wretched prisoners their final and permanent furlough. Hail the conquering hero! Listen to that crowd *roar*, see the confetti rain down in your triumphal ticker-tape parade! Don't be bashful – you *deserve* all this adulation. Because your soul, if it is real and not a figment or fairytale, does the most amazing, most intrepid, most impossible and illogical thing imaginable: *it takes initiative, it acts autonomously*. It brings back "can" into our lives, and without "can" (said Kant) there is no "ought."

When I say your soul acts autonomously, I do not mean to say, of course, that there are no stimuli, no factors or "causes" influencing your soul's choices. *Au contraire*! There are literally *billions* of them. Your soul wasn't born yesterday (it is *not* a post-modernist). It has encountered and assimilated an immense amount of intellectual, emotional and other types of "data" from the surrounding environment. It is an informed soul, and it makes informed decisions. But here's the key point: if it is a "soul" at all, if it is that incredible thing we tend to think and feel that it is, then its decisions are somehow not *coerced* by the data or information accumulated.

In other words, when we say (or hope) that our souls are "free," we don't mean that they are not vulnerable to outside influence – even to pressure. It would have to be a sealed-up, frigid, stupid soul for that to be the case, and "freedom" does not mean abject ignorance or hermetic impermeability in *anybody's* lexicon. Rather, if our souls exist and are indeed free, then they may perhaps be likened to...a college student. Upon arrival freshman year, and throughout her four-year stay at the given institution of higher learning, your average college student encounters a dazzling array of influential experiences. She attends classes and lectures, talks to friends and lovers, plays sports and writes for the paper, goes to frat parties and does the backstroke through two-foot high beer-floods on the floor – the works. But here's what's cool: while allowing herself to be exposed to all these influences and absorbing them, in the end *she and she alone* decides what to do with all that "data," what to accept and what to reject, what to preserve and what to jettison, how to use what she has learned, where to take it and how to put it to work in her future life. *She* is the master – all of those acquired bits of information are her tools, are her *servants*, bent by her will to her yoke. Now, this informed but independent student is *your soul*; the university she attends is *the universe*; and the way in which she handles the environmental stimuli impinging upon her every day is exactly what we mean when we mouth that most wonderful of words in any language: *freedom*.

All that remains, then, dear reader, is to put the positivist proposition to the test. Let's do an experiment to find out where *you* personally stand on the question of your own existence. Let's discover whether you perceive yourself, in truth, to be a conscious, willful, choosing, feeling and essentially *free* human being, or whether you encounter evidence bolstering the position that you are a mindless, soulless tinker-toy. Let's avoid the middle-man and go straight to the source: go have a talk with yourself. Seriously. We'll leave the two of you alone for a moment, and just engage in a little reflexive chat. Take a millisecond to experience your "me-ness." No need to assume the lotus position or breathe in through one nostril and out the other or any of that fun stuff. Just chill, unfocus and let the sides of your lips curl up in a sweet and entirely artless smile, as you meet and greet the one individual who is – after all – your closest friend in the whole wide world. Direct the spotlight inward, as Gandhi would say, and have a tête-à-tête with the dude who sits right behind your eyes, occupies center stage and plays the lead role in your life. Whisper: "Hey – *how ya doin'*?" Inquire: "You are *real*, right?" Knock twice on your skull and ask: "Anybody in there?" Decide: "I'm gonna touch my nose" or "I'm gonna skip around the room" – and then touch it, or skip around the room, or stop just before doing one of these things and spontaneously *re*-decide *not* to do them. Think about your life, your experiences, your dreams, your loves, your private, cozy, wonderful "me": does it feel coerced, compelled, mechanical, automatic? Or do you somehow *know*, dammit, do you *sense in your gut*, that there really *is* a "you," and that that "you" does what it does of its own accord, *freely and independently* and with a whole lot of verve? Go ahead, take the old mind-body problem out for a test drive and see what she's capable of.

"Hold on," you interrupt. "Why is *my* perception of the matter a legitimate barometer? Maybe I am, in fact, a mindless, coerced automaton who just *thinks* he's a sentient and free human being. Couldn't my judgment be clouded or deluded or deceived?"

Why, of course it could. But jeez, man: what have I been doing throughout this whole book – and what has any author ever done throughout any book – except appeal to *your* judgment? There is simply *nowhere else to turn*. And if your judgment is sound enough to be the ultimate arbiter of the cogency of the criterion known as "reason," if it is trustworthy enough to evaluate the merit of the various logical and scientific theories put forward in the preceding pages, then *your* judgment is also sound and trustworthy enough to investigate and draw conclusions about the existence – if not the full nature and workings – of its own consciousness! People's judgments are, at any rate, the *only meaningful barometer that exists for the truth or falsehood of any proposition anywhere*. Now quit stalling and go play with yourself...

...no, seriously, put the stupid book down for a second; what are you, some kind of nerd?

(Pause to permit some expeditious introspection.)

...Well? How was it? Come to any realizations? Do "you" exist? Are you sentient? Can you act willfully? Are you more than just a machine? If I guessed right, most readers will answer these questions with a defiant and resounding "YOU BETCHA!" In which case, you know what's neat? What's neat is that the fascinating and hopefully poignant feelings you just experienced during that little self-communing session entitle you to walk up whenever you feel like it behind any big-name physics professor you encounter and yell: "Hey – *moron*! That's right, I'm talkin' to *you*, mush-for-brains! How'd you get to be such a *dumbass*, anyway?" and other enjoyable expletives to that effect. Because if you actually *do* possess consciousness and act of your own free will, then the chain of causality is smashed to smithereens. And if the law of cause and effect does not govern existence, then all the physicist's attempts to penetrate to the core of reality and understand how it truly works using empirical and logical methods are basically just episode after episode of slapstick comedy. Ha-ha! A real entertainer, that guy.

I'll say it again: if you genuinely believe, in your heart of hearts and mind of minds, that *you exist*; if you believe that you are even the slightest bit capable of doing what we call "taking initiative" and "acting spontaneously"; if you genuinely set store by any of these things, and by the notion that you can truly *want and dream and hope and love*, then at least be aware that your beliefs fly like a lemon meringue pie smack in the face of all that we call rationality and logic, of all that we know as reason and practicality. Neither Newtonian physics nor Quantum physics, neither the worthless joke known as "Chaos Theory" nor the much touted but sorely misnamed Heisenberg Uncertainty Principle, to say nothing of the truly pathetic set of philosophical tautologies currently subsumed under the name "Compatibilism" – none of these brittle crutches can help you reconcile science with sentience, any more than $E = MC^2$ can help the religious apologists reconcile creation with the Big Bang. Indeed, believing in *oneself* is the single most nonsensical notion that could ever possibly be held by anybody anywhere! More than believing in Harry Potter's Hogwarts (where, after all, each spell conjures up the same result every time it is used, the magical version of predictable cause and effect), more than believing in ghosts, more than believing in God – believing in *you* is simply the Himalayan height of irrationality and preposterousness.

And yet: **believe you do**. Indeed, no matter how well I – or Epicurus, or Laplace, or Weinberg, or anybody – would have argued the point, demonstrating step-by-logical-step how when push comes to shove "you" are nothing more than a physically and chemically propelled set of interacting molecules, and how notions like "thought," "independence," "defiance," "passion," "soul," "spirit," "romance" and "love" are all foolish misnomers and meaningless illusions – no matter how well this was spelled out for you by the greatest authorities in the field, you wouldn't buy it for a used Kleenex. You *don't* buy it. None of us does. It's a load of blind, murdering, rationalist bunk.

And therefore, of course, the only way to really *live* – with everything that that voracious verb implies and entails – is to adopt a worldview which is at the very least heavily weighted down on the *il*logical and *ir*rational side of things. And surprise, surprise: that is just what most of us normal, decent, fun-loving folks tend to do! (and, indeed, what most scientists and philosophers do today, as well: it's hard to find many avowed materialists or determinists in their ranks anymore). Ever since the day we were born – by virtue of nothing more than our indomitable, *emotional* need to believe in our own humanness and freedom, to preserve meaning and for crying out loud to *enjoy life* – we have been telling rationalism to take a long hike off a short pier. We all know instinctively from the moment we arrive here on earth, that *rationalism must die so that we might live.*

B. THE WORLD

The scientifically examined life, then, turns out to be no life at all. "To the scientist," said D. H. Lawrence, "I am dead." Nor is this in any way a new, or a purely Western discovery. The notion that we and everything in existence turn out to be – upon closer and more logical inspection – a large load of inertia-governed nothing, has been bandied about for millennia (even before Epicurus himself), and forms the basis of not a few ancient religions and philosophies still thriving today. We ran into one of the oldest of them back at the Los Angeles airport.

Long before my encounter with the Israeli Hare Krishnas, Western seekers were finding Eastern religion. Specifically, more than a century and a half ago, a German philosophy professor by the name of Freidrich Majer introduced a German doctoral student by the name of Arthur Schopenhauer to the wondrous mysteries of the Sanskrit Hindu *Upanishads*. Schopenhauer was bitten and smitten. Till the day he died he never ceased praising the unparalleled virtues of ancient Indian literature, the contents of which heavily influenced the direction of his "pessimistic" thought.

Now, we obviously have no plans here to scratch so much as the surface of that vast and multifaceted mystical-spiritual civilization subsumed under the heading of Hinduism, nor would we presume to delve more deeply than the shallow end of a kiddy-pool into the fascinating, dream-within-a-dream-erected underground complex known as Schopenhauer's philosophy. What I *would* like to do in the following few pages, is to remark with the utmost brevity upon a significant point of intersection where – while East may be East and West may be West – the two intellectual hemispheres nevertheless manage to get together and chill out over a brewsky. For the ironic fact of the matter is that the majority of the schools comprising both Eastern religion *and* Western philosophy have always been dead set on providing humanity – each according to its own peculiar categories and methods – with what the young German poet Georg Herwegh once described as "insight into the nullity of the sphere of appearance." Large sections of both of these overarching intellectual mega-systems are ultimately geared (to paraphrase the Russian writer Vissarion Belinsky) to replacing the "deceptive garden variety of reality" with the "true blue sky of infinity." In a word, at the root of both classical worldviews ultimately lies the notion that the entire gamut of diversity and multiplicity that we see and sense and experience around us *is an illusion* – an illusion that must be overcome. Here we have cross-cultural and interdisciplinary cooperation at its best: East and West, religion and reason, mysticism and science, theology and philosophy – all joining hands and putting heads together in a massive, relentless, history-long quest...for the One. For the Great One that stands behind the meddlesome many. All striving in different ways to transcend this prosaic and variety-plagued existence, and melt back into the arms of the Pure and Infinite Singularity.

In the Eastern religions this "ocean-consciousness" attitude to life and to the world has many names, which I feel no compunction whatsoever about employing here more-or-less interchangeably (doctrines denying all distinction are generally not all that distinct from one another): Chuang Tzu's *ming*, the "Inward Vision" that eliminates all diversity; the Taoist *p'u* or "Uncarved Block," symbol of pristine non-differentiation; the *satori* experience of Zen, in which "I become the uncreated cosmos, and no individual exists"; Sanskrit *nir dvandva*, or "non-duality," rejecting the dichotomy of "I and Not-I"; and many more. But this outlook's most famous formulation (and the one that captivated Schopenhauer) is the Hindu *Jnana Yoga* portrayal of the vast and varying universe around us – and all the objects, beings, activities, sensations, thoughts, feelings and occurrences in it – as mere *maya*: delusion.

Just as it is the Chinese Taoist's duty to peel away the chaotic and conflict-ridden layers of our outer world of experience in order to expose the pure and calm ontological river flowing steadily beneath and through all existence and known to the initiate as the *Way*; just as it is the job of the advanced Buddhist to refocus his mental lens such that all apparent opposites are thrown back into solution, and the phantasm of plurality and contradiction is replaced by the encompassing and homogeneous *Truth*; just so must the Hindu devotee strive with all his might to smash the prism of *maya* responsible for the profane panoply of birds and plants and rocks and fish and sand and hills and rain and people in our universe, the better to be vouchsafed that beatific vision of unsullied and all-consuming Being that is the great white *Light*. And thus together do the Way, the Truth and the Light lead the spirit out of "this body of death," out of the carnal prison of specificity, of desire, of relationship and of passion, and down the holy path of transcendence and world-renunciation. He who loves his life, loses it. But he who hates his life in this world, will keep it for eternal life.

The Hindi term *maya* is etymologically related to the English word "magic," and that is also what it means. Hinduism sees terrestrial reality as a trick, and urges us not to fall for it. The Sanskrit term *Buddha* is etymologically related to an Indo-European root connoting "wakefulness" (in Russian, for instance, an alarm-clock is a *budilnik*). Buddhism sees mundane existence as a bad dream, and urges us all to awaken from it. The Chinese term *Tao* is etymologically related to...who the *hell* knows? It's Chinese! But it basically means "the Way," and I think Chuang Tzu summed up best its overall attitude to life in this world as we know it and live it, in the following recommendation:

> He who needs others is forever shackled; he who is needed by others is forever sad – I would have you drop these shackles and put away your sadness, and wander alone with the *Tao* in the Kingdom of the Great Void.

The corresponding Hindu ideal in this regard is to attain to the realization that the self (*atman*) and the universal reality (*Brahman*) are actually one and the same, to reach the ultimate awareness that *tat tvam asi*: "thou art that." Plurality, on the other hand, is a function of *maya*, the illusory sphere of space and time, which is also responsible for our attachment to earthly delights (*kama*) and our fear of death (*mara*). The practiced Yogi has ascended beyond the ostensible multiplicity and fractiousness of our world, he has "extinguished his ego," he has successfully engaged in "self-naughting," he has "starved his individual personality to death," he has been swallowed up like a single drop in the vast, brimming bowl of Being. Plunging into his own "inner hemisphere" deeply enough to hit the common ground-water irrigating all that exists, he has proudly drowned his uniqueness in it. The notion of distinction in any form is – as usual – the enemy, as we read in a Zen manual describing the highest "stage" an initiate can reach: "All dichotomies between self and others, finite and infinite, good and evil, acceptance and rejection – even life and death – are finally transcended."

Indeed, once the this-worldly, chimeric veneer of *maya* is cast aside, it will become clear – as Schopenhauer himself enthused – "that in truth, we are all one and the same being" (remember: this means you *are* Paula Deen). Here we have the Buddhist *prajna paramita*, the "wisdom of the yonder shore," where the ultimate secret is finally divulged: that the universe is a single, seamless fabric; that division is delusion; that life (as Shelley wrote) "is like a dome of many-colored glass, staining the white radiance of eternity."

Once the Hindu-Buddhist-Taoist-Mystic (again: I lump them together because at least in this matter their aspirations are all but indistinguishable) reaches this vaunted level of total comprehension, doffing those inhibiting garments of individual personality and idiosyncrasy in order to grasp and merge with The All – once this happens, our man is, in effect, dead to the world and everything in it. His kingdom is no longer of this earth, he cares not a whit for its many vanities, he has achieved the Bhagavad-Gita's thoroughgoing "disengagement":

> One to me is loss or gain,
> One to me is fame or shame,
> One to me is pleasure, pain.

The world and all it contains (including his family and friends, if he has any) have receded, have evaporated, and our Nirvana-seeker – who makes Turgenev's nihilist look like a PTA president – has metamorphosed into "a sublime and radically unaffected onlooker, transcending the spheres of the former conscious-unconscious system, aloofly unconcerned with the many tendencies that formerly supported the individual biography." Quoth the Buddha: "As the stars go out in deference to the morning sun, so individual awareness will be eclipsed in the blazing light of total awareness."

OK, now: *were all these people on drugs*? Too much poppy powder, perhaps? A little heavy on the hookah? No. Because you see, whatever complex of motivations led them – and thousands of others like them throughout history, including many Christian, Muslim and even a smattering of Jewish mystics – to develop these highly intricate and deeply spiritual denunciations of our World of Variety in favor of the Great and Uniform Void, one thing's fer damn sure: *their common conclusion is eminently rational.*

The ironic fact of the matter is that all these Eastern metaphysicians, all these yogis and swamis and bodhisattvas and tzus, well, they just happened to have hit the nail *directly* on its logical head. The world-eliminating doctrine that Eastern religion evolved "intuitively" millennia ago – and has continued preaching vigorously ever since – has slowly but surely been confirmed by the rigorous reasoning and relentless experimentation of none other than modern Western science!

How so? Simple. The methodology which is perhaps most characteristic of and essential to logic, science, and philosophy is known in the professional parlance as "reductionism." Reductionism is the cross-the-board imperative-cum-impulse to explain obscure or nebulous phenomena by "reducing" them to more basic, more detailed, more solid, and more readily understandable components. For instance, suppose you were to say to me: "Yo, man, did you hear the new Moby song? It's bug." Now, we will not attempt to analyze what you meant by comparing this entertainer's latest masterpiece to an arthropod. But what do the words "did you hear" and "song" actually refer to? Now *there's* a genuine puzzlement! Rigorously reasoning, scientifically oriented folk will not be satisfied with such vague terminology. They want to know what's *really* going on. And so they "reduce" your interrogative statement – and the rather foggy comprehension of the actual processes of reality it implies – to clearer, more discernable, more measurable elements. "Hearing the Moby song" *actually* means (at an "unplugged" concert, just to make things simpler): the "vocal chords" of the mechanism we will call "Moby" vibrated, and the molecules in those vocal chords collided with adjacent nitrogen, oxygen and other air molecules that collided in turn with further air molecules that themselves displaced still more air molecules until finally a last group of jostled air molecules slammed into the molecules making up your ear drum, causing the latter to vibrate… and so on. *That* is what *actually* happened (although we could, of course, "reduce" it even further). The lazy phrase, "hear that song" is an entirely inaccurate, picturesque, and indeed poetic metaphor for what *really* takes place.

In the West, we "unmasked" this deeper reality of things with the help of technology, with the assistance of tools – like the microscope – which "enhanced" our perception. But now: who's to say that the specific vantage point and particular technique of the electron microscope is somehow "superior" to that of your naked eye? Say your retina registers and transmits images onward that your brain somehow translates into "a rose." The electron microscope – trained on the same object – registers and transmits onward (*via* your retina) images that your brain translates into tiny, identical units of ephemeral matter. Well – why is the microscope's impression privileged? Why is it more "accurate" than that of your naked eye?

Because of another principle informing reductionism: economy. If the rational researcher can discover *one* explanation that simultaneously elucidates *many* different phenomena, he will obviously prefer this to an uncontrollable *cornucopia* of explanations elucidating those same manifold phenomena – the more so as an explanation's cross-the-board utility tends to militate for its accuracy. Before human beings knew about atoms, a rose needed to be explained (if at all) in a *different* way than – say – a chariot. A third explanation was required for the moon, a fourth for a brush-fire, a fifth for your Uncle Lou, and so on. This was a waste of good explaining time. Today, we are on the brink (or so we think) of "reducing" this wide variety of time-consuming explanations down to one all-embracing explanation, a final and unchallengeable Theory of Everything.

It is not far to go from rational reductionism to reach the full-blown philosophical monism presaged in eons past by Eastern religion (and – as we saw before – also by classical philosopher-scientists from Epicurus to Parmenides to Pythagoras to Plato). What's interesting about the trip is primarily the flip-flop involved: what begins in the Western scientific approach as "analysis" – that is, literally, a "loosening up," a separation into pieces – ends up as its opposite:

"synthesis" – a "putting together," a making whole. When the logical mind contemplates aspects of our universe, it automatically begins to "reduce," and – analysis by unsparing analysis – to *break down* the things in our environment that we have always relied upon and taken for granted into so many minuscule building blocks (cells, atoms, monads, quarks, strings, menes – depending on the discipline).

Then, just as we begin to feel like we're living in an Israeli breakfast salad, with everything around us chopped up into fine little pieces, all of a sudden it dawns upon the reductionists in their labs with their computers and their electron microscopes, that since those myriad unchanging little building blocks are in point of fact all *identical* at the most fundamental level, then what we *really* have here in this world of ours – where we once imagined we saw and sensed trees and grass and hats and ferris wheels and farms and families and bulldozers and Breyer's ice-cream – is an infinite, uniform soup of undifferentiated particles, surging without purpose every which way. Analysis has become synthesis: by splitting things into smaller and smaller pieces, we have essentially welded them together. The true face of reality – that is, utter homogeneity – has been unveiled for all to see; the diverse, variegated, psychedelic world we thought we knew exposed for the monochromatic, molecular slime that it really is; and the rainbow tapestry of life replaced by the solid red rug of sameness.

So there you have it, folks: great minds think alike. The mystical metaphysicians of the East and the limber logicians of the West have finally found common ground in confessing "the nullity of the sphere of appearance," the illusory nature of variety, and ultimately: the sheer neutrality and stupefying meaninglessness of existence. "The learned," wrote Nietzsche, "have cold, dried-up eyes, before which all birds lie stripped of their feathers."

Let me clarify. No one with any imagination can remain unaffected by the truism that "there's more to life than meets the eye" or that "things are not always what they seem." Curious people naturally *dig*, they lift up lids to discover what's inside, they take things apart to figure out what makes them tick. Such intellectually driven types are not exactly about to cease and desist plumbing the depths or scaling the heights at some arbitrary line drawn by…*whomever*. And good for them! Their inquisitiveness is the great driving force behind all learning and progress, and who could possibly knock it? Investigating and uncovering "what is above and what is below, what is in front and what is behind" – striving to decipher the secrets of nature and the conundrums of the cosmos – is about as attractive, praiseworthy and beneficial an endeavor as one could think of.

My question is different. My question is: what do you *do* with all that scientifically acquired and therefore undeniably "correct" information, once you've got it in hand? How much weight should the rationalist-reductionist version of reality receive in terms of influencing the way we relate to our surroundings, to ourselves, to others? To what extent should it help us create cultural, social, political or spiritual paradigms?

Suppose I am watching *Seinfeld*, and somebody tells me that if I just sidle up to the TV-set and place my eyeballs *directly* against the screen, I will be privileged to see Jerry, George, Elaine and Kramer dissolve into what they *truly are*: hundreds of little dots in rows intermittently illuminated by a cathode ray. So I do it: I waddle on over, plop down in front of the tube, press my peepers to the glass, and lo! I was not misled. The humanoid images disintegrate and show their true (primary) colors, revealing themselves to be – *in reality* – nothing more than a bunch of phosphorescent points. Congratulations! I've learned something new. I henceforward know more about the "true" state of a certain aspect of existence than I did before.

Now if, in the wake of this momentous discovery, I decide to watch every episode of *Seinfeld* from this point forward sitting one inch from the appliance and smashing my face up hard against the screen, then tell me: *would that make me an idiot – or a stupid idiot*?

It is one thing to "know" that the world looks different, looks homogenous, breaks down into infinitesimal and identical parts, from a purely rational and reductionist (or mystical-metaphysical) perspective. It is quite another thing to *relate* to the world consistently from that vantage point, or to *strive* to do so, or to *preach* such an aspiration! The German-Jewish thinker Franz Rosenzweig once complained:

> Philosophy is eminently incapable of admitting that perhaps somebody somewhere might not want to say that everything 'is' something else...Philosophy refuses to accept the world as world, God as God, man as man! All these must "actually" be quite different from what they seem, for if they were not, if they were really only what they are, then philosophy – God forbid! – would be utterly superfluous.

Sometimes a cigar is just a cigar – *especially if you want to smoke it.* The world is meaningful to us and has value in our eyes only as encountered through the prism of experience. And prisms make for spectrums, and spectrums make for multiplicity, and multiplicity makes for variety, and variety is the spice of life.

People have been trained and conditioned for so damn long to spout the mantra-slogan of "Universal Oneness" – whether this expresses itself in opposition to the nation-state, in the European Union, in the Global Village or in Krishna Consciousness – that most of us by now take for granted almost unconsciously that achieving unanimity in a whole slew of spheres is a really good goal, perhaps the *best* goal. But please, I beg of you: clear your mind for just one moment of all that accumulated mystical, philosophical and ideological cant; leave the mandatory lip-service to Maybelline; and let's just take a moment to genuinely think and feel about this question on a really honest, down-to-earth, *human* level.

Tell me, dear reader: do you *really* want to disappear? Do you *genuinely* crave the extinction of your individual personality and its final merging with and melting into the Universal Mind, or the Infinite Void, or the Primeval Ocean, or the Big Lebowski, or whatever?

Oh, I know you're kind of *supposed* to say you do – at least in many a circle and according to many a catechism – but...do you? *Really*? I mean, even on those rare occasions when you are privileged to experience that wonderful rush of soul-expanding catharsis – you know – when you suddenly feel in touch with everything on the planet and in communion with the entire cosmos, celebrating with the very universe itself the splendiferous amazingness of pure existence – even in such incredible moments, do you really want to…*cease being you*?

Or do you, rather, realize in your heart of hearts and gut of guts that – for God's sake! – it is specifically *you* that is feeling those incredible and fantabulous feelings in the first place! That's right: *you*, that separate, independent and inestimably precious entity; *you*, not an illusion, not a mess of molecules, not a tertiary aspect of the everlasting hypostasis, not a cuticle on the in-grown toenail of the third digit of the left foot of the Great and Terrible Cosmic Singularity. *You.*

It doesn't take all that much contemplation and introspection to recognize that what we human beings really love and truly find beautiful is *the world as it is*, with all its drawbacks and imperfections, and with its plurality and variety quite intact, thank you. You know instinctively, dear reader – do you not? – that if you and your significant other were one and the same entity, sucked up together into some all-engulfing whole, then…*what would become of love*? Because that unparalleled miracle – love, I mean – is all about the *meeting* of things *distinct*! Not for nothing do the words "All One" form the direct etymological root of the adjective "Alone": because when everything is fused and unified, *there's just nobody to be with.*

And many in the East are themselves far from ignorant of this problem (affording us yet another reminder that these are all only generalizations we are using to make a point). As one Hindu *bhakti yogi* put the matter pithily: "I want to taste sugar – I don't want to *be* sugar!"

Further East still, the Malay language happens to possess a sweet little feature that I should like to introduce as a symbol of the indispensable nature and preeminent position of *plurality* in our world. It seems that the word for "two" in Malay is "tanga." The word for "one" is "se-tanga," which means: *half of tanga*. Malays therefore count in this manner: "Half-of-Two, Two, Three, Four…" Singularity is seen as a fraction of the truly fundamental unit and reference constant, *which is duality* – the powerfully anti-monist and therefore anti-rational and anti-mystical message spelled out here being (you guessed it): *it takes two to tanga.*

If we could only get past the pounding propaganda, past the ceaseless Sweet Nothings whispered softly into our ears ever since we can remember, as if we were Bokanovskified babies in *A Brave New World* – if we could only overcome the endless slogans and mind-closing political correctnesses and once and for all be totally truthful with ourselves! I will bet your bottom dollar that in such a case, most of us would rapidly discover that the conclusions reached by Eastern Mystical Pantheism and Western Rationalist Science *both* hold very little attraction for us as glasses through which to view our environment or bases upon which to build our cultures and philosophies. *We don't really aspire to live in a world of Infinite Light, any more than we really aspire to live in a world of quark soup*. These are – once and for all – **not** ideals of ours! So why don't we stop pretending they are? Why don't we stop adducing them as models for the deepest and loftiest outlooks on life? Why don't we stop seeking and searching and attending seminars without end in a desperate attempt to get where we really *don't* want to go? *Why don't we cut it the heck out already*?!

Perhaps – contrary to the claims of almost all philosophies and mysticisms hatched and heralded down the ages – perhaps the most profound and significant type of meditation and contemplation involves our personal encounter not with the One, but with the *many*; not with the empty, but with the *full*; not with the transcendent, but with the *immanent*; not with the infinite, pure and perfect cosmos, but with the *finite and fallible human face*. Maybe the highest spirituality and most magnificent holiness achievable is bound up *not* with detachment – as most of the gurus would have us believe – but specifically with *engagement*, with living *down here* in this wild and wicked and wonderful world with all its intense feelings and focused empathies and social responsibilities and *other people*. Maybe, as the seventeenth-century French theologian Pierre Charron and his near contemporary across the channel Alexander Pope both put it: *La vraie etude del'homme c'est l'homme*; the proper study of mankind – is man!

And maybe, just maybe, dear reader, you'll agree with me that if you were ever vouchsafed a once-in-an-eon opportunity to realize the millennia-old philosophical and mystical dream-goal of contemplating the Vast, Breathtaking and Infinitely Luminous Pristine Magnificence of the Ethereal Majesty of the Inexpressible Beatitude of the Omnipresent Ipseity of the Everlasting Oneness-In-Nothingness on Rye Toast – perhaps you'll agree with me that after gazing in awe and ogling in wonderment and ooh-ing and ahh-ing and maybe even a little exploring, at the end of the day you would already be itching to *go home to the Mrs. and share what you saw.* Otherwise – what's the point?

Here is Plato in the *Symposium*, describing the seeker's arrival at the "final revelation of the mysteries of love" where he finds, essentially, the pristine Platonic "form" of Beauty:

> There bursts upon him that wondrous vision which is the very soul of the beauty he has toiled so long for. It is an everlasting loveliness which neither comes nor goes, which neither flows nor fades, for such beauty is the same on every hand, the same then as now, here as there, this way as that way, the same to every worshipper as it is to every other.
>
> Neither will his vision of the beautiful take the form of a face, or of hands, or of anything that is of the flesh. It will be neither words, nor knowledge, nor a something that exists in something else, such as a living creature, or the earth, or the heavens, or anything else – but it will subsist of itself and by itself in an eternal oneness, while every lovely thing partakes of it in such a way that, however much the parts may wax or wane, it will be neither more nor less, but still the same inviolable whole…
>
> …Starting from individual beauties, the quest for the universal beauty must find [the seeker] ever mounting the heavenly ladder, stepping from rung to rung…and now that he has seen it…he will care nothing for the beauties that once used to take his breath away and kindle such a longing in him…
>
> And if it were given to man to gaze on beauty's very self – unsullied, unalloyed, and freed from the mortal taint that haunts the frailer loveliness of flesh and blood – if, I say, it were given to man to see the heavenly beauty face to face,

> would you call *his* an unenviable life, whose eyes had been opened to the vision, and who had gazed upon it in true contemplation until it had become his own forever?

In a word, Socrates? YOU BETCHA.

If we read further in the *Symposium*, we discover what any avid reader of Plato begins to suspect before too long: that Socrates was really neither heterosexual (despite Xanthippe and the kids), nor homosexual, but *a-sexual* (an inebriated one-time suitor of the Great Gadfly exposes this much to the carousing crowd: "I crawled naked into Socrates' sleeping bag while we were on campaign and… *nothing*"). And is it so hard to see why? Plato was in love with perfection. He saw in the asymmetrical defectiveness of our pathetic sub-lunar realm an impediment to the exact mirroring of that geometrical flawlessness which he conceived to be the ultimate reality and which he ardently adored. Math is Plato's mysticism, straight lines and ninety-degree angles his aphrodisiacs. And those who are in love with perfection (even just as an ideal) cannot but finally fall out of love with human beings, who are by their very nature *irremediably imperfect*. Unlike pristine Platonic Beauty – "unsullied, unalloyed, and freed from the mortal taint that haunts the frailer loveliness of flesh and blood" – human beauty is bound up as tightly as can be with the *asymmetrical*, with the *unpredictable*, with the *non-mathematical*, with the flawed and failing fragility of "sullied" flesh and blood. Once Plato's seeker has feasted his eyes upon the perfect, geometrical "form" of universal Beauty itself, "he will care nothing for the individual beauties that once used to take his breath away and kindle such a longing in him." He will care nothing, that is, for us.

Symposium and Bhagavad-Gita, Western philosophy and Eastern mysticism – two routes leading humanity down the road toward the same despicable destination: *deconstruction and disengagement*.

The rational or scientific description of our world may represent "reality" from a certain vantage point, and we should all unquestionably learn about that reality to the best of our ability in math and science class (and even extend its parameters and applications through vigorous research if we are so inclined). But just as our knowledge of the underlying "truth" that Seinfeld and friends are "in reality" only a bunch of dots on a screen will not cause any sane person to watch the dots every week instead of enjoying the show, so whatever we learn about the ultimate and "true" character of existence – from the scientist, from the philosopher, from the mystic – ought not automatically affect the way we relate to our world. Indeed, far from allowing the logical, materialist or monist interpretation of the universe to function as a spiritual guide or social paradigm; far from permitting it a major say in the domains of aesthetics or politics or religion or love; far from doing any of this, we should instead be *fighting a desperate battle to quarantine these outlooks, and contain their influence with all our might.* We may cultivate rationalist reductionism, may tend science and philosophy and mysticism and esotericism and allow them all to sprout vigorously and bring forth a fascinating crop; but we must finally harvest from this crop only that which will strengthen and deepen *human life* as we know and love it. Otherwise, science will become our guide and math our master, the cart will draw the horse and whither it leads we shall invariably follow – and left to its own devices, the cart of unbridled rationalism and runaway technology will ultimately lead humanity (is *already* leading humanity) straight down the path to inhumanity.

The Midrash tells us that when iron was first created, all the trees in the world began shaking with terror: "Now axes will be made," they whispered among themselves, "and we will all be chopped down." Iron turned to the trees and reassured them with (what else but) an ironic smile: "As long as none of *you* enter *me*" – as long, that is, as no wooden handles are made available upon which to affix iron axe-heads – "you have absolutely nothing to worry about." It is up to us whether (as Emerson lamented) "things are to be in the saddle and ride mankind," or whether we chart our own destiny and arrive there in one piece.

Instead of extrapolating from rationalism to any truly *important* aspects of our individual or collective lives, we must rather nail its ear to the lintel and doorpost and make it our indentured servant for all of eternity; we must harness it to our plow like a dumb ox and crack the whip liberally every chance we get; we must see trees as trees and sky as sky and people as people and love as love, regardless of the messages of mysticism or the microscope; we must – as Nietzsche demanded – "remain true to this earth."

C. THE GOOD

Now that you've been brow-beaten for some thirty-five pages with all this incessant, pie-in-sky philosophizing, I think you will be more than happy to hear that in this third and final sub-chapter, we will be returning to the ground with a thud. William James used to urge that a philosophy be judged *not* by how well it can defend itself logically – for as the Sophists knew so well, almost anything can be proven with sufficient dexterity – but rather by how that philosophy affects the way *human beings live their lives.* Permit me to take one last stab, then, at explaining why I passionately believe we ought to subordinate head to heart and rationality to emotionalism, by discussing what each option holds out for the *moral behavior* of human beings, and the overall prospects for a better world.

Before leaving the realm of philosophy, however, might I interest you in just a few more moments of some perfectly harmless… philosophy? Short and sweet, I promise. Here we go.

Plato has a Dialogue called the *Theaetetus*, in which Socrates and this elderly mathematician named Theodorus are holding intellectual court in the company of a young, beardless prodigy (with whom, were it not for the presence of frigid Socrates, they would subsequently engage in a steamy *ménage à trois*, according to hallowed Greek custom).

The traditional back-and-forth eventually brings us around to one of Plato's pet peeves and nemeses: Protagoras, the late, great "King of the Sophists." Socrates engages in a post-mortem wrangle with this notorious rival, and thereby opens up what will prove to be one of the deepest cans of worms in the entire history of philosophy. We will now try to elucidate this classic polemic by engaging in several exercises, all of which may be easily performed in the privacy and comfort of your very own home. Ready?

Lick your teeth. Go ahead – run the tip of your tongue along the serrated edges of your pearly whites. Have you done it? Great. Now tell me: what did you feel? What thing, what object, what body part was it that you sensed or experienced during that simple procedure?

"My *teeth*, fool."

I hear ya. But think again, dear reader. Wouldn't we be at least as justified, if not more so, in saying that what you actually felt was *your tongue*? That what in truth produced the sensation that was forthwith ferried to your brain, is specifically the nerve endings at the end of your tongue (your teeth are nerveless, so my dentist informs me)? While you are thinking about that question, try something else: pick up your coffee mug, or whatever beverage utensil or household item is readily at hand – go ahead: grab it, caress it, massage its conical contours, the works. *Now* what are you feeling? You weren't going to say the coffee mug, were you? Tut-tut. You are feeling your *fingers*. You are experiencing the activation of the nerve-endings in the tippy-tops of your dexterous digits. Nothing more. It is all about *you* – not about your environment.

Let me ask you another question: is it warm or cool at this moment where you happen to be? Suppose your answer is: "Somewhat chilly, now that you mention it. I think I'll go turn on the heat." Fine. Now, what if a friend of yours waltzes into your presence at this very moment and exclaims: "Damn – it's like an *oven* in here!" Well – which is it? Who's right? Is the room hot, or not? Wouldn't we be correct in claiming that the answer to this question is "in the eye of the beholder" (or – in this case – in the temperature sensitivity of the experiencer)?

Got a coin? Pull it out of your pocket, and place it down on the table in front of you. Now, take a long, hard look at it. What's its shape? "Circular," you say? Really. And just how exactly do you know that it's circular?

"Because I'm *looking* at it, dunce."

True enough. But I can almost guarantee you that from the angle you are currently looking at it, that coin is anything but circular. It's far more likely to be an ellipse – right? Look again. In fact, from only *two* among the many *millions* of possible points of view does our coin really appear circular: from directly above and directly below it. So why give pride of place to those two vantage points, instead of to the legions of others? That sounds unfair to me.

Last example: what color is your chair? Suppose you say "green," but your color-blind friend comes along and swears it's blue. Who's right?

"Well, *I* am," you state confidently. "He's color-blind – *nebuch*."

What? How *dare* you – you prejudiced, egocentric, opticist! Have you at all considered the possibility that it is in point of fact *you* who are "colorblind"? When the lightwaves emitted by the chair strike *your* retina, the resultant impression is forwarded to the relevant section of your cerebrum, where it is somehow interpreted as "green." Your friend's retina (or his cerebrum) is configured somewhat differently than yours, such that when the same light waves strike *his* eyes, the perception that results is described by him as "blue." Why is your retinal (or cerebral) configuration "healthy" and his "defective"? What possible absolute standard could you employ to establish *that* hierarchy of correctness? To *him* the chair *is* blue – just who the hell are you to tell him that no: it's *actually* green? And if you respond by adducing the various state-of-the-art machines clunking around today that can register and distinguish between diverse light frequencies, I'll just ask you again: why is the computer's perspective privileged? *Its* sensors happen to respond *differently* to the light-waves emitted by the source you call green and the other one you call blue. Your friend's sensors don't. In what way is the computer "right"?

Protagoras it is, and no other, who lurks behind all these assertions. His famous motto – as recorded by Plato – is that "Man is the measure of all things." Protagoras is the father of Philosophical Relativism. In his view, there are *as many truths in this world as there are people to hold those truths*. Protagoras – in other words – was a **pluralist**. He believed in many co-existing correctnesses. He believed that "I'm OK, you're OK." He believed that reality and truth are invariably in the eye of the beholder.

Is the Empire State building 1454 feet high, or is it as tall as my index finger? Well, replies Protagoras, that depends on how far away you are when you measure it: from the New Jersey Turnpike this skyscraper is shorter than a thimble. If you stand right next to it, though, it's a big mother. Which vantage point is privileged? Quoth Protagoras: neither. Moving over to more cultural matters, how about

Robert Mapplethorpe's famous "ass-whipping" photograph (if you know the one I mean) – is it art? Well, now, that depends on whom you ask, explains Protagoras. One man's cat-o'-nine-tails-protruding-from-anus is another man's Mona Lisa. And similarly in the matter of modesty: which is the proper norm, the dress code of women in Taliban-run Afghanistan or the (un)dress-code of women on Fashion TV? Neither and both, Protagoras responds: Muslim fundamentalists have their truths, French designers have theirs. We call this overall Protagorean attitude *tolerance.*

Plato thought Protagoras was the world's biggest idiot – and an extremely *dangerous* idiot, at that. Plato believed (and modern science basically concurs) that if we dig deep enough, climb high enough, or study hard enough, we will inevitably discover that in any given case there is only *one* possible truth, absolute and immutable. The notion that *two or more* contradictory truths regarding the same subject can exist concurrently in our universe, said Plato, is obviously and by definition absurd. "The penny," Socrates would have shouted at Protagoras, "is *round*, you imbecile! It can't be *both* round *and* elliptical at the same time! The chair is *green*, your friend is *color-blind*, the room is *hot as a bitch*, the Empire State Building makes King Kong look like a cockroach, and as for those ladies on Fashion TV – well, they're nothing but a parade of shameless strumpets! (What channel did you say that was on?)"

Now, we may justifiably inquire of Protagoras: just how are people supposed to live together and speak a common language if each has his own, individual definition of colors, shapes, temperatures, beauty, decency, morality and so on, and all of these disparate opinions are considered *equally valid*? How are we to reach a viable consensus so that society can function at all? That's easy, Protagoras would have replied: we *vote.* Protagoras was the true father of democracy. If nobody's opinion is considered superior to anybody else's, if there can be no real "experts" in any field (or at least in many fields) because "my truth" on a given subject is invariably as good as "your truth," then the only way we can arrive at a *modus vivendi* is by polling those concerned and adhering to the verdict of the majority. Because *most* people see the chair as green, then we say – for the sake of community and communication – that it *is* green. And that's how we reach the decision that your friend is color blind, too – *democratically*.

Plato, however, despised democracy. Because instead of encouraging those with the greatest aptitude and deepest knowledge to ponder the perplexing problems besetting society and set an effective course toward their alleviation, democracy hands over the community's most crucial decisions *directly to the mob*. Democracy puts the "ignorant masses" in the driver's seat, essentially making the Protagorean claim that the opinion of any member of this roaring riff-raff on the issues of the day is quite as worthy as the opinion of any other member, learned or not. One person, one vote. Far from consulting the wise ones and philosopher-kings, democracy asks advice from the lowest common denominator, making "right" a purely relative term decided by the circus of electoral campaigns. And *there's* the road to society's ruin! – so Plato.

Ok. Now that we've summarized the competing positions of Plato and Protagoras on the subjects of truth, reality, morality and political participation, let's find out where *you* stand, dear reader. Are you a Platonist or a Protagorean? An absolutist or a pluralist? A dictator or a democrat? Inquiring minds want to know.

Let me tell you a nasty story. A *really* nasty story (digest your lunch before reading any further). Ready? You are a British explorer traipsing around India with a company of adventurers in the mid-nineteenth century. One fine evening, while machete-ing your way through the jungle regions of Bihar Province, you stumble upon a group of half-naked, swarthy fellows frolicking in a pond. Inquiring as to their identity, you are informed forthwith that you have to do with members of the Khond tribe.

"Take us to your leader," you venture. The splashing skinny-dippers are more than happy to oblige, and before you can say "Khonds in a pond," you are standing in a lavishly decorated, thatched-roof hut, face to face with the Big Chief himself. He greets you with sincere enthusiasm and amicability.

"Welcome, dear friends – *wel*come! You are the first visitors from the Surrounding Barbarian Darkness to arrive here in our

Island of True Civilization since longer than anyone can remember! And I must say: you certainly have chosen an opportune time to show up. For tomorrow is our great annual *Meriah March*!! How *wonderful* that you will be able to join us! Mahabhardhaharlal – prepare the best hut in the village for our most honorable guests! Gentlemen, take a load off, get some shut-eye, and we'll see you bright and early at the celebration!"

Before retiring, the lot of you interrogate Mahabhardhaharlal about the following day's festivities. He is quite forthcoming. For as long as there have been Khonds – the servant begins – as far back as anyone's memory reaches, there have also been Meriahs. Meriahs are members of a special family within the Khond tribe, the most honored clan in the community, even more so than that of the chief – they are almost royalty. The Meriahs always receive pride of place at tribal events, are reverently yielded the right of way on the road, and are invariably provided with the choicest morsels from the hunt. Meriahs may only marry other Meriahs, and thus do they preserve their pure and sacred lineage.

Every year (Mahabhardhaharlal continues), the Meriah female child closest to the age of twelve is singled out. Thrilled beyond belief that *she* has been chosen to fulfill the duty that each and every Meriah girl is trained since birth to yearn for, the lucky young lady is draped in gorgeous clothing, spun all year long by pious tribespeople. She is anointed with holy oils and pungent unguents, and is brought out with much pomp and circumstance to the village elders, whom she will soon lead in a holiday procession. Well, not actually "lead" – more like "be led," because in a traditional ceremony that takes place just before the procession gets underway, all of the young lady's major bones are bent back the wrong way until they snap, and walking is no longer really an option. Now, the reason the tribesmen break all her bones is because they are not permitted – according to ancient and hallowed Khond tradition – to tie her up or restrain her in anyway.

Why should she need restraining (you ask)? Well: that might have something to do with what happens next. The adolescent Meriah is paraded through the village, stopping at every household along the way. At the threshold of each hut, the head of the resident family greets her with a low bow, then pulls out a knife and slices off an ounce or two of her flesh from wherever on her body he chooses (a knuckle, an ear, an eye, a bit of thigh – first come, first serve). Then, before the living tissue can get cold, he runs through his house, smearing the blood across all of the walls, and finally rushes out back to the field – where he has just finished planting the new crop – and reverently buries the moist piece of flesh in the good earth. After bits and pieces of the Meriah girl have thus been lopped off at every venue in the village, the procession reaches the central square, where the whole populace is out in force, anticipating with electric eagerness the inception of the culminating ceremony.

An altar has been set up in the middle of the square – and it's no *ordinary* altar (enthuses Mahabhardhaharlal, swept up in the telling). It consists of a convex sheet of molten metal that forms a dome over a roaring fire. What is left of the Meriah child is then thrown onto the searing hot surface, across which she rolls in excruciating agony – up and down the slopes, writhing back and forth and screaming to the high heavens as her exposed tissue and dangling entrails are charred black – trying desperately and in vain to find a spot on the metal that isn't a scalding grill.

That's "scalding," mind you, not "scorching" – because the fire is deliberately tempered somewhat so that the victim remains alive and in unimaginable pain for as long as is humanly possible (Khond tradition has it that the more tears she sheds, the more abundant the rain will be this season). When, after a good ten minutes or so of slow roasting, it looks like the Meriah girl won't hold out much longer, four young braves shoot arrows into her body simultaneously from all sides, and the entire crowd rushes at the dying child and tears her to pieces, ripping off limbs, organs, muscle – whatever they can get their hands on – which they promptly send with their kids back home to bury in the yard (for an *extra*-good harvest). Then – the servant sums up – "we party all day and throughout the following night until the break of dawn. It's a blast! My kids look forward to this all year long!"

Mahabhardhaharlal turns to go. "Don't you fellas oversleep, now. As we Khonds are fond of saying: '*the more the Meriah*!'"

You and your buddies stand there dumbstruck. What kind of people *are* these, you ask one another in horror. (The answer – by the way, dear reader – is that they are *real* people. This is a true story, down to every detail except the servant's name and your presence. The Khonds performed this rite until the mid-nineteenth century.)

Well, something must be done, you all agree. Striding over to the chief's hut and waking him up, you and the fellas spend hours trying to convince him that this is a terrible, murderous ritual that has no place in civilized society. The chief, for his part, is absolutely beside himself.

"I am shocked and appalled that barbarians such as yourselves should dare to come to *our* village, to *our* jungle, to *our* land, and tell *us* about civilized behavior! This yearly festival of ours is the central pillar of our holy tribal religion, a religion which has governed and inspired our lives for centuries upon centuries! It ties us to our ancestors and helps us touch the Divine, it is our celebration of the profound agricultural mystery of burial and rebirth that lies at the root of human existence itself, and this celebration uplifts us and gives our lives meaning all the year round and from generation to generation. You could not possibly *begin* to comprehend the fathomless significance to the Khond people of the Meriah March. It is the very soul of our existence!

"You say what we do is wrong. Tell me: just who the *hell* do you think you are to show up here, straight out of the forest, and presume to dictate to *us* what is "right" and what is "wrong," on the basis of *your* "truth," according to *your* society's (I must say) extremely peculiar notions of the ethical? Since when does *your* culture have the monopoly on morality? You have your values – we have ours! I don't come charging into your country to tell *you* how to behave – and you have no right to come charging into ours to do the same. If you have a problem with our annual Meriah March – *there's the door*. Leave! Nobody's stopping you. Now, if you don't mind, I'm going to get some sleep – I've got a big day ahead. Goodnight, gentlemen."

Well, you tried. Gave it your best shot. You all mope back to Hotel Hut in a miserable mood. Suddenly, one of your comrades remembers: "Geez, guys – we got *rifles*. All their primitive weapons *together* are no match for *two* of us, let alone the thirty brave musketeers we are. We can put a stop to this atrocity by the threat of force – force we may not even have to use! I'll just open fire on a nearby tree, so they'll get an idea of what a rifle can do. If necessary, we'll shatter a few knee-caps. Then, we'll simply order them to let the Meriah girl go, and send back to Delhi for reinforcements. Her Majesty's Government will thereafter set up a permanent base here, with the sole and express purpose of preventing the Meriah March from ever taking place again, and teaching these brutes right from wrong! Well – whadya say, fellas? Is it a plan?"

Well – what *do* you say, dear reader? Dawn is approaching, and you have to make a decision – quick! Do you step in and coercively dismantle a millennia-old culture's religion in the name of *your* culture's (comparatively teenage) conceptions of truth and morality? Or do you – rather – opt to follow the famous *Star Trek* Prime Directive, involving a strict *non-interference policy* with regard to civilizations encountered en route across the galaxy? Do you imperialistically force these indigenous tribespeople to abandon a major element of their historical and spiritual heritage, at *your* gunpoint in the name of *your* Truth? Or do you recognize that there is no reason to believe that you have a monopoly on the truth – that, indeed, there *can* be no monopoly on the truth – because there *is* no one truth. They have theirs, you have yours: *live and let live*. In a word: are you a Platonic absolutist or a Protagorean pluralist?

Well, dear reader: which is it gonna be? (And remember: this is a classic hypothetical – there *is* no third way to wiggle out!) It's morning now, and the Meriah March is due to start within the half-hour. Are you going to put a stop to it by force, or not? Why don't you just go ahead and check the appropriate box before reading further (use a pencil – you might want to erase later):

☐ A. I am a pluralist, who believes that there is no *single* moral truth, and even if there were, I couldn't be sure that *I* possessed it. I will *not* interfere coercively and destroy the Khonds' age-old religion and culture.

☐ B. I am an absolutist, who believes that there is only *one* moral truth, and I happen to have it. I *will* interfere coercively and destroy the Khonds' barbarian religion and culture.

Have you made your choice and marked it? Good. Let us proceed.

For those who checked A:

Well, now – you people really are a piece of work. It's hard to know even what to say to you. You are going to stand there and watch (or run away ignominiously) as they mangle, torture, butcher and mutilate a twelve-year-old girl for hours on end. In the name of "pluralism," you will let them crack her bones, you will stand idly by as they cut off her fingers, her feet, her nose, as they rip out her eyes, yank off her ears, tear off her lips, you will listen to her scream in indescribable pain and horror as each householder takes away slice after slice of her life, digs his knife deep into her calf, severs her thumb or her toes and runs off with them, singing. You will take it in stride when they place her on the searing grill, and she writhes and screams and weeps in agony, you will allow them to murder her in front of your eyes, to deprive her – in the most cruel and unusual way ever invented by humankind – of that inestimably precious gift, as they senselessly and sadistically rip her innocent life from her for no damn good reason, these monsters in the form of people, these callous creatures for whom the epithet "animal" is far too good (animals never did anything like that). You will reconcile yourself to all this, in the name of Protagoras, in the name of your dear little principle of "pluralism," in the name of your sweet sounding notion of "tolerance," in the name of your oh-so-politically correct support of the philosophical catechism of "many truths."

YOU SICK BASTARDS! If the Khonds are inhumane villains for reveling in the torture and murder of another human being – what does that make *you*, for letting it all go down right in front of your eyes *when you could have stopped it*?!

"Hey," you interrupt. "Calm down, would ya? Don't you think you're being a bit sensationalist and melodramatic about this?"

EXCUSE ME?! IS THERE SOME **OTHER** WAY THAT I AM UNAWARE OF TO DESCRIBE AND RELATE TO THE PREMEDITATED AND MERCILESS STEALING AWAY OF A YOUNG PERSON'S LIFE BY AN ENTIRE VILLAGE USING METHODS OF THE MOST UNHEARD OF VICIOUSNESS THAN

"SENSATIONALLY" AND "MELODRAMATICALLY"? Do you think we should calm down and discuss this issue "cooly and rationally"? Do you think we should weigh the pros and cons in a subdued and sagacious manner? Do you think that I should stop "playing on your emotions," stop "tugging at your heart strings," stop ranting and raving and treat this subject in an informed and logical fashion (the way you evidently came to your vile and infamous decision to squelch your emotions in the face of the most awful deed ever witnessed, all in the name of an intellectual construct, of an "idea," a "conviction" or a "principle")? Do you think I should stop appealing to your passion and compassion, that I should quit being such a *deplorable demagogue*, and instead entertain this dilemma under the soothing supervision and moderate auspices of reason – quietly and sensibly? Is that what you think?

WELL YOU CAN FORGET IT.

Remember, offended reader: when you are asked to consider a hypothetical situation, what you are *really* being asked to do is hypothesize that the situation being described is *not* hypothetical. You are being asked to imagine that it is *real*, that you are *there*, that you are the very same warm-blooded, sensitive, empathic human being that you are and that you are *actually* experiencing the situation in question at this very moment! And empathy means that *you feel what the victim feels*, together *with* the victim, and *as intensely* as the victim feels it – and (what's equally important) that you let that intense feeling *influence you to your depths*!

In which case would you please tell me this: just how calm, cool and collected of a conversation do you think you would be capable of having – or would want *us* to be having – about this whole complex affair, *if you were a young girl experiencing some of the worst torture ever dreamt up by the malicious inhabitants of this iniquitous planet and about to have all your hopes and happiness eradicated forever as you are destroyed and taken permanently out of this world*? Just how "reasonable" do you think you would be?

And if she begs you? I mean, what if the years of Meriah indoctrination evaporate into thin air as she is hacked to pieces by those she loves and her agony and misery know no bounds, and she turns to all you well-armed knights, the damsel in unspeakable, indescribable distress, and she pleads with you to stop this horror, to *save her life* – would you then regroup in your little policy huddle, go back to the logical drawing board and try to figure out where Protagoras and Pluralism would stand under *these* somewhat altered circumstances? After all (the chief will point out) whereas you visitors may claim to harbor a truth called "individualism" – leading you to attach significance to the girl's *personal* desire not to be dismembered – amongst the Khonds (as in most traditional societies the world over throughout history), the reigning truth is far closer to *communalism*, and as for this new-fangled "individualism" of yours, they have never even heard of it, and it counts for nothing among them. The Khonds have a *different* set of values, according to which the most important unit is the collective, the tribe, and the individual human beings making up this super-significant unit are like the limbs making up the body: if you have to amputate a limb for the welfare of the body, you do so!

Hmmmm, you all wonder (as they slice out the young girl's tongue and cut off her left foot at the ankle) – doesn't the chief have a point there? How should an adherent of the principle of pluralism handle *this* brain-teaser? What would Protagoras do? Does this "communalism" idea qualify as a separate Khond "truth" as well? If so, then why would *our* truth concerning "individual rights" be somehow "truer"? What do *you* make of this, Charlie? We haven't heard your thoughts on the matter yet…

Dear reader: if this is truly how you think we ought to do things; if this is your idea of how to handle a situation like the one just described; if you would really have let that girl be tortured and butchered in front of your eyes (or behind your fleeing back) although you could have saved her – then our relationship has come to an end. Nice knowin' ya (at least I thought it was). Go on, scram. Take your precious little pluralism and hit the freaking road. Go be open-minded and tolerant somewhere else, preferably in another galaxy. Come back when you're a human being.

For those who checked B:

You know, I really thought I had encountered the lowest of the low with those folks back there who checked A – but that was before I met *you* people. Now you *really* take the cake. You've got the Truth, you do – the whole Truth, and nothing but the Truth. And since this Truth is and can be, by definition, the *only* truth; since it is the single and undeniable Truth of truths and brooks no competition whatsoever; since it is, for all intents and purposes, nothing less than a carved-in-stone, finger-of-God, Decalogue-type axiom; then it must be true everywhere at every time and for everyone! And you, my fascist friends – you are prepared to enforce the universal application of this categorical imperative of yours at the point of the good ole' bayonet, now aren't you? Since truth can never be relative – can only be absolute (say you) – you feel justified as can be in coercing people on pain of death to act according to the One Truth, which also happens to be *your* truth.

Funny – why does all of this conjure up in my mind vague pictures of rice paddies and rolling fields and Khmer of a crimson kind? Or of mass starvation and collectivization and gulags and execution chambers and another guy with a rather "steely" pseudonym? Or of hundreds of thousands of thirteen-year-olds sent out to the Iran-Iraq border to serve as human mine-sweepers by an octogenarian True Believer in a turban? Or of Jesuits baptizing Aztec babies and then bashing their heads against the wall? Why do all these fuzzy images jump to mind? Oh, yeah – *I* know: because these are only the most recent installments in a history-long series of the world's most unspeakable atrocities, all carried out – not least of all by biblical Israelites, who preceded Plato himself in their uncompromising Monism – in the name of the One Truth, the Absolute and Infallible and Only Truth, the Pervasively Applicable Truth.

And now, dear checker of "B" box, *you* have opted to throw your full support behind this well-worn way of doing things, to magnanimously undertake your White Man's Burden by stepping in and *forcing* your own ethnocentric ideas, values and truths on indigenous cultures, the better to turn all of them into *you*. Everybody must believe the same things, everybody must act according to the same principles, and all deviants – as Arthur Koestler famously said of Soviet policy – must be either reformed, deformed or liquidated. By interfering in and ultimately outlawing the Meriah March at gunpoint in the name of your Truth, you are upholding the *very same absolutist principle* that led to all those unimaginable religion- or ideology-based historical horrors in which thousands and millions were eliminated because of what they believed (hey: that's some nice company you keep). In fact, you are supporting the very coercive mentality that serves the Khonds themselves so well as they socialize and ultimately force Meriahs to undergo the aforementioned ordeal. And, of course, you are declaring that "might makes right." After all, what if the Khonds had invented gunpowder first, and believed that *they* had the One Truth? What would the world have looked like then? (Think Meriah March down Park Avenue.)

"Hey, now: what kind of cockamamie comparison is that?!" you fume. "*My* principles are *noble* – the Khonds' are execrable! Those people are murderers – I'm trying to *save* lives!"

Sigh. Do you think there is *one* Islamic suicide bomber in the entire exploding lot who does not believe that "his principles are noble"? Do you imagine there is *one* abortion clinic attacker who does not say: "Those people are murderers – I'm trying to *save* lives!"

And tell me: what if it *weren't* ritual torture and murder of the Meriah – but only ritual torture and rape? Would you *still* step in with rifles locked and loaded? How about just torture? Just rape? An annual ceremonial flogging? Clitorodectomy? A parental spanking? *Where do you draw the line*?

Once you've established and acted upon the Platonic principle that there is only one Truth, and all else is manifest error, you're well on your way down that slippery slope to intolerance of the coercive and decapitative kind, as practiced by most of the world's religions and ideological-political movements at one point or another in history. What's to stop you telling people what to do in *all* types of different situations, lethal or otherwise? Where does your Reign of Terror in the name of "right thinking" end? Under the shadow of your gun we'll all dress, eat, sleep, talk, sing, dance, work, play and worship our gods in the same "acceptable" manner, and you'll call in the guard and shoot us dead if we don't (or send us to reeducation camp). Wow – you're the real enlightened type, aren't you? I think there are still a few diehard military dictatorships scattered around the planet where they might be in need of your services – why don't you just pack up your gear and *git*?

...Damned if you do, dear reader, and damned if you don't. The positions of both men – Plato *and* Protagoras – if taken as they are, lead us straight down the well-paved path to bloodshed and catastrophe. Adhering to the Protagorean theory of *many truths* makes you a heartless, gutless, relativist wimp who will stand idly by as murder is committed. Subscribing to the Platonic theory of *one truth* means sanctifying the brand of rigid intolerance that breeds monstrous, narrow-minded, totalitarian tyrants who may well carry out more murders than can possibly be counted. How do we extricate ourselves from this moral morass?

Let me suggest a solution. It's a solution that will definitely not be palatable to everyone, may even sound like sheer babble to some or reckless insanity to others, but neither you nor I will have any fun or make any progress if the author just sticks to rehearsing positions that have already long ago assumed the guise of conventional wisdom. Besides, I have this sneaking feeling that the solution I am about to propose is not mine – it's yours. It's all of ours. It's the way most of us decent people behave on a regular basis – and the way we would *really* act at the Meriah March – but it is nevertheless rarely granted the formal recognition or legitimacy that I for one deeply believe it deserves. So let's call a spade a spade, and dig it:

WHO GIVES A GOOD GODDAMN WHETHER THERE IS ONE TRUTH, OR MANY TRUTHS, WHO COULD CARE LESS ABOUT PLATO OR PROTAGORAS OR ANY OF THOSE OTHER ATHENIAN BLABBERMOUTHS? TO ABSOLUTE HELL WITH ABSOLUTISM, AND PLURALISM CAN STICK IT WHERE THE SUN DON'T SHINE – THERE IS A YOUNG GIRL ABOUT TO BE TORTURED AND MURDERED IN FRONT OF MY EYES, AND **MY HEART CAN'T ABIDE IT**, WON'T SURVIVE IT, WILL EXPLODE LIKE A HYDROGEN BOMB, WILL FORCE ME TO FORCE THEM TO CEASE AND DESIST IMMEDIATELY AND WITHOUT FURTHER ADO. ANYBODY WHO CAN WATCH SUCH AN ABOMINATION TAKE PLACE IN FRONT OF HIS FACE AND NOT INTERVENE IS NO PERSON, IS NO HUMAN, PRACTICALLY DESERVES TO BE THE NEXT VICTIM HIMSELF.

But here's the catch: I intervene, all right. But I intervene – we intervene – *not* in the name of Plato and the "One Truth" that I happen to possess. I entirely ignore the philosophical, intellectual and rational issue of how many truths there can or can't be, and *do what my emotions tell me to do*, when those emotions are unhampered by considerations of "creed" or "principle." I follow my heart, without being guided by some sterile, logically-derived philosophical "truth" concerning how many truths there are or aren't, and my intervention is entirely unconnected to (and therefore in no way implies) support for Plato's position. And in acting thus – in acting admittedly and emphatically in the name of my emotions, and *not* in the cause of moral absolutism and a categorical imperative – I thereby refrain from endorsing either side of this argument, neither joining the pathetically disengaged relativists, nor adding strength to the cause of fascist monism or establishing a Platonic precedent that can be used in the future to ban all kinds of differences in thought and behavior. I have transcended this classic, rational argument – which never had any business involving itself in moral issues in the first place – and reinstated on its rightful throne the legitimate monarch in such matters: *my feelings*. By ignoring – when the chips were down – the logic-based, academic argument about "truth" between Plato and Protagoras, I effect a major coup in myself, ultimately *bending my head to the will of my heart*.

Finding the way out of the impossible dilemma set up for us by Plato and Protagoras in the *Theatetus* requires first and foremost a super-heroic effort on the part of the reader to suspend what is probably the most deeply ingrained axiom (or at least the most oft-spouted slogan) in all of human history, ideology and religion. And that axiom is: *that Truth has value in and of itself.* I doubt any set of syllables in any language has ever received as much attention, as much adulation and as much adoration as this one little word: "Truth." There is probably no term anywhere that so automatically elicits unbridled praise and ecstatic worship, that has been the object of so many quests and the subject of so many paeans, that can bend entire societies to its will and reverse the course of history at the drop of a hat. There is no notion, no concept, no idea I know that is so immediately associated in the minds of the many with all that is good, right, awesome, powerful, worthy, fine and essential. Too bad that "Truth" – forsooth – has nothing *whatsoever* to do with *any* of these attractive adjectives.

Sometimes we use a word so many times in our lives in conjunction with a particular set of sentiments that that word eventually becomes almost indistinguishable in our consciousnesses from those same sentiments. Thus, for most people, "Truth" – which means "what is" – has become synonymous (and is used interchangeably) with "good" or "right" – which mean "what should be." It is hard to imagine a more miserable mix-up than the conflation of these two *diametrically opposed visions*, and in the next few pages we will do our damndest to try to tear them apart and build an impregnable wall between them fifty miles high.

(Let me preface the up-and-coming diatribe by saying that our target here is "Truth" with a capital T, meaning the revelation or determination of what existence is actually like, the discovery of what's "really going on" in our universe or in ourselves, and stuff like that. We most decidedly do *not* have "truth" with a *small* t in our cross-hairs: there will be no preaching of prevarication in the service of ostensibly noble ends in these pages. The Talmud relates the story of an estranged couple that lived on opposite sides of a house and employed their lone offspring for communication. When the husband would request – through his son – lentils for dinner, the wife, out of spite, would cook him peas, and on the occasions when he would ask for peas, she would invariably send him lentils. One day the child came bounding into the room bearing peas – just the dish his father had requested!

"How did you pull *this* off?" queried Dad.

"Simple," replied his shrewd progeny. "When you asked for peas, I told Mom you wanted lentils."

"Smart kid," said his father. "But you are never, *ever* to do that again, you hear? Because the way you are going, you'll eventually get mixed up in insider trading!"

I updated the last sentence, but the Talmud definitely does *not* harbour an "ends-justify-the-means" attitude to lying – or to much else, for that matter – and neither does this book. Caveat duly delivered, we now return to the bigger fish we have to fry: Truth with a capital T...)

The problem with the positions taken up by Plato and Protagoras regarding the singular or plural nature of Truth is that instead of relegating this debate to its proper status – a fun intellectual exercise on a fine Athenian afternoon – both men were thoroughly convinced that their dispute had major implications for how all of humankind should conduct themselves forevermore. And their disciples on both sides of this polemic have been striving ever since to convince us that we should set up one or the other of these classical conceptions of Truth as a guide for our individual and collective actions. In recent centuries the breakdown has run more or less along hemispherical and religious-secular lines, with (to engage in gross generalization) the modern, secular North and West leaning toward the Protagorean position of "many truths," and the traditional, religious South and East (especially the Middle East) emphasizing the Platonic position of "One Truth."

But whatever their disagreements, then as now, the philosophers, mystics, clerics and ideologues on *both* sides of the Platonic-Protagorean divide have always been agreed on one thing: that *knowledge is virtue*, that cognizance of the true state of affairs (whether that state is singular or plural) is the steering wheel of ethics, that awareness of the actual nature of reality leads to (or is itself) moral behavior. Plato – like his older contemporary, the Buddha – famously maintained that the exercise of reason precludes sin, and that evil is solely a function of ignorance. "The bad man," agreed the Stoics, "is false to facts. The good man is one who possesses a body of true propositions." "And you shall know the Truth," echoed the Galilean, "and the Truth shall set you free." "To understand something," declared Benedict Spinoza, in his suggestively titled *Ethics Demonstrated According to the Geometrical Order*, "is to be delivered of it" – and so on and so forth down the generations, until this very day. (Many, following Aristotle, have gone further still, worshipping knowledge and the "contemplation of reality" as veritable ends in themselves, the loftiest and most beautiful pursuits available to man. Sang the poet Arthur Clough: "It fortifies my soul to know, that though I perish,

Truth is so…") And because the truth about any aspect of existence is arrived at via rational reasoning, this latter process, too, has been sanctified from earliest times. Here is the eighteenth-century Scottish philosopher David Hume:

> Nothing is more usual in philosophy, and even in common life, than to talk of the combat of passion and reason, to give the preference to reason, and to assert that men are only so far virtuous as they conform themselves to its dictates. Every rational creature, it is said, is obliged to regulate his actions by reason; and if any other motive or principle challenges the direction of his conduct, he ought to oppose it, till it be entirely subdued, or at least brought to conformity with that superior principle. On this method of thinking the greatest part of moral philosophy, ancient and modern, seems to be founded; nor is there an ampler field, as well for metaphysical arguments as popular declamations, than this supposed pre-eminence of reason above passion. The eternity, invariableness and divine origin of the former have been displayed to the best advantage; the blindness, inconstancy and deceitfulness of the latter, have been as strongly insisted upon.

Now, the really strange part of all this, is that for some unfathomable reason, only a very few thinkers since the beginning of time (chief among them Hume himself) thought to ask the seemingly simple question *what in hell does "Truth" – whether united or divided, Platonic or Protagorean, divine or scientific – have to do with how people should live and how they should act in this world*?!

Does my knowledge of a given truth about a given subject ever really *motivate* me in any way? Let's check it out. Here's a truth: "vegetables are nutritious." Now, this statement is about as rational and factual as they come – researchers in the laboratory (and parents across the planet) can attest to the scientifically proven salutary effect of green-beans on the human constitution. But let me ask you a question: is it really the knowledge of this indisputable fact that *motivates* you to feed your child vegetables? Do you feed your child vegetables *because* vegetables are nutritious? I daresay you do not. You feed your child vegetables because… *you love your child.*

The truth-statement "vegetables are nutritious" is inert, is meaningless, is in itself nothing, it packs no punch, stimulates no response, induces no deed, is possessed of no intrinsic positive or negative charge – it is dead. What motivates you to *make use* of this entirely uninspiring, totally value-neutral piece of information is not knowledge, but *feeling*, is not an intellectual truth, but an *emotional desire*: your solicitation for your child's welfare, which derives from your **love of your child**. Now *there's* the galvanizing power-pack in this story, there's the prompter, the impeller, the prime mover, the drive. A statement of fact in splendid isolation is perforce and by definition *completely devoid of emotional content*, and as such is quite as useless as a hammer when there is no desire to build anything. (And just as hammers can be employed to smash as well as to build, plain information simply *has no valence*, is entirely nonpartisan, can be manipulated every which way: the knowledge that vegetables are nutritious could even conceivably be exploited in order to *deny* such produce to someone whose health one is interested in wrecking!) Impressive and interesting as they may be, intellectual statements are nothing but dumb instruments, unprovocative, unmotivating, impartial and thoroughly insignificant – until emotional instigators arrive upon the scene, snap up these hapless truths in their powerful paws and employ them to achieve the goal of a particular passion.

Subtle or simple, this point is not easy to get across, perhaps more than anything due to the conventions of language. We say, "awareness of this new piece of information *led* me to do X," or "the discovery that [God exists, Copernicus was right, roses are red, the market is down] *caused* me to change my original plans…" Now, no doubt there are many who would insist on the accuracy of such formulations in portraying what actually takes place in our psyches. Permit me to suggest, in contrast, that the process is much more akin to driving down the highway, when you suddenly spy a sizeable boulder in the middle of the road. "I was forced to swerve by a boulder in the road," you might comment afterward. But, of course, you were not. The boulder didn't force you to swerve – it's a *rock*. Your deep desire to keep on living forced you to swerve. The boulder doesn't act upon you – *you* act upon you. Without the impetus provided by feelings, facts in themselves are a whole lot of neutral nothing.

The opposite, however, is not the case: no one truth-statement is essential to the strength or meaningfulness of a given emotion. While "vegetables are nutritious" loses all significance unless at least somebody somewhere cares about the welfare of someone (even just himself), *love for one's children* will continue to energize and motivate in ten thousand different directions, whatever "facts" may be generated and decay in this world and in our cumulative collective consciousness. "Vegetables are nutritious" is dead meat without love; but love lives on even if broccoli is declared carcinogenic. Rationality is an ass (albeit, a nice ass) ever doing emotion's bidding. The head is the tool of the heart.

Is all this just casuistic, semantic hair-splitting? The kind of analytical nitpickery that contemporary philosophy seems to engage in without cease? It probably would be, if it weren't for one minor little point, and that point is that *the vast majority of the world's religious systems, mystical "ways," philosophical schools and ideological movements throughout history* – that is to say, **almost all of the really smart people who have ever lived** – have been consistently urging us since the very dawn of time to **reverse this master-servant relationship,** and to channel or subdue or remake or eradicate our emotions in the light of one or another particular "Truth." "You may *feel* X," most every cleric, scholastic and commissar on record has at one time or another pontificated to his flock. "But you must nevertheless *transcend* your unreliable emotions and uncontrollable inclinations, and *do* Y – for that is the imperative of The Truth."

How strange, though, that anyone should ascribe an imperative to Truth! Because statements of fact – as we have just tried to show – are not in the least bit capable of motivating, and indeed: are not even privileged to participate *passively* as a *dead tool* in a given action unless *a live emotional impetus* steps in and takes charge of the whole business! How then can we be told that our emotions should *step aside* to make way for a truth-statement, for a principle, for an idea, for a product of reasoning or an aspect of knowledge? How did statements of fact all of a sudden climb into the driver's seat? And how did our emotions become the ass?

Plato and Protagoras (and Aristotle) it was – among others – who made all this possible. For they not only planted in our minds the perverted notion that rational truth-statements should somehow determine the direction of all human behavior and endeavor. They went further still, adding insult to injury, and presented humankind with what each perceived as *the* truth-statement *par excellence* that must govern our very attitude to the formulation of truth-statements: in Plato's case – that there can be only one of these at a time; in Protagoras' case – that you can have many of them side by side. In choosing to reject the motivating power these men and their manifold philosophical, religious, ideological and political followers have attributed to statements of fact and declarations about "what is," we are reversing the hierarchy that they have set up for so long. "No longer," cry we, "shall 'wanting, feeling and aspiring' bow and scrape before 'reasoning, calculating and knowing,' the former serving the latter with abject truculence. From now on "wanting" is reinstated as rightful ruler, and "knowing" – its epaulets ripped off in righteous anger – demoted to the rank of humble advisor. From now on our emotions call the plays. We have recognized, with Hume, that "Reason is, and ought only to be, the slave of the passions, and can never pretend to any other office than to serve and to obey them."

Granted: putting the emotions in command of the rational faculties is, at first glance – even at last glance – a recipe for a really big mess. Nevertheless, as problematic as it is, the heart-over-head approach remains the lesser of evils. Giving the intellect and the various Truths that it settles upon charge over the passions is – as it turns out – far, *far* worse.

We often tend to imagine evil in the guise of seething, frothing, hot-blooded people violently acting out their emotions of rage. And sure, there's definitely no shortage of that. Human beings do all sorts of awful things in states of advanced fury and frenzy, and were we to put emotion in the driver's seat unchecked, we would certainly live in a wild and wanton world. But the lion's share of the *really* horrific deeds that have been done throughout history – the repressions, the enslavements, the inquisitions, the terrorisms, the genocides – have been carried out for the most part not in *hot* blood, but in *cold* blood; not in boiling anger, but in calm calculation; not as a result of emotions on fire, but as a result of emotions *extinguished*; not in response to persistent, uncontrollable, passionate feeling, but in obeisance to dispassionate, droning, unfeeling "Truth."

I still remember an excerpt from Victor Frankel's *Man's Search for Meaning*, in which a survivor of the Babi Yar massacre (I think) who had crawled out wounded from under hundreds of bodies, wrote about the moments just prior to the execution of his family. When their turn came to strip naked and stand at the edge of the mass grave – as thousands just before them had already done – the author glanced at the German soldier on killing detail. He sat there with his tommy gun on the edge of a ridge smoking a cigarette and dangling his legs, and on his face the writer saw – not anger, not hatred, not even disgust – just boredom.

Fierce anger and hatred – of the caliber required to kill – are highly intense, all-consuming emotions that cannot but subside rather quickly, else their bearer will burn up and collapse. It takes incredible amounts of energy to maintain a constant, malicious, murderous fury. It also takes "motive." If you come home to find your dearly beloved spouse rolling in the sheets with someone not you, your wrath and hatred will be real and focused, and you may even be capable of maintaining that high level of negative emotion long enough to go get the shotgun from the garage and blow the one or the both of them to kingdom come. Such a reaction might conceivably warrant the plea of "temporary insanity" or at least "extenuating circumstances." It constitutes, at any rate, a "crime of passion."

Not so the systematically planned and executed killing of hundreds, of thousands, of tens and of hundreds of thousands of anonymous innocents. In such a case, there is no *specific* motive to vehemently hate each and every one of your victims separately, and – especially *without* such an immediate and recurring stimulus – no human being could ever pull it off. No man born of woman could possibly maintain the magnitude of hatred that induces murderous madness for hour after day after week after year, toward each and every one of the myriad and anonymous human targets that passes in front of him like an endless train. *Rage runs out.*

And there's a further complication: emotion cuts both ways. German soldiers had not been brought up prior to the war to be especially bad people. They had no sinister, Marquis de Sade-type "evil" training. They were more or less normal human beings. If the Nazi extermination machine had relied solely or primarily on these boys' feelings of passionate hatred (yes, even toward the Jews), not only would operations have closed down after a few weeks when the immediate perpetrators ran out of anger gas, but the same cultivation of emotion that brought out hate would have inevitably brought out compassion, too. People who *really* hate – that is to say, not those whose hatred is *taught*, and thus derives from a generalized, ideological truth-statement that *dampens* emotions, but those who hate because of *specific* wrongs committed by a *specific* culprit upon whom one can take *specific* revenge – people, I say, who *really* hate, are more often than not just as capable of feeling *other* strong emotions as well, like pity, or empathy, or anger at injustice, and the like. No smooth killing operation can afford all these risks, or run efficiently with all these obstacles and complications in the way. What you need for the job are emotional zombies.

And so another method is found. A "Truth" is propounded, in the light of which *all* emotions (even hate) count for very little, are to be reigned in and tamed. And when feelings *do* count, it is only in the context of love of and service to this Truth. Negative emotions (*all* emotions) are expressed collectively, in a *channeled* and *controlled* and *generalized* way – those mass rallies and Hitler harangues preserved for posterity on film – and these emotions are no longer caused by the natural human responses of the individual and directed at the particular objects of his hatred, but are engendered by the Great Truth and aimed nebulously at the Great Truth's enemies. Murderous rituals are then prescribed by this Truth for its adherents, which by their very repetition help dull the emotional edge and dim the fire of the heart (like our blasé executioner at Babi Yar). While feelings are blunted and harnessed, the claim is simultaneously cultivated and accepted – sometimes aboveboard, sometimes below – that the Great Truth is in fact the *motivating force* behind the entire collective project, which in a sense it has in fact become, in that it has neutralized the individual's emotion-based ability to make free decisions and go against the grain (and this is the ultimate emasculation and humiliation of emotion: it is to be ruled by a master that strictly speaking *has no power to command*).

Now the problem has been solved. Because remember: Truth, unlike intense emotion, is inert – it is quiet, it makes no fuss or bother, causes no seizures, requires no effort. No one ever gets exhausted adhering to the Truth. It lies there motionless in the background of your brain, solidly and steadily supporting and soothing you as you move from outrage to outrage. And you – the loyal servant of the Truth – soon imbibe its ways yourself, and settle down into a calm, cool, untroubled and efficient regimen of following orders. Emotionless crimes – that is, crimes perpetrated in the name of Truth – are the easiest crimes to commit on a mass and continuous basis. And because their perpetrators cannot even excuse themselves as having acted out of genuine personal rage, they are also the *most evil of all possible crimes*. The greatest atrocity committed by the Germans in World War Two was not that they murdered six million Jews because they hated them. The greatest atrocity committed by the Germans – the abomination for which they should lower their heads in ignominious shame for the remainder of all human history – was that they murdered six million Jews because they *did not* hate them.

When I say that the heart should rule the head, I am not trying to put a damper on cogitation, God forbid. Rational thinking has always contributed an immense amount to the bettering of the human condition, and the proverbial *Yiddische kop* – the "Jewish Genius" – has spearheaded humanity's intellectual struggle ever since anyone can remember. *So keep on thinking*! Keep on researching and scrutinizing and theorizing and analyzing and hypothesizing and demonstrating and evaluating and inventing. Doing so is critical for our future, and besides: it's a blast! This is a book about the primacy of emotion, but it could never have been written (or read) without the help of at least a modicum of grey matter. Putting emotion in the driver's seat isn't worth much if the car isn't running, and hey: why settle for less than a Lamborghini?

We are also not suggesting that our passions be our constant and immediate moral guides in all situations, nor are we envisioning an anarchistic society a la *Lord of the Flies*. Rules, principles, socialization, hierarchy, authority and the remaining trappings of an organized political order or social contract – when they coalesce over time *as a product* of demands made by genuine feelings – perform essential tasks in our daily lives, allowing us (if you will) to suck on the intellectualized and institutionalized popsicle of what were originally heated emotional impulses, to inure the heart to discipline and accustom it by rote to doing good. No one is talking here about getting rid of the structures by means of which we transmit, foster and even enforce these ultimately emotional-based "values." But those structures must never forget where they originally came from, for that is when tragedy really strikes. They must be made to understand – via vigorous civil disobedience if necessary – that they represent nothing more than a technical means to the achievement of goals established by the Big Boss: *our feelings*.

In other words, we must always ensure – in every individual and collective situation – that emotion remains the Sultan, and rationality its Grand Vizier. The Sultan gives the overall tone, points us in the general direction; and the Grand Vizier is responsible for the orderly, day-to-day implementation of the Sultan's mandate. The Grand Vizier can also function as high council (when summoned), and may even perform the important role of calming down the volatile Sultan before he goes off half-cocked in one of his moods and does something he'll later regret. But just because the Grand Vizier is granted pervasive powers to carry out the wishes of the Sultan and advise him, *that does not excuse delusions of Sultanhood on his part.* And if and when the Vizier gets too uppity, or – carried away by the logical momentum and symmetrical loveliness of his own legislation – begins taking actions no longer in accordance with the Sultan's will, well: over waltzes the sovereign with his executioner to the Grand Vizier's offices, and it's *off with the refractory bastard's head.* A new, more docile Vizier is installed, who keeps to his place and understands his relatively modest role in the overall scheme of government.

That is what happened in our encounter with the Khonds of Bihar Province: the inability of our eminently rational (pluralist or monist) principles to reflect our real emotions and create the world we desired, shone forth on that occasion like a supernova. So we dismissed and dispatched our Platonic or Protagorean Grand Vizier, took care of some extremely pressing business (stopping the Meriah March – because that was the immediate firman of our feelings), and our next job would have been to *hire and train new intellectual officers, of the type that will better bend their necks to the yoke of our sovereign emotions, instead of presuming to dictate to them*, and to keep tabs on these new appointees regularly to see that they maintain this servile attitude without a glitch (which someone forgot to do in the case of Greek – and much of modern – philosophy). We have thus demoted rationality to its proper status of servant, and promoted feeling to the highest rank of Master. We have humbled the pretensions of the head, appointing it premier executor of the injunctions of the heart.

We have dethroned the king – and crowned the clown.

Chapter Nineteen

Being alive, being human, feeling free, finding meaning, finding fulfillment, having fun, living in this world, loving in this world, behaving ethically, fighting the good fight against the bad guys – all of these desiderata gradually disintegrate into empty nothingness under the cold and sterilizing spotlight of rationalism. This is, more than anything, what we have been striving to demonstrate in the preceding chapters. The long-term survival of *everything that we really care about* depends directly, therefore, on a one hundred and eighty degree reversal of the much-touted and deeply entrenched ideal of intellect-over-emotion. Unless we perpetrate a truly courageous coup, ending the tyrannical reign of reason over romance (or the widespread aspiration toward the same) and installing feeling as our undisputed sovereign, there will ultimately be a diminished self, a colorless world...and no goddamn good.

The burden of the previous pages has been to lay some serious stress on a point that any reader not currently in a coma already knows as well his own name: that pretty much everything we value deeply in our lives – our dreams, our desires, our loves, our passions, our ambitions, our imaginings, our very selfhood – partakes not of the realm of the rational, but of the realm of the irrational. The really good things in life are the ones you can't justify logically, can't explain empirically, can't assess pragmatically, can't measure mathematically. Human beings (as Erasmus of Rotterdam put it) owe their existence to folly. **We live by, and for, unreason.**

I hear tell that phylacteries these days cost double what they did when I bought mine, and I can only hope the price keeps going up. Because the willingness of Jews – or any people – to spend their hard earned money buying things that afford them no rationally explicable returns, restores my faith in human nobility, and encourages me to believe that we will yet win the fight against the lethal reductionism that would strip our lives down to necessity and pleasure. Tefillin, by the way, are a bargain compared to your average thirty to fifty thousand dollar Torah scroll, which Jewish law stubbornly and indefensibly insists must be hand-calligraphed on parchment, five hundred years after Gutenberg and a millennium after the invention of paper. And if there's one thing that lifts my spirits even more than wasting money, it's wasting time: the countless hours I spend every week memorizing the complex chant melodies for the public recitation of the Torah portion, only because age-old tradition unreasonably prohibits adding musical notation to the text in the scroll – well this makes me feel like nothing less than a Hero of the Resistance, holding off the homicidal onslaught of generic, logical, utilitarian, superficial living. Try building a sukkah from scratch and then sleeping in it: now there's an activity with no practical benefits to speak of! And we've got lots more where those come from. An active Jewish life is the best antidote I know of to sensibleness and pragmatism, which together, when allowed to dominate and dictate, empty life of its best parts.

And so we come full circle, dear reader: back to Ofer's original airport allegation, which we summarized so baldly at the outset of this tirade by declaring that "Judaism is nonsense." Ofer, as we strove so mightily to show, is completely correct in this assertion. Judaism is indeed nonsense…*right up there with all the other worthwhile and wonderful things in life*. We ought to take Ofer's censure as the greatest compliment we've ever received!

Remaining or becoming an active, committed Jew in modern times – living the lifestyle, participating in the peoplehood – is not by any stretch of the imagination the rational thing to do (so we have argued). Indeed, almost everything about being Jewish today requires a conscious or subconscious *subjection of the head to the heart.* Jewish ritual and Jewish nationhood are – on the whole – a lot more bound up with feelings and goose-bumps than they are with practicality or rationality. Jewish practice and Jewish affiliation in this, our rationalist and universalist age, fly directly in the face of reason. So far from being a function of logical or pragmatic thinking, Jewishness today is both a product and a producer of *passion*. Which, as it turns out, is perfectly swell, because hey:

PASSION FOR PRESIDENT!

As luck would have it, you see, all the wild and crazy sentiments, all the poignant and powerful emotions, all the fierce and fiery feelings and yes: all the unrepentant *irrationality* that form such a major part of being Jewish – all of these drives, emphases, and enthusiasms just happen to comprise, at the very same time, the *premier characteristics of the life-force itself.* They happen to represent the wellspring of humanity and the supply closet of significance, not to mention the ultimate source of every single thing that gets us up in the morning.

Coincidence? Not hardly.

Being a connected Jew has always meant being on fire. Sometimes we simmer softly over a low flame, other times we are all but consumed by a roaring conflagration. But we always burn. How could it be otherwise? As "essentialists" *par excellence* – for whom history is a continuum and each generation imbibes thirstily from its predecessors, drinking down the bitter with the sweet – we have accumulated over the ages fuel reserves so vast they make those of Saudi Arabia look like a grease stain. Each century that elapses in our fathomless history, every event we experience, ordeal we endure, and lesson we learn, all that we have done and all that has been done to us, flows unceasingly into our oceanic and incendiary reservoir, an ever-widening, ever-deepening cache of combustible emotion emanating from generations gone by to feed our *ner tamid*, the eternal flame of Jewish Passion in the present. Our past ignites us. It adds fuel to our fire.

This cumulative stockpiling results primarily from the uniqueness of the Jewish phenomenon – a uniqueness that we discussed in earlier chapters, in connection with our "tribal" nature. Let me explain. Together with his older contemporary, J. G. Herder, George Wilhelm Friedrich Hegel constructed a theory of nations involving three stages of national development: (1) birth and maturation, (2) a great contribution to humanity, and (3) decline. Greece grew, bestowed the aesthetic and philosophical spirit upon the world, and then tumbled into the dustbin of history. Rome rose, donated to humankind its political and juridical institutions, and then faded away. And so on for the lot. Hegel's theory would have worked just fine, had it not been for those ubiquitous troublemakers, those annoying and incorrigible miscreants, the Jews, who – as usual – "messed up the row" by obstinately refusing to disappear, by continuing to flourish for centuries with no end in sight even *after* having made their "great contribution to humanity" (monotheism, according to Hegel). By such *chutzpadik* defiance of his theory, we drove Hegel to rug-chewing distraction.

Here is what Hegel, "the Father of History," did not understand. True, we Jews have unquestionably created and contributed much down the millennia. We have made books of great beauty and wisdom, offered the world sons who shone like suns and daughters who gleamed like stars to illuminate humanity's forward march, hatched ideas and evolved institutions so powerful they have changed the face of the globe. For this, few would deny us credit. But with all that, this has never been our primary focus or *raison d'être*. Rather, **our most important oeuvre has always been ourselves**. The Jewish People's preeminent masterpiece is…*the Jewish People*.

Unlike Truths, which are designed to remain fundamentally static – and have often managed to do just that over history, functioning as so many eternally immovable rocks upon which endless churches have been built – unlike such immutable ideologies and crystallized doctrines, a *people* is by nature a dynamic phenomenon, a living organism that constantly grows and evolves. A living nation – just like a living person – is an ongoing "work in progress," is an entity expanded and deepened by the endless accrual of its collective experiences, is a bringing to bear on a fleeting present of an ever-lengthening and increasingly multifaceted past. A people is unavoidably and quintessentially the cumulative product of everything it has ever been through.

And we Jews, dear reader – do you know what *we* have been through? Do you know where we have been, what we have seen, how we have dreamed, and felt, and built? The things we've known and loves we've lost and hopes we've carried in our breasts? How we have tried, and died, and striven, how we have fallen and arisen, how much we felt and fought and wrestled, how much we suffered – and created? *Do you know all this*? Not just in your head, as history – that's easy! – but in your **heart**? Does your *heart* remember and comprehend these things? Does it *feel* them? Does it internalize, identify, react, ignite…*explode*?

No, we won't start ticking off incredible and "flammable" Jewish experiences throughout history – we'd simply never finish. But at the risk of being accused of kitsch, or demagoguery, or "Holocaust Judaism," or any number of other crimes against academic detachment and blasé sophistication, I *will* offer up at some length the following passage from the conclusion of Andre Schwarz-Bart's *The Last of the Just*: read it and weep. (No, really: *weep*. The heart is a muscle like every other, requiring constant exercise and training to stay in shape. Unless we teach it to shed tears faster than a hero of a Balzac novel, our emotional and empathetic fitness goes straight to pot):

> There, under the showerheads embedded in the ceiling, in the blue light of screened bulbs glowing in recesses of the concrete walls, Jewish men and women, children and patriarchs were huddled together. His eyes still closed, Ernie felt the press of the last parcels of flesh that the SS men were clubbing into the gas chamber now, and his eyes still closed, he knew that the lights had been extinguished on the living, on the hundreds of Jewish women suddenly shrieking in terror, on the old men whose prayers rose immediately and grew stronger, on the martyred children, who were rediscovering in their last

agonies the fresh innocence of yesteryear's agonies in a chorus of identical exclamations: "*Mama*! *But I was a good boy*! *It's dark*! *It's dark*!" And when the first waves of Cyclon B gas billowed among the sweating bodies, drifting down toward the squirming carpet of children's heads, Ernie freed himself from the girl's mute embrace and leaned out into the darkness toward the children, invisible even at his knees, and he shouted with all the gentleness and all the strength of his soul, "Breathe deeply, my lambs, and quickly!"

When the layers of gas had covered everything, there was silence in the dark sky of the room for perhaps a minute, broken only by shrill, racking coughs and the gasps of those too far gone in their agonies to offer a devotion. And first a stream, then a cascade, an irrepressible, majestic torrent, the poem that through the smoke of fires and above the funeral pyres of history the Jews had traced in letters of blood on the earth's hard crust – that old love poem unfurled in the gas chamber, enveloped it, vanquished its somber, abysmal snickering: "SHEMA YISRAEL ADONAI ELOHENU ADONAI ECHAD... Hear, O Israel, the Lord our God, the Lord is One. O Lord, by your grace you nourish the living, and by your great pity you resurrect the dead, and you uphold the weak, cure the sick, break the chains of slaves. And faithfully you keep your promises to those who sleep in the dust. Who is like unto you, O merciful Father, and who could be like unto you...?"

The voices died one by one in the course of the unfinished poem. The dying children had already dug their nails into Ernie's thighs, and Golda's embrace was already weaker, her kisses were blurred when, clinging fiercely to her beloved's neck, she exhaled a harsh sigh: "Then I'll never see you again? Never again?"

Ernie managed to spit up the needle of fire jabbing at his throat, and as the woman's body slumped against him, its eyes wide in the opaque night, he shouted against the unconscious Golda's ear, "In a little while, I *swear it*!" And then he knew that he could do nothing more for anyone in the world, and in the flash that preceded his own annihilation he remembered, happily, the legend of Rabbi Chanina ben Teradyon, as Mordecai had joyfully recited it: "When the gentle rabbi, wrapped in the scrolls of the Torah, was flung upon the pyre by the Romans for having taught the Law, and when they lit the fagots, the branches still green to make his torture last, his pupils said, 'Master, what do you see?' And Rabbi Chanina answered, 'I see the parchment burning, but the letters are taking wing…'" "*Ah, yes, surely the letters are taking wing,*" Ernie repeated as the flame blazing in his chest rose suddenly to his head.

With dying arms he embraced Golda's body in an already unconscious gesture of loving protection, and they were found that way half an hour later by the team of *Sonderkommando* responsible for burning the Jews in the crematory ovens. And so it was for millions, who turned from *Luftmenschen* into *Luft*. I shall not translate. So this story will not finish with some tomb to be visited in memoriam. For the smoke that rises from crematoriums obeys physical laws like any other: the particles come together and disperse according to the wind that propels them. The only pilgrimage, estimable reader, would be to look with sadness at a stormy sky now and then.

And praised. *Auschwitz.* Be. *Maidanek.* The Lord. *Treblinka.* And praised. *Buchenwald.* Be. *Mauthausen.* The Lord. *Belzec.* And Praised. *Sobibor.* Be. *Chelmno.* The Lord. *Ponary.* And praised. *Theresienstadt.* Be. *Warsaw.* The Lord. *Vilna.* And praised. *Skarzysko.* Be. *Bergen-Belsen.* The Lord. *Janow.* And praised. *Dora.* Be. *Neuengamme.* The Lord. *Pustkow.* And praised…

Take a few moments, dear reader, to recover from *that.* (Better yet: take an entire lifetime *not* to recover from it.) And then remind yourself: that's *us* he's writing about. This happened to *us.* Elie Weisel once argued, in a book called *Legends of Our Time,* that if anyone were ever to gain so much as a minuscule glimpse of genuine understanding of what actually happened to our people over there in the concentration camps of Europe during World War Two – then such a person should go completely insane, and never come back. Now: take all of the deep and dark, all of the beautiful and powerful, all of the terrible and ineffable emotional elements in the lines of Schwarz-Bart's words, above; take everything they do to you and everything they evoke in you and every visceral chord they strike in your soul; take all this and *multiply it ten thousand times*. Multiply it by the myriad adventures and odysseys, triumphs and tragedies, nightmares and dreams, hatreds and loves that, because we're a *people* – and not merely class after class of pupils passing through a school of static Truth – *each and every one of us essentially experienced*, as part of that living, growing, beaten whole: *Am Yisrael*, the organically contiguous Nation of Israel. Multiply the feelings elicited by Schwartz-Bart's excerpt exponentially, and you begin to understand why the involved Jewish heart is permanently and inextinguishably ablaze; why we suffer from a deep-seeded (indeed, a codified) collective manic-depression; and why we Jews will never be appropriate candidates for "inner peace" seminars. The poignancy and power of all that we have been through – as a nation unique among the nations of the world, as a people whose temporal reach is almost as long as history itself – means that we cannot but burn brightly and fiercely. It means that *we are a passionate people*. It means that our motivations, when they are genuinely Jewish, emanate far more from our warm and throbbing hearts than from our cold and calculating cerebrums. Sure, Jews may be smart – but they simply *must* be irrational. Aware of it or not, committed members of our tribe live lives animated first and foremost…by romance.

But being Jewish not only *entails* being irrational – it is also specifically and designedly *about* being irrational, or better yet: it is about designating the rational as draft-horse, and the irrational as droshky driver, the rational as Vizier, the irrational as Sultan. You may remember that way back at the beginning we attempted to demonstrate that the rabbis of the Talmud used rationality merely *as a tool* through which to achieve objectives that were – in the majority of cases – highly irrational. We made much fun of the rabbis on that score, yes we did, and meanwhile all the time *it was they who had the ratio right*, they who were tuned in and turned on to what makes all of us truly human: **rationality in the service of irrationality**. Rabbinic methodology, in the end, is none other than the very methodology of life itself.

And this, by the way, reminds us of the single greatest offense committed by scholastic apologia, the one we let slide back in our polemical tirade of chapter three. We Jews, you see, were once upon a time plugged in and logged on to The Power – not exclusively, mind you, but we certainly had some major bandwidth – we were hooked up to the juice that makes everything go, we were nourished by the very gravity that counteracts inertia, that reanimates dead logic and makes life wonderful and miraculous: the propelling force of the immeasurable, the unpredictable, the nonsensical and the romantic, the proper proportion and hierarchy between intellect and emotion. We possessed that priceless treasure, oh yes we did, and praise the Lord we still possess it, but no thanks to the purportedly pious apologists, who strove and still strive so relentlessly to take it from us, by cutting our cords to the irrational. The beating Jewish heart will always vanquish them, for they bow to a false messiah – Truth – and to a foreign god – Euclid – the cult of both of which represents the very *definition* of idolatry in Judeo-classical sources: worshipping and surrendering to the eminently powerless.

The Schoolmen taught: Strive to be perfect, as the Lord your God is perfect. Before classical rationalism showed up and corrupted it, however, the Jewish outlook could be read as essentially the opposite of this: strive to be *imperfect*, as the Lord your God is *imperfect*. By creating us in His own fully fallible image, the Deity of the Bible granted human beings the greatest and most unique gift in the entire universe: "the privilege of absurdity," the ability to rise above or fall below or simply ignore the rigid rules of mathematical symmetry, and do the most illogical things imaginable if we so desired. We are children of the Lord our God: just as He is jealous and zealous, loving and hating, incomprehensible and incorrigible (or was, before all the Hellenized PR guys and apologetic image-makers got to Him); just as He is emotional and impulsive and gets things wrong and even loses; just as He is neither omniscient nor omnipotent, neither a flawless robot nor an errorless computer – so we, too, dear reader. We have been granted the right to do wrong. Rejoice! Our Creator has been kind enough to share with us the *divine privilege par excellence*, the privilege of **imperfection**, which is nothing less than the privilege of life and liberty. Over our dead bodies will the apologists take this from us!

But the talmudic subjection of rationality to irrationality is not limited to the legal realm of fleshing out heavenly commandments. The taming of reason and harnessing of truth, the manipulation of the real in the service of the ideal – this tendency has flourished most widely as part of a more general phenomenon: the rabbinic methodological magic known as *Midrash*.

Permit me to illustrate. It is a soft summer's afternoon in the land of Canaan, some four thousand years ago, and an unprepossessing pavilion of goat's hair forms the sole expression of verticality on the otherwise desolate Negev flats. A rustling is heard, a flap is thrown up, and our dashing forefather Isaac emerges from his tent to take a little fresh air. He is a comely cloud-gazer this one, a shepherd from earliest youth, and no stranger to the desert vastnesses. His long, curly locks sweep playfully across his broad shoulders, and his tunic – made from the skin of the lion he caught harassing his sheep last month – is draped just so, nonchalantly, over the lithe muscles and tanned skin of his imposing form. He stretches, saunters, sits down on a rock and lights a fire. A tinge of troubadourian melancholy washes through his voice as he sings a song of shifting sands, while raising his eyes heavenward and skillfully strumming his oud.

Just at that moment, his father Abraham's servant Eliezer rides over a nearby ridge, accompanied by a pretty young damsel all decked out in spangles and silk and seated on the camel next to his. Throughout the entire journey, our nubile foremother Rebecca has been wondering, imagining, hoping and mostly fearing: what would he be like, this desert man she was to spend the rest of her days and nights with? Would he resemble the hard and coarse Bedouin she had often seen as a girl, riding through her hometown of Haran to procure some necessities, grunting and spitting and speaking only of their wares? Would he be bent and deformed by the arduousness of his nomadic existence, shriveled by the hot sun, perhaps gnome-like, or one-eyed, or bald? Thus had she wracked her mind in tearful suspense throughout the seemingly endless southward trek. Now, as they crest the hill and she espies this fine figure of a man with the full head of cascading hair and the well-fitting lion-skin tunic, strong and handsome and serenading the open spaces with a voice full of pathos that could melt the very stone of the mountains, Rebecca's heart leaps within her, and she falls – not only in love at first sight – but *directly off her camel* in a rapturous swoon.

Wow – what a scene! What an image! What passion, what ardor, what romance! Rebecca was so blown away by her husband-to-be that she actually plummeted straightaway off the hump of her dromedary, landing splat in the hot sand below. *Amazing*! Countless generations of Jews have woven fantasies around this dramatic first encounter between our second matriarch and patriarch. Stimulation and speculation, imagination and fascination, warmth and sweetness and not a little *amour* have accompanied this anecdote down through the centuries, wherever folks have read or retold it.

Imagine my surprise, then, when one day I was perusing a scholarly English translation of the Bible, and came upon the following:

> And Isaac went out to meditate in the field at eventide; and he lifted up his eyes, and behold, there were camels coming. And Rebecca lifted up her eyes, and when she saw Isaac, she descended from the camel.

What? *Excuse me*?

> And she said unto the servant: "What man is this that walketh in the field to meet us?" And the servant replied: "It is my master." And she took her veil and covered herself.

My righteous indignation knew no bounds. What kind of impious claptrap was this? I sought out other translations: "And she alighted from the camel," "and she dismounted from the camel," "and she climbed down off the camel." A veritable conspiracy!

A little investigation turned up the source of the rank heresy which sought to dash all my dreams to pieces. The original Hebrew verb describing Rebecca's reaction upon seeing Isaac is *va-tipol*, which in biblical parlance could denote either "and she fell" or "and she got down" – in the latter case replacing an accidental with a deliberate act (as in "to fall on your face," which in the Bible means to bow prostrate). Add to this semantic latitude the fact that – according to the order of the verses – our bonnie lass did not yet know that the singer she saw was her intended when she *tipol*ed; that in the ancient Near East it was the widespread custom to dismount in honor of a personage approaching from the opposite direction; and that after you fall off a camel you do not so much proceed to ask courteous questions and cover yourself with a veil as you do go directly to the nearest emergency room – all of this taken together makes the possibility that Rebecca actually pitched sideways and plunged headlong to the earth rather remote. The text in context really couldn't mean that. Indeed, many of the great medieval commentators insist that our modest foremother did little more than politely nod her head on that occasion. The translators were right – and I was absolutely miserable.

Where, then, did I get my admittedly somewhat Hollywoodish take on this whole affair in the first place? That's easy: the notion that Rebecca actually *fell* from her mount when she first saw Isaac was brought to us a couple thousand years ago by what is known as the Midrash. "Midrash" is a general term for a vast body of literature written in talmudic and medieval times (and in a certain sense still being written) that evinces a singular approach to the Book of Books – an approach that, in truth, informs most all rabbinic endeavor, legal, legendary, or otherwise. Midrash is as bold and creative a method of textual exegesis as one is likely to come by, the more so given the target of its interpretive salvos: none other than the explicit Word of God Himself. Daring to dismiss divine "authorial intent" with the wave of a hand and taking scandalous liberties with the content of sacred scripture, Midrash grabs hold of the supposedly black-on-white, hard and fast, hallowed and immutable phraseology of the Bible, and turns it into psychedelic silly-putty. Just as the miraculous manna in the wilderness tasted (according to the Midrash) like whatever the Israelite eater was craving at the moment, so the same sentences in the Bible were flavored by the rabbis with a hundred and one different and even contradictory meanings, each in accordance with what a particular interpreter sought to convey at a given time. "Seventy faces hath the Torah," was the brash midrashic motto: *choose your point of view*! This is ultimately, I think, what old Ben Bag-Bag had in mind when (if you will recall) he exhorted his listeners regarding the Torah: "Turn it over, and turn it over again, for *everything* is contained in it" (Avot 5:25).

Everything is contained in the Torah, you see…*because* we turn it over and over again! Because we gaze at it from an infinite number of possible and impossible angles, because we "find" ever new ideas and institutions in it, because (let us not mince words) we *put* those ideas and institutions in there, generation after generation. The Torah testifies about itself: "It is no empty thing for you; for it is your life…" (Deuteronomy 32:47). By a slight punctuation alteration, the Midrash amplifies this point: "If it is an empty thing – it is because of *you*." It is because *you* did not actively and aggressively *fill* it. The Book becomes the object, the maker of Midrash the subject, and the ancient scriptural stories clay to be molded into endlessly diverse shapes at will. The "*pshat*" or literal meaning of the text becomes little more than a launch-pad for the "*drash*" or intrepid midrashic exposition, which is liable to blast off to the furthest reaches of anywhere. In the fluid and fantastic world of Midrash, trees become scholars, stars become candles, tears become exiles, the Deity dons phylacteries, and Canaanite grapes grow to the size of bowling balls. Holy writ in midrashic mode functions as the almost-anything-goes playground of the talmudic rabbis (albeit with purposes often serious enough) and the slightest linguistic ambivalence is seized upon as an excuse to weave wild and enchanting narratives *ex nihilo*. Did the text state that Pharaoh's daughter sent her "*amah*" to fetch the baby Moses out of the Nile, employing a Hebrew homonym that denotes not only "handmaiden" but also "arm"? Then the princess' upper appendage veritably shot out of its socket, extending fifty feet long like a giant eel in order to snatch the future prophet from his basket. Does the verse in Exodus depicting the second plague declare that the "*tzefardeah*" came up and covered the land, utilizing the singular for "frog" to indicate the entire species? Then no: we actually have to do with *one gargantuan, Godzilla-take-a-back-seat frog* whose country-size torso blocked out the entire Egyptian heavens from horizon to horizon. Did the newly manumitted Israelites stand "*betachtit*" Mt. Sinai, a usage signifying "at the foot of" but derived from the root *tachat* meaning "under"? Then the Lord no less than *lifted up the entire mountain* and held it dangling over the heads of the Hebrews there encamped: "If you accept My Torah, well and good; if not – I drop the mountain."

Now, it's not that our rabbis of blessed memory were unaware of the *pshat* – the literal meaning of the pentateuchal passages in question. They were aware and how. It's just that at the time of *drash* or interpretation, they had a totally different agenda to push. They had points to make and lessons to teach and stories to tell and ideas to impart, and they unabashedly took the canonical text and bent it to their will and all out of shape in order to achieve those ends.

Midrash, however, is not just a hermeneutical device for use in scriptural studies. It represents an all-encompassing attitude and worldview, as well. Remember Seinfeld? Now, the intelligent viewer is well aware that he has to do – *literally speaking* – with a cathode ray and a whole bunch of phosphorescent points on a grid, but he *chooses* to allow these comparatively prosaic elements to be something else, to be something more, something meaningful and enjoyable to *him*. He elects to employ the scientific *pshat* as a base for the unscientific *drash*, to exploit the technical mechanism for the sake of the non-technical goal: *the fun of watching the show*. Each of the two possible perspectives offers a "reality" of its own: the literal or rational for discovering *how* to do things (the inner workings of a TV), and the interpretive or irrational for discovering *why* to do them (that's entertainment!).

Similarly, we are all pretty well aware of the *pshat* or the "literal reading" of the universe around us – the scientific analyses of (say) particle physics, which atomize and demystify everything in existence – but we *choose* to maintain that world as an object for our subject, we *choose* to enthrone our own relatively "romantic" view of ourselves and of our environment, and we do so despite all the logically irrefutable evidence and rationally persuasive arguments to the contrary. Is this "tender-mindedness"? Perhaps. Is it errant? If so, then it is *knight* errantry. Is it Midrash? You betcha.

Like all people everywhere who wish to live a meaningful existence, the Jew *darshens* the world (which term, if it please, is a Yiddishized verbal form meaning "to do Midrash to"). The Jew aggressively interprets his current surroundings and his historical experience with a prejudicial purpose in mind: to inject them with significance, and to fight with all his might against the constantly encroaching hollowness of realism. The world is the Jew's text, and the ways of "Judaism" his Midrash on that text. And to the extent to which this interventionist attitude is institutionalized in Jewish thought and practice, it is indeed rather unique. For unlike the Greek philosophical, Eastern mystical, and modern scientific approaches, Jewish tradition is less desirous of *analyzing* and *deciphering* existence, than it is of *fantasizing*, *manipulating*, and *reinventing* existence; we are not so much interested in *understanding* the universe, as we are in *taking*, *shaking*, and *making* the universe into what we want it to be, into what we think it *should* be. This is the wellspring of what has always been known far and wide as Jewish *chutzpah*. It is why we make such good revolutionaries. It consists of the Kantian (if not the Berkeleyan) subjection of "what is" to "what ought to be." It consists of the emotions telling the intellect: "that's a really interesting discovery, sweetheart – now run along and play!" It consists of the defiantly irrational life-force baring its teeth and activating its survival instinct in the face of the relentless rational attempt to sap its sap.

Remember the New Testament's take on rain? How it comes pouring down equally upon the righteous and the wicked? Well, would anybody deny that – scientifically speaking – that assessment is one hundred percent on the button? Of course it is. Jesus was just being rational. But here's the problem: rational rain is also morally meaningless rain. And so we Jews up and *darshened* it ("hylozoically," so to speak): we made the rain come alive, and rendered it ethically relevant – as we did and still do with the rest of the cosmos – creating the weather in our own image and endowing it with all those quirky human traits of irregularity and preference, just as this was once done for us. Just as God (according to one Midrash) "hurled truth to the ground" in order to create man, so we, too, laid the literal meteorological reality aside and whipped up a wet and wild fantasy of conditional irrigation – in order to create meaning.

Does righteous rain represent the "fact" of the matter? Well, the fact of the matter is *that we don't really care all that much* – anymore than the Midrash gave two hoots whether Rebecca "really" fell off that camel. That's not to say that the empirical mechanism of, and explanation for, rainfall (the meteorological *pshat*) is of no interest to us. One of my students is a particularly pious air force pilot who has nevertheless been involved in frenetic cloud-seeding all this past month (to no avail, I'm afraid – the Sea of Galilee currently remains at rock bottom). Precipitation technology is just terrific on the literal level. But when we are in midrashic mode, well: the "truth" of the matter just doesn't matter, and rain exists on a different plain. The midrashic outlook on the world privileges an alternate – a less "logical" and less "reasonable" – vantage point. It leaves science to the scientists (among whose ranks we Israelites are quite satisfactorily represented anyway, thank you!).

As should be clear from all that has been said so far, the Jews have no monopoly on this outlook. Most people in most places at most times have looked at life through such irrational, "midrashic" glasses, and have thus furnished their existences with meaning and their hearts with happiness. It was the Jewish People, however, who more than anyone else turned this resistance to the ramifications of rationality and this cultivation of invigorating *ir*rationality into a bona fide, codified, national pastime. Jewish perspectives on the world – and activity *in* the world – are designed more than anything to struggle against the logical, against the cynical, against the cold and meaningless conception of life that so easily creeps up and snatches our souls from us. While most strands of Eastern religion and Western philosophy – and *all* strands of modern science – have always been busy striving to figure out and array before us "what is *really* going on" (and in many cases – from Hinduism to Taoism to the Stoics to Spinoza – preaching passive acceptance of and/or ecstatic merging with that same inexorable reality), Jewish tradition has devoted most of *its* energy in the opposite direction: toward a deliberate and ongoing *idealization* of, even confrontation with, existence, toward an active re-envisioning of, and *interference* with, the workings of the world. **We are an unrealistic people.** If the Buddhists seek to awaken from their dream, we Jews seek to dream while awake, with eyes wide open: to dream the dream of life as it should be, of meaning and romance and falling off camels. We will it (as Herzl would say) – and it is no longer a dream.

We Jews (I say again) are a family, and "Judaism" – that is, the process of aggressively *darshening* the world with the help of traditional law and lore – is our quintessential family business: the way we manipulate our environment to turn a *bissele* profit. The way we inject meaning into nihil and cosmos into chaos. The way we have found to make life worth something – worth everything. It takes a boat-load of impressive logic to discover the *pshat*, to see things as they "really" are; it takes a freight-train of fearless feeling to superimpose the *drash* on that *pshat*, to see things as they could be, should be, ought to be. We Jews allow our emotions to color our environment. And the greatest emotion by far is love, and love (as we were reminded by the movie *Shallow Hal*) paints even the plainest things beautiful.

Every Jewish story we tell and pentateuchal rite we perform – on top of its specific and individual significance – is a blow struck for the forces of irrationality and impracticality (Ofer asserted this long before I did, and he was right). Blowing a *shofar*, waving a *lulav*, lighting Hannukah candles, singing Sabbath songs, wearing *tzitzit*, masquerading on Purim, casting bread-crumbs on Rosh HaShanah, fasting on Yom Kippur, sleeping on the floor on Tish'a BeAv, hugging a tree on Tu Bishvat, lighting a bonfire on Lag BaOmer, studying all night on Shavuot, sanctifying the moon, blessing a rainbow, not wearing linsey-woolsey, getting married under a *chupa*, pronouncing benedictions over various enjoyments, learning Torah, engaging in prayer, circumcising, reciting *kiddush*, eating bitter herbs – these and a whole slew of other uniquely Jewish acts of commission and omission (if done up right, with maximum enthusiasm) are some of the best ways to make the world a less rational and more romantic place to be. These observances and performances take the texture of existence and rewrite it for us midrashically.

But such ceremonial strikes for irrational idealism would indeed mean little, were they not all reflections of and conduits toward the single most powerful and significant form of irrationality known to humankind: love. Preferential love, that is. Love of self, love of family, love of clan, love of nation. *Kinship*.

You see, if **love is a better motivation than Truth** (this book's thesis in seven words), then – all other things being equal – tribal ties are *indeed* a better basis for affinity and solidarity than common faith or ideology. Here's a syllogism for you: if (1) passion ought to rule the world, and (2) love is the prince of passion, and (3) preference is the lord of love, then (4) preferential love ought to rule the world, and nothing on earth or in heaven ought to be more sacred in our eyes than those we love the most. Vladimir Jabotinsky was not one to mince words. When a reporter once asked him if he believed in God, he replied curtly: "My God is the Jewish People."

I, too, love the Jews. Love 'em something fierce. Tried meditation, hypnotism, reflexology, tai-chi – nothing helps. I'm a basket case. And since love is the world's greatest all-time motivation, I am proud to proclaim that more than for any other reason, I personally perform "irrational" Israelite ritual and stuff my life silly with Jewish law and lore, because it brings me closer to the folks I love, binds me to them throughout all their generations and habitations, resurrects them for me and lets me clasp them in my arms. Like so many of my crazy fellow Jews, I live an eminently "impractical" life – chock full of every weird and wacky observance from Sabbath dinners and synagogue services to *sukkah* building and torture *tefillin*. These things I do not just because I have found them to comprise an incomparably stimulating and enjoyable lifestyle in themselves (and I have). These things I do, more than for any other reason, because *I love my people so incredibly damn much that I want them to be around forever.*

Yes, I want the Jews to be around forever, and I know that "more than Israel has kept the Sabbath, the Sabbath has kept Israel." I know that "as long as she fulfills the commandments, Israel will never die." I know that the Torah and its prescriptions constitute the single greatest national survival blueprint history has ever seen. (The early twentieth-century Russian-French philosopher Nicholas Berdyaev once commented that "the continued existence of Jewry down the centuries is **rationally inexplicable**." He hit the nail on the head: what accounts for this continued existence is specifically our endless and pertinacious insistence on the *ir*rational.) However one prefers to look at it – metaphysically or sociologically – it cannot be denied that Jewish observance has managed to instill an immediate, coherent, distinct and powerful cultural identity in generation after generation of Jews, allowing us to stick around as a nation for three millennia and counting. You gotta love it!

And I confess: I do. I love irrational Jewish ritual – the more irrational, the better. Out there in those Judean mountains six months ago, climbing down that cliff at sunset with the fellas to fetch that notorious "now it's kosher, now it's not" magic matzah baking water, the hills of Eretz Israel fading off into the distance like so many pregnant ladies tanning by the day's last rays, and that sublime sense of sweet sadness and indescribable *déjà vu* that comes from somewhere so deep inside you it feels like it preceded your birth, a warmth and a wonder and a love so overwhelming...as if all...as if you...well. Let's just say that I'll be diving in again this coming Passover.

So: Jabotinsky loved the Jews, and Ben-Gurion loved the Jews, and Herzl loved the Jews, and I love the Jews, and that's the main reason I am here in the Middle East doing as many *mitzvahs* as I can in the Jewish State that they were kind enough to create. How about you, dear reader? Have we convinced *you* to love the Jews, too? Have our pages upon pages of philosophical pleading – all those claims and contentions and anecdotes and illustrations – have they helped you to make up your mind to enlist in the hoary Hebrew brigade? Have we argued our case well enough to persuade you to throw in your lot with us, to mull matzahs, make *hamantaschen*, marry within the fold, move to Israel, multiply your *mitzvahs* by the fourteenth power? Well: *have we*? Jeez – I sure hope not.

You see, had you been convinced by our piling up of arguments to identify and involve yourself with the Jewish People, then those same arguments would have failed miserably. For in the end, this whole long polemic has striven to establish one point above all else: *how ineffective such polemics should be*. Sound paradoxical? It isn't. We've been arguing for giving feelings an exclusive in the matter of motivation, and we've also been arguing that the Jewish phenomenon in history and today is not primarily a religion or an ideology, but an affection-based tribal affinity. Add up and superimpose these two assertions, and it ought to become rapidly clear that in this writer's mind, at least, being a Jew is not so much an idealistic act as it is an *emotional state*: the state of loving your extended national clan like the dickens. And there's nothing I could ever write that would "convince" you to do that. Love doesn't arise out of conviction. Neither philosophies nor arguments nor "isms" nor truths can genuinely motivate. Only emotion can motivate: and you can't learn to feel a particular emotion from a book (although it can conceivably throw some logs on your fire). You may find the claims I have made to date compelling, or you may find them spurious – I am frankly not always sure myself which they are. But no matter how well I would have argued the case for "Judaism" in these pages, if it were just about the cogency of the particular claims put forth, then tomorrow a smarter guy than me would write a *more* persuasive plea for the moral and intellectual virtues of Hinduism, and you'd be asking me to buy a psychedelic book in an airport. Intellectual arguments do not (and should not) carry the day. *We don't love our families because we were convinced by intellectual arguments to do so.*

If in your heart of hearts you genuinely don't give a flying farthing about the Jews; if they mean as much to you as the Malaysians or the Mormons or the Aztecs or the French; if you feel no special connection, if you can honestly say that there is no privileged place in your heart reserved for this specific bunch that you happen to hail from and belong to; then believe me, neither this book nor any other will change that one iota.

Luckily, however, the fact that you've read this far would seem to indicate that you *do* have a unique emotional and clannish connection to the Jewish People; that you *do* feel inside that you are a Jew and that the Jews are your kith and kin; and that this aspect of your identity is highly significant to you. All this book has attempted to do is clear away some of the more obnoxious modern and post-modern ideological obstacles that so often prevent such feelings from blazing forth in all their heartwarming glory. We have endeavored to plug up that canister of "truth spray" – all those accumulated piles of rationally inspired principles subsumed under slogans like "use your head and not your heart" and "love everybody equally," which weaken the gravitational pull of passion – in order to legitimate the contemporary Jew's *indulgence* of the gravitational forces of irrational romance and preferential love that attract him to his people. **Go ahead, man: love away!**

One more thing in this connection, and it's important. We all know what a major beating the notion of "love of nation" has taken in the wake of the ostensible emotionalism of the twentieth-century fascist movements. How can we respond to those who would wield the horrors of World War II as a club with which to beat down nationalism? What shall we say to those who have the nerve to use the example of the Nazi extermination of six million Jews to argue now that the Jewish People should disband?

We shall say two related things to them. First, that we have tried our best in pages past to demonstrate that – despite appearances and conventional wisdom to the contrary – Nazism and its various counterparts on the right and left were *anything but* genuinely "emotional" movements. They were, as we said, the very opposite: sophisticated frameworks for taming and controlling human feeling, for diluting, directing and thereby ultimately *withering* the emotions. To be fooled by the rhythmic chants and collective catharsis of a National Socialist rally into believing that here we have thousands of people giving free reign to their individual feelings and following the genuine dictates of their fiery hearts – is to be fooled badly indeed. Those rallies rather represent manipulated, mass-produced pseudo-sentiment whipped up in the name of a particular *principle* (Aryan Supremacy, The Jews are our Misfortune, etc.). They are a drug-induced, herd-like bleating of elation and euphoria – growing out of emotional *equanimity* – at having *crushed* one's individual feelings and *surrendered* one's personal inclinations at the feet of the all-powerful overlord of a given Authority or Truth. There is nothing romantic or emotional about any of this (at least not in the sense that we have been consistently defining these adjectives here).

Well, then: what is the difference between German nationalism and Jewish nationalism on this score? May not the same accusations be leveled at us? Has not our historical togetherness involved the same subjection of sentiment to principle? I hope you will remember my hard-earned anti-apologetic credentials and give me the benefit of the doubt when I declare: *absolutely not.*

We strove to show earlier in this chapter that the Jews are "essentialists" *par excellence*, that we form an organic continuum across centuries and continents, that – in a word – *we have hung out with each other for a very long time*. We have perceived ourselves as an *am*, as a nation, as a commonly descended family and naturally knitted tribal unit for as far back as anyone can remember. This much cannot be disputed.

German, as all European nationalism, is, on the other hand, a relatively recent phenomenon. Many of these movements were not so much inspired by as they did *create* the national entities on behalf of which they proceeded to labor. Modern nationalism is one part nation, two parts "ism": one third genuine filial feeling based on common historical interrelationship or experience, two thirds *the theoretical principle* which defines and consolidates this heretofore amorphous collective entity. When you barely have a nation, you need a whole lot of "ism." When, on the other hand, you are a well-defined tribal grouping going back almost four thousand years, a grouping that never for an instant throughout all that time had the slightest doubt about its familial relationship and communal solidarity and responsibility – when, in short, you've got a nation and how – you needn't take "isms" too seriously.

Does the Goldblatt family have any use whatsoever for "Goldblattism," or for "familyism"? Do they need such ideologies as *raisons d'être* in order to keep them together? Does *your* family? Well, neither do the Jews. We have been a nation since the Bible, and our sense of nation*hood* has grown stronger with every era that we experienced and endured together down the centuries. By the modern period we were indubitably *three parts nation* – no "ism" required, thank you. ("Zionism" was a necessary neologism: we needed two parts "ism" to make up for the zero parts Zion we were working with at the time.) While German and European nationalism is still largely an ideology, then – barely holding its own at this writing against the onslaught of more "universalist" ideologies – traditional Jewish identity and group feeling certainly is not. *We're just us.*

Why is this important? Because isms and Truths are not just unhealthy for feelings – they also have another bad habit: the creation of an intrinsic intolerance and inevitable sense of superiority. If

Islam is right, then all other systems are wrong (or at least less right). The same goes, perforce, for doctrines, philosophies, and scientific conclusions of all shapes and sizes (including "Judaism"): if they are correct – and their adherents generally believe them to be so – then most if not all of the others are in error (this is true even for Protagoras: if he is right about there being many coexistent truths, then those who believe in only *one* truth are clearly wrong). In turn, this knowledge of one's own indubitable "correctness" naturally leads those who are possessed of it to view themselves as superior, and often sanctions, encourages and even *requires* them to impose their doctrines to the furthest ends of the earth. This is *Jihad.* It is also Imperialism, Communism, Nazism and lots of other nastiness.

But families are not like ism-based groups in this matter. Because while Truths must necessarily vie with one another for King of the Mat (for that is the nature of Truths), emotions – and especially the lion-king of all emotions, love – can pretty much live and let live. I hope, dear reader, that you love your family a lot, but if you do, this certainly in no way precludes or diminishes anyone else's affections for *their* family, does it? You and I *can't* both be right about the truth, but we *can* both love our spouses and our children. No family's sentiments of affection-based solidarity are in any way more "correct" than those of any other's (we ventured earlier that in the matter of emotions, not even God can claim superiority). And even if while growing up, many of us were convinced that our parents were "the best parents in the world," we never really meant to imply by this the existence of some rigorous absolute standard, according to which other kids' parents couldn't be "the best in the world" too. *Love is the greatest pluralism.*

I'm nuts about my family the Jews. This doesn't require in any way that Jews represent some master race in my mind or have the corner on the truth market (even way back in the Bible, on the occasions when the Hebrews evinced that monotheistic intolerance of which we basically own the copyright, we did so solely within the confines of our own home. Our beliefs were never really universal "categorical imperatives" in our eyes). Sure: at times I am overcome by this wave of – you know – "we're the best!" But this in no way leads me to begrudge other national communities the same powerful affections for and fierce pride in their own people. Why would it? It's no skin off my back. It doesn't diminish *my* sentiments in any way. *Love and let love.*

If German nationalism had evinced any of *these* characteristics, believe me: there would have *been* no World War II. So please: let's hear no more of this "emotionalism leads to fascism" rubbish. For there is no greater antidote or preventive medicine for fascism than the cultivation and preservation of genuine emotion.

There is another not-so-fringe benefit of our "natural," kinship-based nationhood. Two Jews, three opinions – twelve million Jews, a googolplex opinions, and a people that is almost irremediably factionalized these days. This bodes ill for us. The Jews can continue to be a people (a goal the merit of which we strove to show throughout this book) based on one criterion only: unconditional, family-type love. We Jews will never agree with one another, but hey: neither do most siblings or married couples. Rather than focus all our energy on trying to win each other over to a unified outlook on theology or the world – a mission beyond impossible – we Jews must re-emphasize our tribal affinity, and demote our ideological predilections to their proper status. Only thus will we continue to have the privilege of truly reflecting Theodor Herzl's declaration: "We are a people, one people." Only then will we be assured of staying together forever.

(Let me just stop here and say this: you may have formed the impression by this point in our travels that all I have been doing in this book is simplistically and superficially piling up almost every philosophy, mysticism, science, ideology, political system and religion anywhere in existence [including "Judaism"] on one side of the scale; throwing genuine, preferential, all-too-human love by itself alone on the other side; and rashly proceeding to declare that *omnia vincit amor* – love conquers all. If that is your impression of my overall argument, then you have hammered the nail directly on the head: that is *exactly* what I have been doing.)

The Jews are a family, and as we said before: bewitching the world through Torah and *mitzvoth* (commandments) is our number one family business. Not everybody in the family excels at the business.

Even those who go through all the proper motions sometimes make no profit. Magic can become routine like anything else after a long enough while, and once ideals are structured and charisma is classicized, the stuff of dreams can become as practical, as boring and as insignificant as balancing your checkbook. The Jewish challenge – and, I would insist, the human challenge, the human *imperative* – is to do everything in one's power to avoid such an eventuality, to sustain awe and cultivate passion, to feel fiercely and imagine like mad. Our lives are not empty, unless we fail to fill them; our experiences are not neutral, unless we neglect to charge them; our world is not profane, unless we cease to sanctify it, unless we allow it to deteriorate into apathy, into habit and inertia. "Do not make your prayer routine," enjoined the rabbis. Do not make anything routine.

But there are other – and certainly better – reasons why many members of our family today do not exactly shine at certain aspects of the family enterprise. You see, it's all well and good to celebrate the irrational by participating in discourse and ceremony that is meta-sensible. Bringing logic to heel by employing it in the service of matzah-baking is – at least to my mind – a meritorious act in more ways than one, and humiliating reason by refraining from cheeseburgers is totally OK by me (difficult, but OK). Cheeseburgers, however, have no feelings, and neither do their leaven-laden buns. Dietary law and Passover restrictions injure no one.

But not every Jewish injunction is so easily swallowed. Laws against homosexuality (for instance) are another matter. Or the restrictions put upon women. Or the predicament of a *momzer* – a child of an incestuous or adulterous union – who suffers through no fault of his own. Here people's *selves* are involved: their feelings, freedom, lives, loves. It's not that simple anymore. What can we do, then, if and when some of the by-laws of our family business wreak major havoc with our consciences?

That's a tough one. I'd try to wiggle out of it, or change the subject (How 'bout those Mets?), but that would make me exactly the creature I railed against early on: the ugly apologist. There are those Jews who can gloss over such problems, who can ignore them or explain them away or deny their existence altogether, and thereby preserve traditional theology intact. There are those Jews, at the other end of the spectrum, for whom the presence of such unpalatable prescriptions undermines the very foundations of traditional theology, and leads them to abandon or ignore everything Jewish. If you belong to either of these categories, dear reader, then I wish you Godspeed and *Gesundheit* – for I have little if anything to offer you. You have either found or lost the Truth, and developed your servile or inimical relationship to "Judaism" accordingly. There is a third group, however, to which I myself am proud to belong, and I would imagine I'm far from alone. That is the group of those for whom – whether they admit it out loud or not – **love supersedes Truth**, and for whom, therefore, the state of Judaic theology and our personal attitude to it is (get out your smelling salts) *of lesser importance* than our emotional bond to our national family. Such Jews are searching for a way to clasp hands with that family, even though they are not so proficient at certain aspects of its business, even though its traditional code of conduct is not and probably never will be fully acceptable to them.

How can people of this latter persuasion achieve that goal? How can they tie in to their people and promote its prosperity, on the one hand, while loyally obeying the dictates of their heart, on the other? Well, they can start by making a major contribution to Jewish longevity and to their own personal depth and connectedness by participating in as many of the *mitzvoth* as do *not* mess seriously with their notions of morality. Why? *Why not*? It couldn't hurt, as my grandmother used to say, and it comes highly recommended: *Jewish study and practice is a blast of epic proportions.* Throw yourself into it with reckless abandon.

But what to do with pentateuchal or talmudic precepts that "our hearts cannot abide"? How can we, in such a case, remain true to our feelings and conscience, and simultaneously bend ourselves to the "yoke of Heaven"?

We can't. If you were looking for a quaint rationalization, look elsewhere. One of these loyalties has to go in such cases – either the call of our emotions or the yoke of heaven – and you probably know by now how I feel about yokes (don't even like 'em in eggs). Active rebellion or at least civil disobedience is the only option in such a case. All I can offer in the way of comfort – for those not too keen on going fifteen rounds with He of the Mighty Hand and Outstretched Uppercut – is the following midrashic fantasy of my own. I call it a midrashic fantasy, because to call it anything else would be to invite excommunication (on the one hand) and accusations of apologia (on the other). The fantasy goes like this:

We all know about the age-old, classical conundrum of "freewill versus predestination" (we side-swiped it briefly in the beginning of chapter eleven). The question whether life and history are "determined" ahead of time by a deity or by the laws of causality or whether (alternately) our actions are totally up to us, the product of our sole and independent initiative – this is one of the oldest and most unyielding intellectual stumpers on the books. Rabbis and Church Fathers, Gurus and Sufis, Manicheans and Neo-Platonists, Kabbalists and Kalaamists – an endless procession of sages, philosophers and clerics from the early Roman period onward have measured their wits against this mystifying poser (before that time, most formalistic conceptions of reality of which we are aware could be deemed "deterministic," with the early Greeks obsessing about *moira* or fate, the Babylonians and Egyptians essentially averring that "the fault lies in the stars, dear Brutus," and the Indians – well, we've talked about them). The thousands of treatises penned down the centuries to illuminate this murky subject evince a broad spectrum of opinions and conclusions, spanning from full-fledged fatalism to absolute freedom.

Now, it should come as no surprise to anyone who has not been listening to Iron Maiden while reading, that of all the major religious, philosophical and scientific systems we have mentioned so far in this book, it is Jewish tradition that comes down most heavily and clearly on the "freewill" side of the spectrum. This is true primarily because – as Immanuel Kant argued so brilliantly – the indispensable *sine qua non* of human freedom of choice is a suspension or at least a demotion of the rational. And hey: *that's our specialty*. Indeed, the Jewish worldview has always been so heavily steeped and soaked in the fundamental idea of freedom, that even the greatest of all Jewish would-be rationalists – Moses Maimonides himself – simply could not hold back:

> Let not that enter your head which the fools of the nations of the world and many of the ignoramuses of Israel say: that the Holy One, blessed be He, decrees for each person at the outset of his creation whether he shall be righteous or wicked. For the matter is not thus. Rather, it is within the power of every human being to be as righteous as Moses or as wicked as Jeroboam, to be wise or foolish, merciful or cruel, miserly or openhanded, and the same for all the other qualities. And there is no one who compels him or decrees for him or pulls him in one of these two directions, but rather he himself of his own free will turns toward whichever path he desires… This conception is a great fundamental, and it is the pillar upon which the Torah and its commandments stand, as it is written: "Behold, I place before you blessing and curse" (Deuteronomy 11:26) – meaning: the choice is placed in your hands…And we must know without the slightest doubt, that the deeds of man are in the hands of man, and that the Holy One, blessed be He, neither impels him nor decrees upon him any course of action. (*Hilkhot Teshuva*, 5:2–3, 5)

So concerned was the Lord (explains the Midrash) with ensuring our full-fledged freedom of choice, that for the sake of this end He was willing to decree *death for the righteous* as well as for the wicked – when the original plan saw this bitter pill prescribed for the wicked alone. Why the change of policy? So that no one should ever choose to be upright for fear of death – because that would not be an entirely unconstrained choice! (See Genesis Rabbah, 9:5)

Right: so we're free. Now, here's the point: the idea that we were granted all that truly miraculous liberty and independence, all that wonderful autonomy and the responsibility that comes with it – just so that we could then turn right around one hundred eighty degrees and ungratefully hand it back to Sender by simply following orders from On High no matter what we may think or feel about the matter; the idea that God was gracious and loving and *imaginative* enough to share with His human creatures the extraordinary divine prerogative of choice – solely in order that we should in every circumstance and on all occasions "choose" obsequiously to obey God's commandments and do whatever He says; the idea that (in the traditional formulation) we were "freed from Egyptian slavery in order to enter into divine slavery"; this rather pervasive notion that makes the rounds in religious circles has always seemed to me...well...not entirely thought out. If all God wanted was a herd of bootlicking lackeys, He already had the angels – why create us? And if (as they say) He created us unfettered because He craved the pleasure of being chosen *freely* as an object of adoration, or because He wanted us to "acquire merit" by *electing* to serve Him of our own accord – in that case, I'm sorry, O Lord, but You can't have Your cake and eat it, too. If you want the lady to love you freely, she simply *has* to have the *legitimate* option of refusal, and without fear of punishment! All in all, this whole "born to be a slave" theory just doesn't wash.

True, Moses quotes the Lord to the following effect:

> And now, O Israel, what doth the Lord thy God require of thee, but to fear the Lord thy God, to walk in all His ways, to love Him, and to serve the Lord thy God with all thy heart and with all thy soul, to keep the commandments of the Lord and His statutes which I command thee this day, for thine own good? (Deuteronomy 10:12)

There's no denying the fact: the Torah is here demanding of us an absolute and unqualified compliance with the ordinances of the Creator. We are indeed required by this and other scriptural passages to employ that amazing gift of freedom we were given, solely and simply in order to *do what we are told*.

Well, now: should we listen? The answer to that depends on how we perceive and relate to the Deity who is making the demand: in the Greek philosophical manner – as a perfect, logical, symmetrical, transcendental, super-computer in the sky; or in the Jewish biblical and midrashic manner – as a loving father. If God is the cold and calculating cogitation machine that the religious rationalists say He is, then He will clearly be no more amenable to the notion of disobedience or rebellion than is your average booby-trap: cross the tripwire and *bam*! – like a reflex, like an equation, automatically and inexorably – you get zapped. If, on the other hand, God is the mushy-gushy, lovey-dovey, let-Me-show-you-My-wallet-stuffed-full-of-My-kids'-pictures paternal super-softy that Jewish tradition (when read without Greek glasses) almost invariably describes Him to be, then the situation is vastly different. Then God is not dead – He's Dad:

> When Moses prayed at length for Israel's deliverance at the Red Sea, the Lord interrupted and said: "Wherefore criest thou unto Me? I need no asking when it comes to My children! As it is written: 'Wilt thou ask Me concerning My children?' (Isaiah 45:11)". (Mechilta 30a)

> When Israel feels uneasy about having to stand in judgment before God, the angels say unto them: "Fear ye not the judgment – know ye not Him? He is your next of kin, He is your brother, but what is more: He is your father." (Tanchuma 118:10)

> But now, O Lord, Thou art our father… (Isaiah 64:7)

> You are the children of the Lord your God… (Deuteronomy 14:1)

If our heavenly Father is anything at all like an earthly father – if, that is, the thousands of anthropomorphic descriptions of God-as-Parent in Jewish literature are indeed intended to convey the idea of common qualities linking divine and human progenitors – then we have a much better idea of what's going on here in stern biblical verses like the one quoted above. Human fathers are always saying stuff to their kids like: "What do I ask of you, for cryin' out loud, except to do what you're told? If Daddy says 'no,' that means *no*. Remember: this is for your own good!" Yes, fathers are always making such statements, but think about it: does Dad *really* want his children to spend the rest of their lives doing *everything* he tells them, never deviating so much as an iota from his dictates, never defying, never challenging, never displaying the slightest independence?

I daresay he does not. *Yuk*. No father or mother worthy of the title truly desires this, mouth-off as they might while momentarily peeved. We don't want truculent, toadying, carbon copies of ourselves for offspring – any decent begetter would view such an outcome as a tragic failure. Good parents are more likely than not to be *happy* at the first signs of some genuine backbone in their children, even (and perhaps especially) when that involves standing up to Mom and Dad themselves, and yes: breaking some of the rules. Nor is it unheard of that the older generation may occasionally even *learn* something from the civil disobedience of the younger, and *reverse its position*.

So, now: does the Jewish Dad-God really want submissive, spineless sycophants for children, forever doing His bidding without emitting so much as a peep? Is there no possibility that He will ever even *entertain* a petition from His growing boys and girls to amend a particular precept in the light of changed circumstances or passionate protest? I guess in certain places He pretty much *says* He won't (like most dads) but – *won't He*? Does the Jewish Deity really never change His mind? Is He never influenced by His creatures? (The non-Hellenized Torah and Talmud both show repeatedly that He does and is.) Is the Divine-human relationship so completely unidirectional, is the interaction between the two such a one-way street, is our Pa such a rigid, brittle, immutable, inflexible, heedless Aristotelian robot that He simply cannot and will not even *listen* to His children? Is it so completely clear and certain to all concerned that God has *absolutely nothing to learn from us*?

All of this would indeed be the case, were there no analogy to be made between the Jewish God and a human father – but again: the lion's share of our greatest literature stresses over and over again *that there is*. (Nor do the endless rabbinic descriptions of the intimate relationship between God and Israel confine themselves to the notion of "child": almost every single term of endearment found in the Hebrew language – sister, brother, mother, bride, lamb, calf, dove, eye, ewe, gazelle – is drafted to convey the exceptional closeness between us.)

Now, not only do we expect that the Lord, as an *Abba*, will allow His compassion and mercy to unseat His strict justice about one hundred times daily and all throughout the night (as Judeo-classical sources constantly emphasize that He does), but more than this: we expect that He will *welcome* a little rebellion here and there, even laugh with delight and exclaim: "My children have defeated Me, My children have defeated Me!" (Baba Metzia 59b).

"Objectionnnnnn!!!"

Welcome back. What can I do for you?

"You can give me a break, is what you can do! This is all a bunch of pie-in-the-sky theo-babble. You know damn well God is not going to come down out of the heavens tomorrow in order to consider or refuse some petition of ours! Let's be honest with each other: you can bluster about like this and goad the Deity in print only because we're both supremely confident that *that's never going to happen.* It's easy to taunt the lion when you are on the other side of an impenetrable fence. This is all just talk."

Dear reader: if this is what you were thinking, then I congratulate you – *you are an atheist.* Or at least you do not believe in the personal God of the Jewish sources. In which case: *yay*! – you are truly in great shape as far as this whole issue is concerned, and have absolutely *nothing* to worry about. You can adopt and discard whichever Jewish practices and precepts you damn well please (based on the criterion of Jewish survival, personal enrichment, whatever – take your pick!). There will be no "metaphysical" consequences to speak of – and the problem is solved! You can be a committed Jewish nationalist without worrying about how to deal *mit der Aybershter.*

But as for those who have yet to give up on Our Father in Heaven, let me close with this. To be truly created in the image of God means to resemble Him closely – by *not* resembling Him *too* closely. It means to follow His lead – by *not* following His lead in *everything.* Just as God is independent, be *ye* independent (even, when necessary, of Him); just as God is creative, be *ye* creative: of your own path (even when it diverges from His); just as God makes His own choices un-coerced by any authority, so make ye *your* own choices, un-coerced by *His* authority (as Maimonides explicitly demands). Carve out your own path: give Dad some *nachos* (not the potato chip; this is Yiddish for "parental pride and pleasure").

All of this is, as I admitted earlier, a rather far-fetched fantasy and *chutzpadik* Midrash of my own on the text and on traditional Jewish theology, and I don't expect it will find many supporters. There is certainly no lack of passages in our sources that militate for the difference and even incomparability between God and His creatures: "To whom then will you liken God? Or what likeness will you compare unto Him?" (Isaiah 40:18); "For My thoughts are not your thoughts, neither are your ways My ways" (Ibid. 55:8).

However that may be, though – Deity or no Deity, Doting Dad or Divine Device – we must never forget that we are free. That we are free we know, not just because Jewish sources tell us so, but because if we are *not* free, then in the most fundamental, ontological and essential sense, nothing anywhere means anything at all, and there's no point in continuing to write or read these lines (let's go hit the strip clubs).

Now, then, if we are free; and if we *know* we are free; and if we choose to *exercise* that freedom; then all of our decisions in life are perforce our own, are ultimately the exclusive business of our private consciences – including the decision whether or not to obey divine commandments. And since the fundamental force and final criterion underlying all of our decisions is inevitably going to be not rational but *emotional*, then if and when we do find ourselves face to face with a commandment enjoining us to do something we simply cannot ethically abide – something that really cuts our heart to ribbons – then I'm afraid there is simply no other way out: *just say no*.

And don't say "no" the wimpy way, under your breath behind the closed doors of some isolated inner chamber. Nah. Go all out. Make a scene. Here's what I propose for such situations (if it backfires, don't tell 'em I sent you): first, learn all you possibly can about the offending issue. Become a veritable expert on it. Dig down deep into the classical sources (in the original, dammit – learn your nation's mother tongue!), discuss the subject with all types of people in the know, read commentaries and super-commentaries, search out studies of the question in question, turn it over and over in your mind (and in your heart!) – gather your ammunition but good. Meanwhile, during the time you are busy increasing your level of understanding and your ability to take on all possible comers…go to *schul.* That's right: start attending synagogue services regularly, master the liturgy and ritual to a T, and see to it that you always arrive before the rabbi, thereby quickly establishing a reputation for unrivalled piety. Wait for the Sabbath on which the Torah Portion of the Week will be chanted which contains the unbearable clause that got you started in the first place, and arrange things ahead of time with the gabbai/sexton. Get all *fapitzed* on the morning in question, don *tallis*, grab prayer-book, and head on over to the house of worship (walking, please – for remember: not riding on the Sabbath is a romance-increasing ritual that simultaneously hurts no one, strengthens the staying power of our beloved tribe, affords you the opportunity to smell the flowers, improves your circulation and lowers carbon-monoxide emission levels). Perform all the prayerful stuff with verve and vigor: wash your hands thrice, sing the psalms sweetly, sit, stand, bow, swivel, shout, fall silent, cover your eyes during the *shema*, and kiss the *tzitzit*, raise your heels during the *kedushah*, and embrace the Torah scroll as it comes around. Heck: learn the special melodies, prepare the proper portion, and be nothing less than the Torah reader him or herself in the flesh. Chant out the chapters and verses with passion and feeling. Point with your little finger as the scroll is lifted high in the air afterward and unfurled like the glorious stele of our nation's soul that it is. Listen to the minor tones of the *haftorah* and absorb its powerful message into your bones, respond "amen" with gusto to its after-blessing, serenade the Big Book like a troubadour – and kiss and embrace it like a long lost sibling – as it winds its way back to the ark.

Now, it's your turn. You have been slated – at your own request – to give today's learned sermon on the Portion of the Week. The congregation assumes they are going to hear another ordinary speech, praising the pious protagonists of the *parashah* and extolling the goodness of the Lord and the wisdom of His words. They settle in for a good twenty-minute snooze…

"***J'accuse***!!" you thunder, shaking a clenched fist heavenward and glaring furiously down at the audience (they get Haydn's Surprise Symphony instead). "I most vehemently *protest* – against God for issuing this unconscionable injunction, and against *you*, my fellow

Jews, for letting it slide by this day without so much as a murmur! Woe unto ye, cynics and sycophants, callous ones all!"

They sit there wide-eyed and open-mouthed, as you relentlessly rip into your target, fiercely denouncing the rank injustice of commandment and Commander, passionately condemning the placid acceptance, the pious inattention, the complete lack of true engagement by the People of the Book with their glorious Book. "Where's the *response*?" you demand to know. "Where are the cries of 'unfair!' during the reading, where are the whistles and cat-calls and boos – is this text taken seriously? Does everything just go in one ear and out the other, perhaps crossing the mind but bypassing the heart? In the name of Heaven, *did you listen to what was just read*?! Can you really gloss over it so easily? Is that how we give honor to our greatest national treasure, to the Wellspring of our Wisdom and Tree of our Life – *by ignoring it*? For what is this perpetual head-nodding and rubber-stamping, this passive endorsement and apathetic acceptance of everything chanted out week after week, if not – essentially – disregard? Is there a greater insult to a text and its author than to manage to read through from beginning to end without being provoked in the slightest degree? Wake up, you servile slumberers! Criticize! Fume!! *Attack*!! Wrangle and tangle and grapple and wrestle with what is being read out to you, picture it, think about it, *feel* about it – and respond! For God's sake: *is this a monologue*?!"

Don't let up: spray your listeners with an impressive series of citations evincing a breadth and depth of knowledge that sends the rabbi scurrying to his study. Point by pulverizing point you build your case against the Heavens, angrily demanding redress like the Israelite – the "he-who-fights-God-ite" – that you are. And then – just as they're all expecting you to perform the old hermeneutical one-two, the famous "bait-and-switch" trick where you turn the whole story around and make it all better; just as they're beginning to wonder how on earth you're going to extricate yourself out of this major entanglement and bring the entire business to a happy and reverential ending in which the Lord and His problematic precept come out shining like a newly polished diamond; just as they're waiting for you to go and pull that old shenanigan – *don't.*

Yeah, do the opposite. Tell them that, as far as you're concerned, this aspect of the Jewish national constitution is anathema, is out of bounds, is beyond the pale, is *wrong*, and you're not willing to have anything to do with it, no matter how observant you may or may not become in a hundred other areas; challenge them to show you why you should feel or act differently, challenge them to show cause why *they* shouldn't act like *you* in this matter; turn the synagogue into a modern day *Bet Midrash*, a cacophonous house of study and seeking and no-holds-barred debate (attendance will go up). Suffer the argument to accompany the entire congregation out to *kiddush* after services – where you will, no doubt, recite the proper benedictions with the fervor of a free individual making an independent decision to perform a benign, irrational and benevolent precept – and let the issue ripple and reverberate into the houses of each congregant as they sit down to *se'udah shniyah*, the second Sabbath repast. Walk (don't drive) back home, accompanied the whole way by an honor guard of your *qvelling* ancestors, remonstrators and theomachists all, in whose fiery footsteps you've just followed with such courage and aplomb: on your right, Abraham ("Will the Judge of all the earth not do justice?!"); on your left, Moses ("Erase me from that Book which You have written!"); in front of you, Gideon ("If the Lord be with us, why then has all this befallen us?"); behind you, Elijah ("Oh Lord my God! Hast Thou also done evil to the widow with whom I sojourn, by slaying her son?"); and hovering high above you, the proud Father Himself – who prefers rebukers to flatterers any day of the week, and can take it just as well as He can dish it out. There He is, shaking hands and handing out cigars, shining His countenance upon all and sundry, beaming with pleasure at His successfully created chip-off-the-old-Block, and exclaiming with delight to anyone within earshot: "That's my kid!" Head home smiling, the happy heretic.

No, I can't guarantee you that that's how things will pan out. You might get thrown off the synagogue stage in mid-harangue, hauled out of the building by two burly guys in polyester suits and chucked into the street, where you will be forthwith struck by lightning. I really don't know how such an affair would end up. But regardless of whether you make synagogue scenes or not, it is essential when dealing with matters Jewish (as with any other matters) to bear in mind at all times and under all circumstances just who exactly is in charge here: **you**. Do Daddy's bidding whenever you can, and buck His authority whenever you must. How else can a free and feeling person proceed? Daddy doesn't want no fawning Mamma's boys.

The *pshat* of Jabotinsky's statement, "My God is the Jewish People," is rather clear. He was a dyed-in-the-wool nationalist, head-over-heels in love with his people – and an avowed atheist. Here's a *drash* on the same. In the book of Exodus (25:8) God commands Moses: "And they [the Children of Israel] shall make Me a sanctuary, and I shall dwell among them." From the Hebrew for these last five words – *ve-shachanti betocham* – arose the notion of *Shechina*, the "divine presence" that virtually inheres in Israel: "The Lord thy God walketh in the midst of thy camp" (Deuteronomy 23:15). Since that time the *Shechina* has stuck loyally with the Jewish People, everywhere we went: She trudged with us through the torrid desert, returned with us to the Promised Land, went out with us to battle our foes, never abandoning us for a moment, even (the Talmud tells us) accompanying us into exile and weeping together with us by the rivers of Babylon. The *Shechina* has been there in our midst through it all, across all the generations, registering upon Her person our victories and defeats, our sufferings and celebrations, our dispersions and redemptions. When we fall, the *Shechina* falls, when we arise, so does She. Our glory is Her glory, our shame Hers, too. If you prick us, She bleeds. The consistent identity of actions and interests is uncanny, mirror-like. I wonder: is someone trying to tell us something?

Doron
The Challenge of Inertia

"How can you be so naïve? Look around you, *habibi* – get with the program! The world is constantly imploding, getting smaller all the time. The distances between societies are diminishing everywhere, and the borders that divide us one from another are evaporating like a thousand Berlin Walls tumbling down. It's *happening*, man – whether you like it or not! The world is progressing, moving forward, toward oneness..."

Chapter Twenty

As we enter the homestretch, here's the upshot. The two forces working hardest today to undermine the Jewish national future – harder even than Hassan Nasrallah or Isma'il Haniya – are the twin ideologies of Universalism and Rationalism, with which we have saddled poor Shira and Ofer respectively, and at which we have fired what ammunition we possessed. These two have decimated Jewish ranks in the Diaspora for generations, and they underlie, as well, nearly all of the corrosive trends and attitudes currently eating up the State of Israel from the inside. This being the case, the worldwide Jewish agenda today ought to envision and enshrine one imperative beyond any other: *an all-out campaign on every front imaginable to unseat Universalism in favor of Preferential Love, and to subject Rationalism to the sovereignty of Romance.* This is the Jewish mission of the hour, and probably will be for years, decades and even centuries to come.

If things were that simple, though, my guess is we'd be home free. Most people I know prefer variety to monotony, prefer preferring to not preferring, even prefer passion to pragmatics. If we banded together and gave it the old college try, we'd probably have

Universalism and Rationalism on the run in no time, and could get started rebuilding all the invigorating relationships and essential institutions they have ravaged and ripped to pieces over the years.

But we aren't banding together and giving it the old college try. Why? Because Shira and Ofer are not exactly poor, defenseless orphans with whom we can do as we please: they have a Papa. They have a Papa, alright, a progenitor who is far more forceful and persuasive than they, and without whose constant support they would neither of them be very long for this world. This Father of Universalism and Rationalism is no one to be trifled with. Unlike His offspring, He cannot be shaken by arguments. He is not an idea, He is not a doctrine, He is not a feeling or a passion. He is neither "what is" nor yet "what ought to be," but a force ten thousand times more irresistible than these. He is here all around us, everywhere and in everything. He is the Great and the Terrible, the Omnipotent, the Inexorable, the Relentless, the Merciless, the Unyielding, the Invincible. He has been the genuine Unmoved Mover since the beginning of time, and the entire universe bends its knee and bows its head in trembling submission before His awesome and crushing power.

Would you like to meet Him? Very well. Fill a big bowl two thirds of the way up with water. Taking care not to spill, pick up the bowl and give it a little whirl, a little shake, a little swirl, then immediately place it back down on the table, and watch what happens. Do you see how at first, the surface of the water is agitated and uneven, wavy and tempestuous, how one side is up, the other down, one part rippled, another bubbled – you know what I mean. Now, notice what takes place only seconds after the vessel and contents are left to their own devices: the agitation quickly calms, the tempest tosses less, the waves subside in favor of placidity, and we finally arrive back at a smooth, uniform and undisturbed surface from wall to wall.

Dear reader: you have just participated in the single most important scientific experiment known to humankind. No, really. And your big bowl is a more powerful crystal ball than ever possessed by any warlock or sorceress: with it you have just peered *trillions of years into the future*, and witnessed the swan song of the universe. You are now officially a prophet for all the ages, next to whom famous foreseers like Isaiah or Jeremiah couldn't predict a horse race. You are, after all, *His* prophet – so you know everything.

OK, I'll cut the cryptic stuff. You already know what I'm talking about. The water in your bowl has just rendered homage to and thereby illustrated for us Newton's Second Law of Thermodynamics, known for short as "Entropy." Loosely defined, Entropy is the persistent tendency of all things in existence to move from a state of variety and complexity, where matter is distributed "unevenly" and "asymmetrically" (like the turbulence of the water in your agitated bowl), to a state of uniformity and homogeneity, where matter is distributed equally (like the unruffled surface of the water afterward). Viewed from another perspective, Entropy is the process whereby energy gets lost, or rather: is converted from the type available for work to the type unavailable for work. For while it is indubitably true that the amount of energy outputted by any event or reaction will precisely match the amount of energy inputted (this is the *First* Law of Thermo-Dynamics), the energy that emerges "splits up" into a number of different forms – e.g., heat, light, sound – only *some* of which can be harnessed for subsequent jobs. This is the irreversible enervation and metastasizing fatigue that makes a perpetual motion machine impossible.

In short, Entropy is the inexorable tendency toward rest. It is exhausted existence seeking RwR (Rest *without* Recreation). It is the inevitable winding down of everything. It is the incessant quest of all there is for peace and tranquility, which is achieved when multiformity (which requires a lot of energy) is finally replaced by uniformity (which requires none).

It may be helpful to analogize this one-way procession – which has characterized the universe since its explosive debut and will continue to do so until the bitter finale – to the way my grandfather used to drink tea. The beverage was too hot for him, and patience wasn't his forte, so he would spill out some of the liquid from the cup into the saucer, where it would immediately spread out and cool down. Well, last month it became official: my grandpa's cup-to-saucer trick is the way the universe will end. Just like his tea, the whole shebang is expanding, cooling off and breaking down as we speak into ever tinier and more equidistant particles. A bunch of big-time astrophysicists recently held a press conference at MIT, where they outlined the demise of existence stage-by-stage: from the "stelliferous era" (that's us), to the "degenerate era" (when, as Gordon Lightfoot sang, "one by one the stars will all go out"), to the "black-hole era," to the "dark era." In this last phase everything will have analyzed into its component particles, there will be no more agglomerations or "nonconformist" clumps of matter, there will be no more motion or activity of any kind: just an infinite, tenebrous, everlasting, uniform stillness. *Shantih Shantih Shantih.*

Who cares about any of this? After all, the unstoppable process of cosmic decay will take somewhere in the realm of ten thousand trillion trillion trillion trillion trillion trillion trillion years (to update the famous reassurance of Woody Allen's family doctor in *Annie Hall*). What does all this have to do with us and our subject?

Only everything. First of all, in case you've forgotten, we human beings are a part of this universe, too, and as such we are subject to Entropy just like anything else. We each have our initial Big Bang, as we are fired out of the maternal cannon into the awaiting world, and we surf the resultant momentum till the wave crests and crashes (if you will pardon the mixed metaphor). It is then that variety is exchanged for uniformity, complexity bartered for simplicity, hot traded for cold, and particles that were once involved in diverse and unique matter clumps arrive at the ultimate placid solution of homogeneity and equilibrium. We call this *you're dead.*

None of this should be in the least bit strange to any of us. We spend almost all of our lives fighting the battle of Energy versus Entropy, even on a daily basis. And Entropy, not surprisingly, usually has the upper hand. Even when we can get up the gumption to exercise, our activity is – I would venture – most often performed with a mind to eventual *inactivity*, to the hours *after* the run or the treadmill when we plan to sprawl onto a love-seat with a beer and a bag of Doritos and watch the game. Indeed, we often spend the majority of our aerobic huffing and puffing envisioning, dreaming of and longing for that exceptionally *an*aerobic moment that will ensue just as soon as we're done. We exert ourselves for the sake of *not* exerting ourselves. We quest after the great *ahhhhhhhhh* that follows the effort, the relief and release after the discomfiting tension. We spend our week working and waiting for the Sabbath, spend our history working and waiting for the messianic Day That Will Be All Sabbath. Individually and communally, religiously and culturally, we sanction the search for the "rest that precedes the Great Rest," and hallow and even seek to hasten the Great Rest itself.

And because for so many thinkers throughout history, necessity has always been the mother of...well...*everything*, cultures, religions and philosophies the world over have rarely waited for the onset of decomposition to begin worshipping the Master of Masters, the Theos of Thanatos, the Enlil of End. Nah, we get our dibs in early. We know how to recognize the inevitable when we see it – and we know how to resign ourselves to it and grovel in the dust before it in writhing, sycophantic adulation. *Pre-emption by means of acceptance*: if you can't beat it, embrace it. Feel your limbs go limp, feel the stress and agitation flow out of your veins, feel the serum of submission calm and soothe your raging heart. "The desire for peace waxes stronger as hope declines," wrote Joseph Conrad in *Lord Jim*, "till at last it conquers the very desire for life." It is then that we are overwhelmed by the "extreme weariness of emotions, the vanity of effort, the yearning for rest." The seduction of this most indomitable of Dictators is such that human beings have always devised for themselves foreshadowings of our ultimate digestion in its boundless bowels: an endless array of ideological and institutional man-made extinctions-before-extinction. "The consumptives of the soul," railed Nietzsche, "they are hardly born before they begin to die, to long for doctrines of weariness and renunciation...Everywhere resound the voices of those who preach death."

While Papa Entropy preaches a persistent doctrine of "spread out and slow down" to all of existence, his twin children – Rationalism and Universalism – are ever at their father's beck and call. The first runs bowing and scraping before the Old Man's retinue, and prepares the way for His entry into the minds of men. Calling causality to the colors, Rationalism proves step by logical step the scientific inevitability of the decline of all things, and thereby lulls or cows us into resignation: *go quietly and gently into that good night.* Hell: make a party of it! Celebrate!! Turn the "way of all flesh" into a positive spiritual paradigm. Isn't dying a terrific model for life?

Rationalism is not done helping out the family, though. It simultaneously canters before the cortege of its sibling, Universalism, smoothing *its* path to world domination by intimating that were we only to think "reasonably," all human aspirations everywhere would swiftly become identical. Without this harmony of purposes, after all, no Eschaton of equality and equanimity would ever be possible, as Isaiah Berlin points out:

> The very idea of universal fulfillment presupposes that human beings as such seek the same essential goals, identical for all, at all times, everywhere. For unless this is so, Utopia cannot be Utopia, for then the perfect society will not perfectly satisfy everyone.

How, then, do we ensure that everybody's ends are the same? By teaching them all to be rational, and to value truth above everything else. For there is (with apologies to Protagoras) only *one* true answer to any given logical query. If we all think rationally, we should all ultimately arrive at the same conclusions. In art class we may be individuals; in math class we are a *Gestalt.* Thus is Rationalism his brother Universalism's keeper, paving the way for today's ever-expanding unanimity and global sameness. And as the emotional energy required to maintain multiple, distinct, independent and *sui generis* societies is increasingly sapped, Papa Entropy's ravenous black-hole is fed by humanity's exponentially increasing uniformity. "Ach!" He sits back in his chair and pats His huge stomach, stuffed to the gills with delectable empty. He smiles down on his progeny's promising handiwork, reflected in *realpolitik* statements that urge us to take wing and fly the way the wind is blowing, like the one made by Doron at the airport: "The distances between societies are diminishing everywhere, and the borders that divide us one from another are evaporating like a thousand Berlin Walls tumbling down. It's *happening*, man – whether you like it or not!"

Wake up and smell the rotting stench of the ineluctable, my man! "What is" *is indeed* "What should be": they are birds of a feather. Anyway, the bottom line is: there's nothing to be done! Nothing to be done about any of it. Just accept fate, says Doron, and go with the flow. The world is moving away from the notion of nation, away from the "irrational solidarity group," away from kinship- or tribal-based communities. Humanity is "progressing" by leaps and bounds in the direction of more rationally defensible geographic, political, ideological and even economic associations; the population of the planet is streamlining, collectivizing, unifying and heading toward global oneness. This trend is irreversible, says Doron (says Entropy) – why bother fighting it? The Jewish People and the Jewish State are both untenable anomalies in an age surging pell-mell toward the lowest common denominator; they are both doomed. Just accept the inevitable, and surrender to it: you are, at any rate, helpless to combat it.

Back in those pious days when I used to chant the Torah from the pulpit in synagogue, one weekly portion in particular would give me extra special trouble. Near the end of the yearly cycle of readings, there are a few chapters in the book of Deuteronomy known traditionally as the *tokhekha* (the rebuke) or the *qelalah* (the curse). These paragraphs enumerate in the most excruciating detail the disasters that will befall the Children of Israel if they neglect to behave properly in "the land which the Lord hath given you." Rain, of course, will be out of the question, but it gets worse:

> The Lord will bring a nation against you from afar, from the ends of the earth, which will swoop down like an eagle – a ruthless nation, that will show the old no regard and the young no mercy. (Deuteronomy 28:49-50)

> And she who is most tender and dainty among you, so delicate that she would never venture to set a foot on the ground, shall begrudge the husband of her bosom and her son and her daughter the afterbirth that issues from between her legs and the babies that she bears; she shall eat them secretly, because of

> utter want, in the desperate straits to which your enemy shall reduce you in your towns. (Deuteronomy 28:56-7)

> You shall be left a scant few, after having been as many as the stars in the sky, because you did not heed the command of the Lord your God. And as the Lord once delighted in making you prosperous and numerous, so will He now delight in causing you to perish and in wiping you out; you shall be torn from the land which you are about to enter and possess. (Deuteronomy 28:62-3)

There's a lot more where that comes from, and it gets so you have to take a break and walk outside to compose yourself before preparing further (the more you know of subsequent Jewish history, the harder these verses are to read). But there is one particular passage in this portion that used to give me the chills more than any other. It goes like this:

> You shall betroth a wife, and another man shall lie with her; you shall build a house, but shall never live in it; you shall plant a vineyard, but will not eat of its fruit. Your ox shall be slaughtered in front of your eyes, your donkey shall be seized in front of your face, your flock shall be handed over to your enemies, and there will be none at all to save you. Your sons and your daughters shall be delivered unto another people, while you look on; and your eyes shall strain for them all the days, but there shall be no power in your hand. (Deuteronomy 28:30-2)

The greatest curse in all the world is helplessness. The worst nightmare imaginable is the one in which those you love are being harmed in front of your eyes, and you can do nothing about it. There is no greater exile than the exile from control over – or at least influence upon – what takes place in your life and your surroundings. We all know about this nightmare: it was the Jewish People's curse for two thousand years, and we relived the scenes described above by the Pentateuch over and over and over again throughout those many horrific centuries, unable to stem the tide of outrages or alter our miserable fate.

When I first moved to Israel ten years ago, my stone-age laptop refused to acclimate itself and immediately went on the fritz. The computer industry in Israel at the time was not yet the sprawling high-tech paradise it is today, and I was forced to proceed to actual IBM headquarters in Tel-Aviv to get my machine fixed. While the technicians operated, I wandered around outside. The IBM building stands directly opposite the Ministry of Defense, and soaring up some fifty stories out of the midst of that ministry's grounds is an edifice that completely dominated the Tel-Aviv skyline until very recently. It is a colossal communications and they-could-tell-you-what-else-but-they-would-have-to-kill-you tower, and it is unmistakably designed to resemble a sword ("unmistakably," commented a friend of mine who works inside it and with whom I just got off the phone, "only in *your* disturbed brain").

You may be surprised to hear that the sword speaks. I first discovered this while strolling outside the IBM building a decade ago, and since then, wherever I am in this bustling ocean-side Hebrew metropolis, and whatever mundane monkey business I am preoccupied with at the time, if I look up and listen, I can still hear it. It whispers three times daily across the skies of our fair city by the sea, above the din of bus engines and car horns and construction racket, over the heads of the heedless and industrious remnant, beautiful brands snatched from the ravenous fire. The sky-scraping scimitar whispers sweet somethings, whispers and comforts, whispers and promises. It says, "No one will ever hurt you again. No one will starve you, or beat you, or gas you, no one will rip up your mothers with child, no one will force you to dig your own graves, or freeze you, or burn you, or put you in ovens. You are safe, and you are blessed. Blessed are you in the city, and blessed are you in the country. Blessed is the issue of your womb, the produce of your soil and the offspring of your cattle, the calving of your herd and the lambing of your flock. Blessed is your basket and your kneading bowl. Blessed are your comings, and blessed are your goings, and blessed is the work of your hands. *You are home.*"

In the light – in the darkness – of events these past few years, the sword's outgoing message can sometimes ring a bit hollow. But that will change. We will change it. Because the real message of the sword – and of the book it is quoting – is something even deeper than security and prosperity. It is the message of freedom, and power, and will, the message of agency, of choice, of the ability and duty to overcome even the supposedly insurmountable: "I call heaven and earth to witness this day: life and death have I placed before you, blessing and curse. *Choose life...*" (Deuteronomy 30:19). The Voice of Choice says: Choose to conduct an undying battle against the Death Wish, in all its many institutional and ideological guises. The Voice of Choice says: *Spit in Entropy's face.*

Many are those who do not heed the Voice, so powerful a temptress is helplessness. Even Nietzsche, that *Lebens-Philosoph* with a capital LP, could not help being captivated by the life-sapping charms of this paralyzing siren and her seductive goat-song. Thus did Nietzsche go on about *amor fati* – about "love of fate" (*Et tu Brute*?). See how powerful is the pull of the path of least resistance; how pleasant finally to stop fighting the current and let it wash you softly out to sea; how cathartic the individual and cosmic "*ahhhhhhh*"; how aesthetic and sensual suicide. Such is the allure of "the supreme day and the inevitable hour." Such are the enticements of the heavy chains of telos. "*Far vos men bagropt a toyter*?" asked the famed Rebbe of Kotzk – "Why do people bury a dead man?" "*Vile er lozst*," he answered – "Because he lets them."

But we must not let them. "It is easy to go down to the underworld," explained the Cumaean Sibyl to Aeneas. "The black door of Dis stands open night and day. But to retrace your steps and escape into the upper air – that is the task, that is the labor." *Pros kentra laktizein*. To go against the grain, to run against the wind, to flow not downward, to the ocean to be submerged, but back upstream, to the source, to be revived. Mimic and sanctify the process toward the inevitable? Never! *Never*! But rather blaspheme it, profane it and rage, despise it and loathe it and render it *evitable*. Revile and repulse the inertia-propelled juggernaut of foredoom, take up the gauntlet thrown down by Entropy, preach power and dreaming and the realization of dreams. Preach love of life and **hate of fate**.

There is an old kabbalistic (and Neo-Platonic) belief that God continually creates the world anew, every day, every minute, every second. The story goes that a *Misnaged* and a Hassid – the latter presumably a devotee of Kabbalah, the former less so if at all – were asked how the Holy One, blessed be He, would go about destroying the world if He so desired. The *Misnaged* answered by speaking of fire and lava and hurricanes and tidal waves; said the Hassid simply, "He would stop creating it." Just as He, so we. Like parent like child: we know what we have to do, if we want the greatest love story of all time to keep on being told.

We have to make the conscious and collective decision to gird our creative loins, to recover the guts and the confidence, the romance and the idealism, the wildness and the midrashic *chutzpah* that alone enable human beings to create; and we have to reclaim the capacity to really dream, to dream big, to dream as a team, and along with it the courage and stamina to struggle like sled dogs for the *realization* of our dreams. We Jews are far from finished. If we will it, our little family can once again reach down into its fathomless well of experience, knowledge and power and draw up the resources to rebuild itself. If we revive the fire and the fascination, the study and the practice, the passion and the love; if we come home to our people with the world in our backpacks and combine what we've learned with all that we are; then the Jews will again shine their light on the nations, on the countries and cultures that refuse to disintegrate, on the great Persian rug of variety and color that we all weave together for the sake of our kids.

Imagine *that.*

About the Author

Ze'ev Maghen is a professor of Arabic Literature and Islamic History and Chairman of the Department of Middle East Studies at Bar-Ilan University. A senior fellow at the Shalem Center in Jerusalem, he has lectured around the world and in Israel, where he lives with his wife and four children. He served in the Tank Corps of the Israel Defense Forces until his discharge in 2005. He was the 1983 International Frisbee Golf Champion (Junior Division).

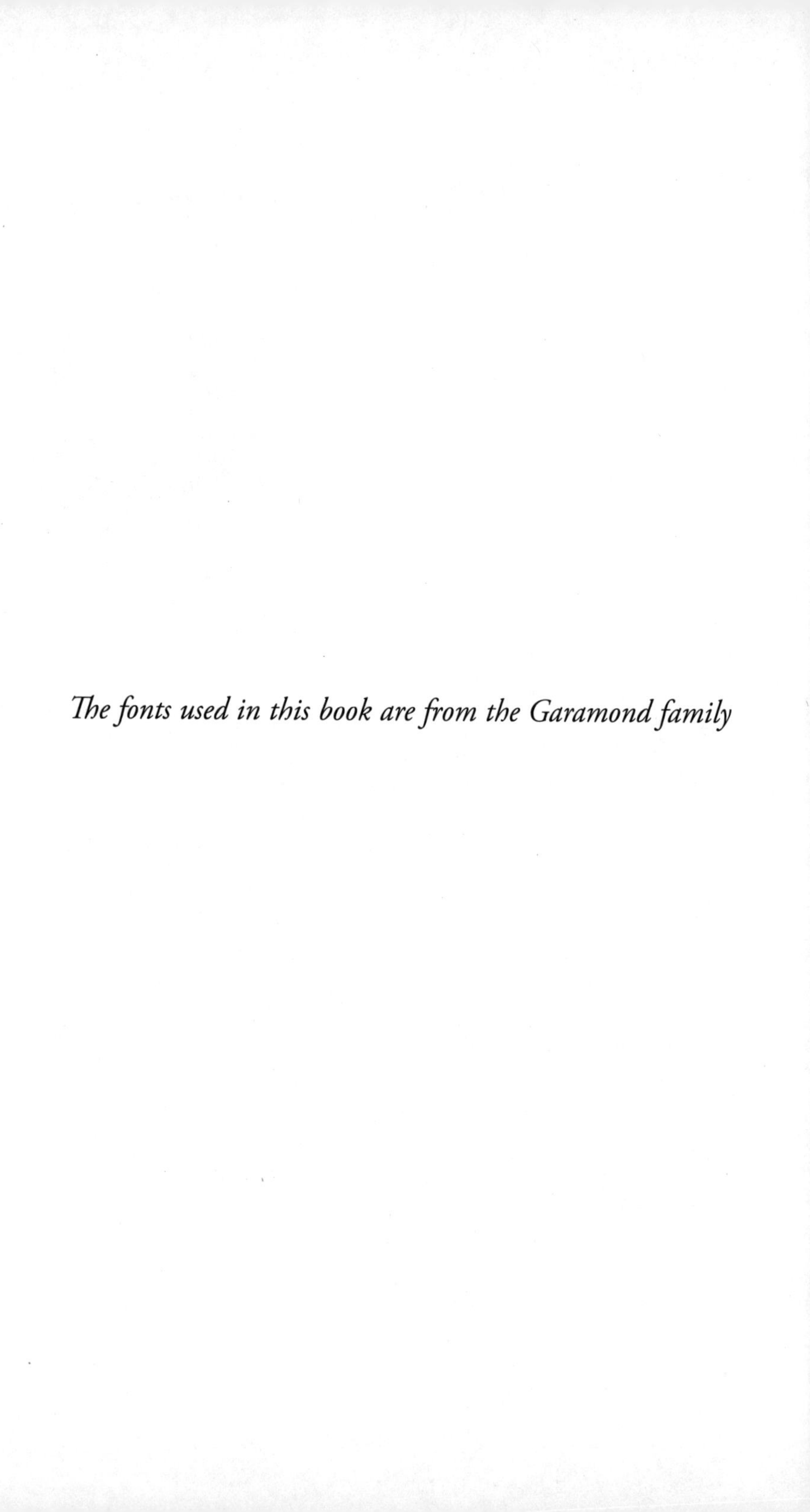

The fonts used in this book are from the Garamond family

The Toby Press publishes fine writing
on subjects of Israel and Jewish interest.
For more information, visit www.tobypress.com.